IMAGES of America

YORK COUNTY TROLLEYS

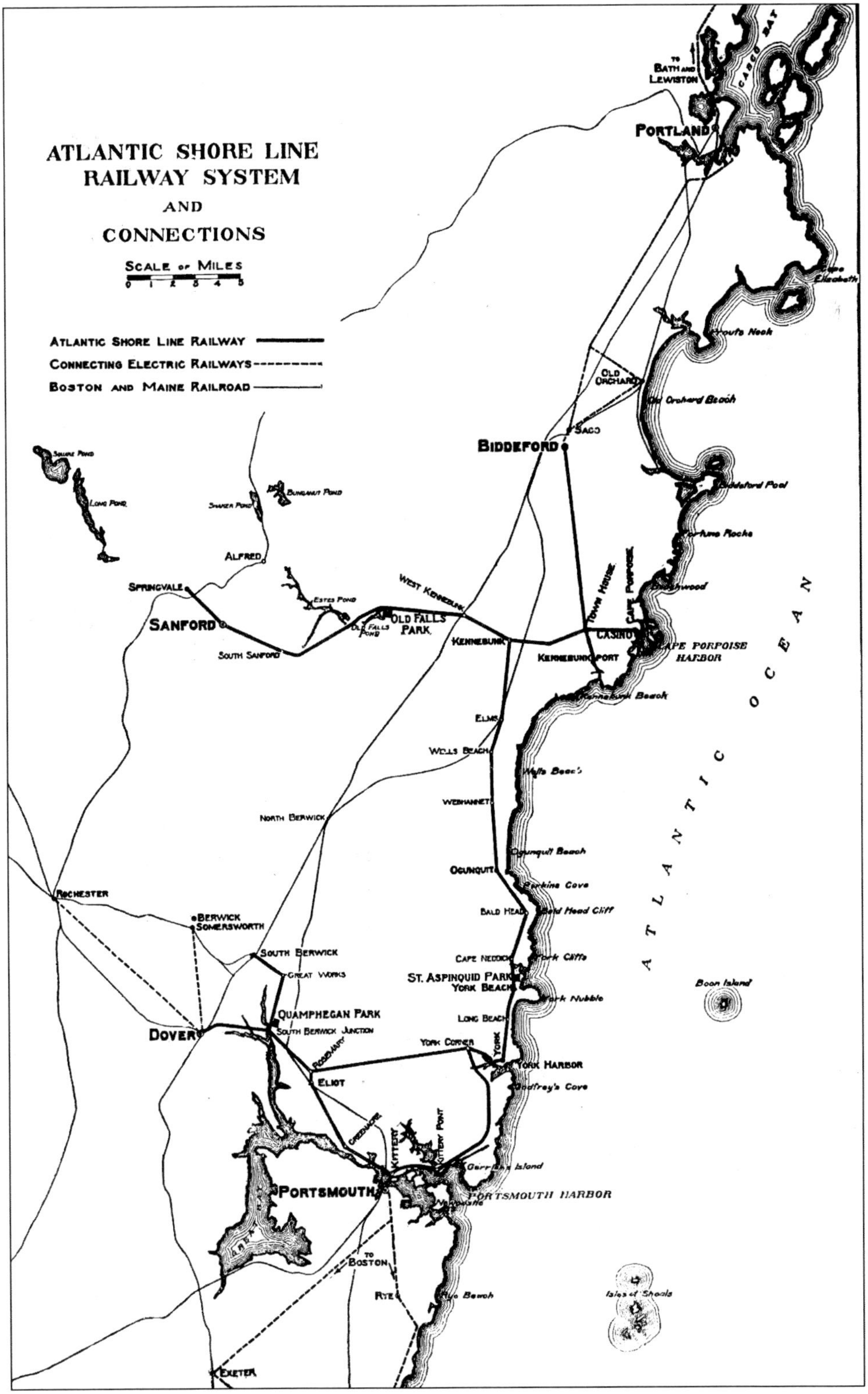
ATLANTIC SHORE LINE RAILWAY SYSTEM AND CONNECTIONS
SCALE OF MILES
0 1 2 3 4 5
ATLANTIC SHORE LINE RAILWAY
CONNECTING ELECTRIC RAILWAYS
BOSTON AND MAINE RAILROAD
TO BATH AND LEWISTON
CASCO BAY
PORTLAND
Cape Elizabeth
Prouts Neck
OLD ORCHARD
Old Orchard Beach
SACO
BIDDEFORD
Biddeford Pool
Fortune Rocks
ALFRED
SPRINGVALE
SANFORD
SOUTH SANFORD
Estes Pond
WEST KENNEBUNK
OLD FALLS PARK
KENNEBUNK
KENNEBUNKPORT
TOWN HOUSE
CAPE PORPOISE
CASINO
CAPE PORPOISE HARBOR
Kennebunk Beach
ATLANTIC OCEAN
ELMS
WELLS BEACH
Wells Beach
WEBHANNET
NORTH BERWICK
OGUNQUIT
Ogunquit Beach
Perkins Cove
BALD HEAD
Bald Head Cliff
ROCHESTER
BERWICK
SOMERSWORTH
SOUTH BERWICK
GREAT WORKS
CAPE NEDDICK
York Cliffs
ST. ASPINQUID PARK
YORK BEACH
Boon Island
York Nubble
QUAMPHEGAN PARK
SOUTH BERWICK JUNCTION
LONG BEACH
DOVER
YORK CORNER
YORK
YORK HARBOR
ROSEMARY
ELIOT
Godfrey's Cove
GREENACRE
KITTERY
KITTERY POINT
PORTSMOUTH
PORTSMOUTH HARBOR
TO BOSTON
RYE
Rye Beach
Isles of Shoals
EXETER

IMAGES
of America

York County Trolleys

O.R. Cummings, Historian
New England Electric Railway Historical Society, Inc.

ARCADIA
PUBLISHING

ISBN 978-0-7385-0137-6

Published by Arcadia Publishing
Charleston, South Carolina

Printed in the United States of America

Library of Congress Catalog Card Number: 9961841

For all general information contact Arcadia Publishing at:
Telephone 843-853-2070
Fax 843-853-0044
E-mail sales@arcadiapublishing.com
For customer service and orders:
Toll-Free 1-888-313-2665

Visit us on the Internet at www.arcadiapublishing.com

Contents

ACKNOWLEDGMENTS

O.R. Cummings, 75, a retired journalist, has been a trolley enthusiast since 1940 and has been a member of the New England Electric Railway Historical Society Inc., owner of the Seashore Trolley Museum, since 1942. He has written and had published histories of several Maine electric railways, including ones on the Atlantic Shore Line, the Biddeford & Saco Railroad, the Portland Railroad Company, and the Portland-Lewiston Interurban, and has amassed a large collection of photographs, postcards, and other memorabilia of the trolley era in New England.

Among those who years ago or more recently contributed to this collection were: Howard T. Moulton of Portsmouth, New Hampshire; the late Lee H. McCray of New Bedford, Massachusetts, general manager of the Atlantic Shore Railway from 1911 to 1918; the late Garland Patch of Portsmouth; the late John D. Bardwell of York; the late Edward D. Leavitt of Biddeford; the late Charles D. Heseltine of South Portland; the late Russell Goodall of Sanford; John Martin of Kennebunkport; the late Forest L. Horton of Brentwood, New Hampshire; Norman Sullivan of Portland; Edwin B. Robertson of Westbrook; the late Gerald F. Cunningham of Silver Spring, Maryland; the late Charles A. Brown of Sutton, Massachusetts; the late Roger Borrup of Warehouse Point, Connecticut; and the late Charles A. Duncan of Danvers, Massachusetts.

INTRODUCTION

Maine's York County boasted more than 100 miles of trolley lines from mid-1907 through 1922. Among the three operating companies, the largest was the Atlantic Shore Line Railway, incorporated in 1900 and succeeded on January 1, 1911, by the Atlantic Shore Railway. This system, which operated 90.41 miles of main track at its peak, served part of the city of Biddeford and the towns of Kennebunkport, Kennebunk, Lyman, Alfred, Sanford, Wells, York, Kittery, Eliot, and South Berwick; the system also extended into Dover, NH, and maintained ferry service across the Piscataqua River between Badger's Island, Kittery, and Portsmouth, the Granite State's only seaport. Its various lines consisted not only of those built by the company itself between 1900 and 1907 but also those constructed by several predecessors: the Mousam River Railroad Company, the Sanford & Cape Porpoise Railway, the Portsmouth, Kittery & York Street Railway, the Kittery & Eliot Street Railway, and the Portsmouth, Dover & York Street Railway from 1893 through 1903.

After 1908, there were two operating divisions, the Eastern and the Western, with the former consisting of lines connecting Sanford and Springvale Villages in Sanford and extending from Sanford to Cape Porpoise, Kennebunkport; from Dock Square, Kennebunkport, to City Square, Biddeford; and from Kennebunk southerly through Wells and the present town of Ogunquit to York Beach. Routes of the Western Division, formerly the Portsmouth, Dover & York Street Railway, extended from Portsmouth to York Beach via Kittery Foreside, Kittery Point, York Village, and York Harbor; from Portsmouth to Dover via Kittery, Eliot, and a corner of South Berwick; from Dover to South Berwick village; and from Dover to York Beach.

Constructed as a horsecar line in 1888, the Biddeford & Saco Railroad, which extended from Biddeford through Saco to Old Orchard Beach, was electrified in 1892; after the construction of a large loop in Biddeford in 1900, there were 7.61 miles of main track. The Portland Railroad Company commenced running through cars between Portland and Saco via South Portland and the town of Scarbough, 16.66 miles, in July 1902. A similar service was inaugurated between the Forest City and Old Orchard Beach, 15.26 miles, on Independence Day in 1903. It owned 4.72 miles of track in Saco and 2.71 miles in Old Orchard and connected at both points with the Biddeford & Saco Railroad. Until hard-surface, all-weather thoroughfares were constructed and private automobiles became numerous, residents of York County depended on the trolleys for local transportation the year-round. Many were those who regularly commuted to and from work on the electric cars, which also carried large numbers of schoolchildren from September through June, and in the winter, when streets, roads, and highways were buried under deep drifts, powerful snow plows cleared the street railway tracks swiftly after severe storms so the trolleys could get through. It was in summer, however, that the street railways enjoyed their heaviest patronage. In addition to the ordinary day-to-day travel of York County folks, there was a large amount of pleasure riding to and from such resorts as York Beach and Old Orchard Beach, and trolley touring was a popular pastime from Memorial Day until Labor Day. Indeed, both the Atlantic Shore Line and the Atlantic Shore Railway encouraged such riding by offering special round trip excursion fares over a number of routes.

Representative of summer schedules was that maintained by the Atlantic Shore Railway in 1912. Half-hourly service was maintained between Portsmouth and York Beach, between Portsmouth and Dover, between York Beach and Kennebunk, and between Dock Square, Kennebunkport, and City Square, Biddeford. Cars ran hourly between Dover and York Beach and between Sanford and Cape Porpoise Village in Kennebunkport. The Portland Railroad Company, which had been leased to the Cumberland County Power & Light Company earlier in the year, operated a 30-minute headway between Portland and Old Orchard Beach, which also was the destination of Biddeford & Saco trolleys leaving Biddeford every 15 minutes.

Also carried by the Atlantic Shore Line and the Atlantic Shore Railway were substantial amounts of freight, express, and mail. Carload freight shipments were interchanged with the Boston & Maine Railroad (B&M) at Kennebunk, West Kennebunk, and Springvale, while the express service over the system was operated under contract from 1908 on by the Tarbox Express Company and its successors, the Hoyt-Tarbox Express Company and the Atlantic Express Company. Most of the mail was moved in closed pouches and sacks on regular passenger cars but a railway post office car was run between Badger's Island and York Beach, the York Harbor & Beach RPO schedule generally calling for four round trips daily except on Sunday in the summer and two round trips in other seasons.

While both the Portland Railroad Company and the Biddeford & Saco were profitable undertakings, the Atlantic Shore Line and the Atlantic Shore Railway very definitely were not, largely due to sky high interest charges on an astronomical bonded indebtedness. The latter was placed in federal receivership on November 1, 1915, and on May 1, 1917, its Western Division was turned over to a separate receiver for operation as the Portsmouth, Dover & York Street Railway. What remained of the Atlantic Shore system was taken over by the newly organized York Utilities Company on February 1, 1923. The World War I years were difficult ones for street railways throughout the United States for a variety of reasons and soon after the conflict ended, automobiles began rolling off assembly lines in ever-increasing numbers and at progressively more attractive prices. As the nation entered the "Roarin' Twenties," more and more residents of York County acquired motor cars and forsook the trolleys that had served them so faithfully for such a long time. First to succumb was the Portsmouth, Dover & York Street Railway, which discontinued operation on March 17, 1923, by order of the U.S. District Court. The York Utilities Company absorbed its Kennebunk-York Beach route on March 31, 1924, and on September 15, 1927, it discontinued all rail service outside of Sanford. Retained were trolley lines between Sanford and Springvale Villages via River Street and Main Street.

Trolley service between Portland and both Old Orchard Beach and Saco ended on April 16, 1932, and on April 2, 1935, the York Utilities Company substituted buses for electric cars on the Main Street route between Sanford and Springvale via Main Street. Rail passenger service over the River Street route ended April 1, 1947, but electric locomotives continued to haul freight between the Springvale interchange with the Boston & Maine and Sanford Village until June 1949, when a diesel locomotive took over. Yet one can still ride an electric car in York County. The Seashore Trolley Museum, founded in 1939, is situated in both Kennebunkport and Arundel and runs daily demonstration trips from late spring until early fall on part of the Kennebunkport-Biddeford line of the Atlantic Shore Line and its successors. Six cars once owned by the York Utilities Company and two from the Biddeford & Saco Railroad are preserved at the museum. Attractions include two exhibit barns, a restoration shop, and a display of street railway photos and artifacts in the orientation room of the visitors center.

One

The Atlantic Shore Line Railway: Kittery and York

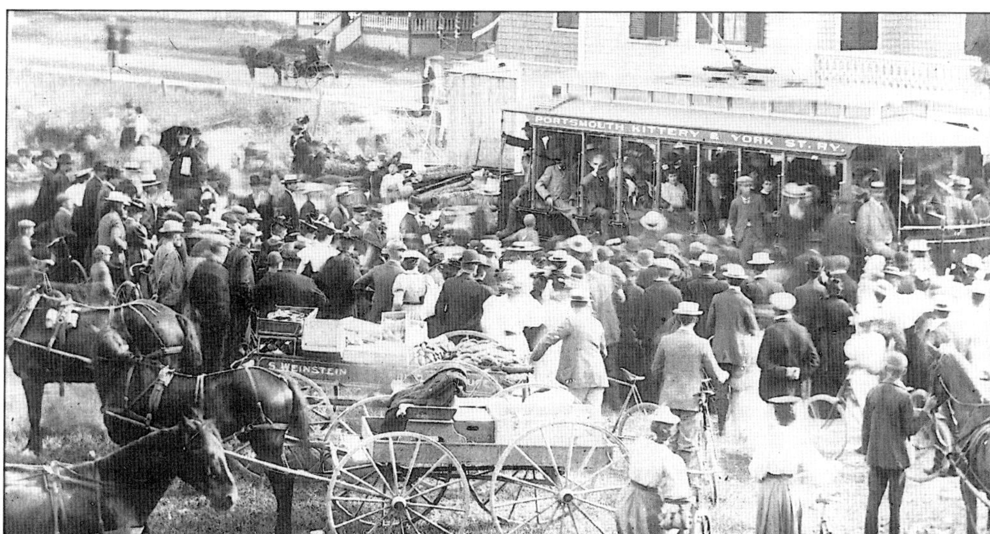

The Portsmouth, Kittery & York Street Railway (PK&Y) operated its first through trip from Badger's Island, Kittery, to York Beach via Kittery Point, York Village, and York Harbor on Friday, August 27, 1897. The four-wheel open trolley was greeted by a sizable crowd when it arrived at the resort around 3:30 in the afternoon. The PK&Y was absorbed on November 1, 1903, by the Portsmouth, Dover & York Street Railway, which was consolidated with the Atlantic Shore Line Railway on February 1, 1906, and became the latter's Western Division. All trolley service between Badger's Island and the resort ended March 17, 1923.

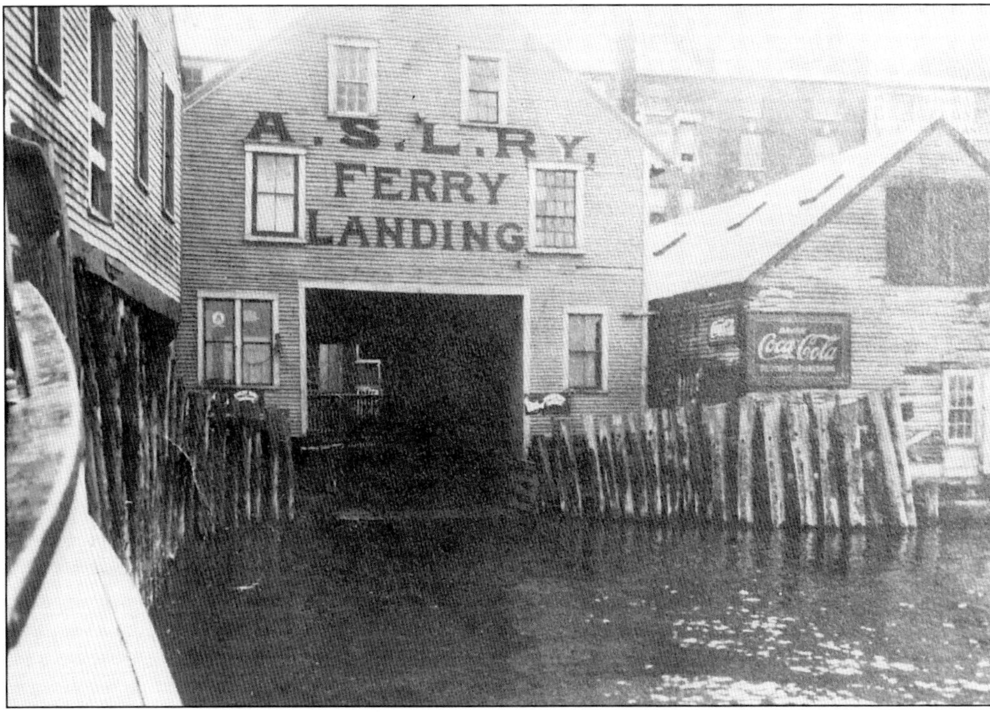

The Portsmouth ferry slip of the Portsmouth, Kittery & York was situated in the leased old Spring Market building off Ceres Street, just a few steps from Bow Street. A waiting area and a lunchroom were provided for the convenience of passengers and after 1899 the slip was just a short walk from the trolley tracks of the Portsmouth Electric Railway on Market Street. An upscale restaurant now occupies the ferry landing site.

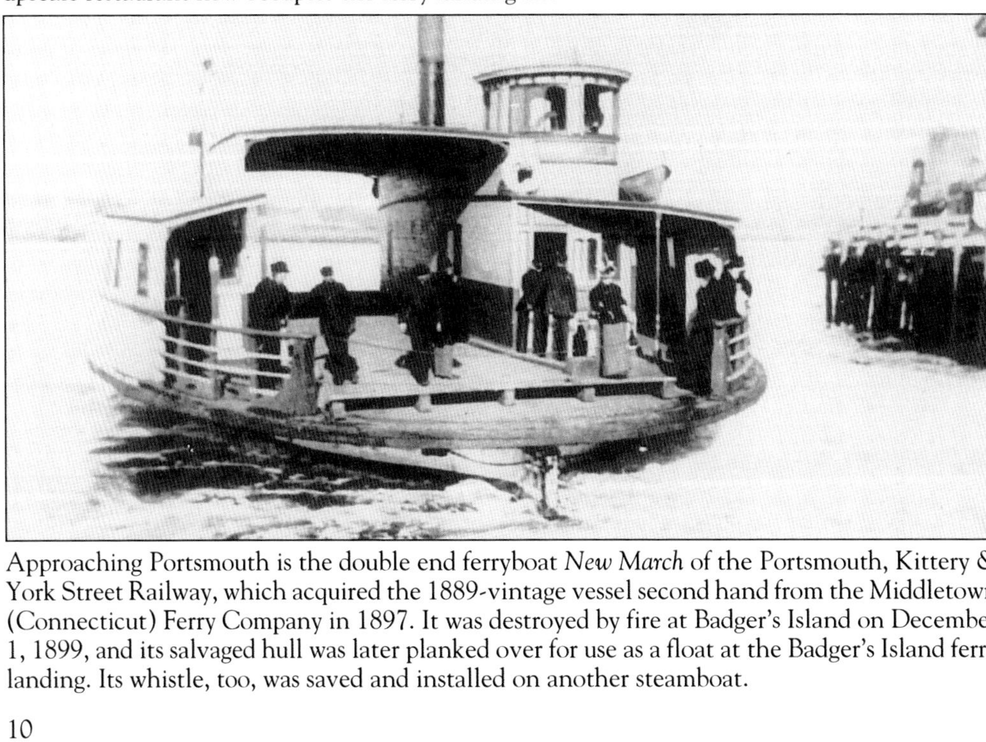

Approaching Portsmouth is the double end ferryboat *New March* of the Portsmouth, Kittery & York Street Railway, which acquired the 1889-vintage vessel second hand from the Middletown (Connecticut) Ferry Company in 1897. It was destroyed by fire at Badger's Island on December 1, 1899, and its salvaged hull was later planked over for use as a float at the Badger's Island ferry landing. Its whistle, too, was saved and installed on another steamboat.

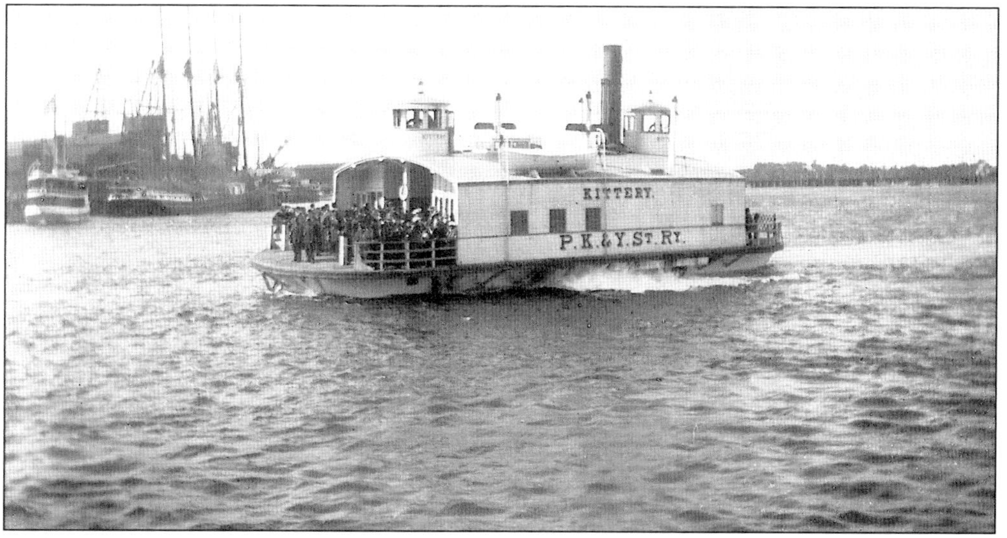

Replacing the *New March* was the ferry *Kittery*, built in 1900 at the David Clark Shipyard in Kennebunkport and placed in service on August 18th of that year. More powerful than its predecessor, it made the Piscataqua River crossing in five minutes and schedules called for it to leave Portsmouth at 25 and 55 minutes past the hour to connect with trolleys leaving Badger's Island on the hour and half hour. It was sold to the Grand Isle Ferry Company of Lake Champlain in 1918.

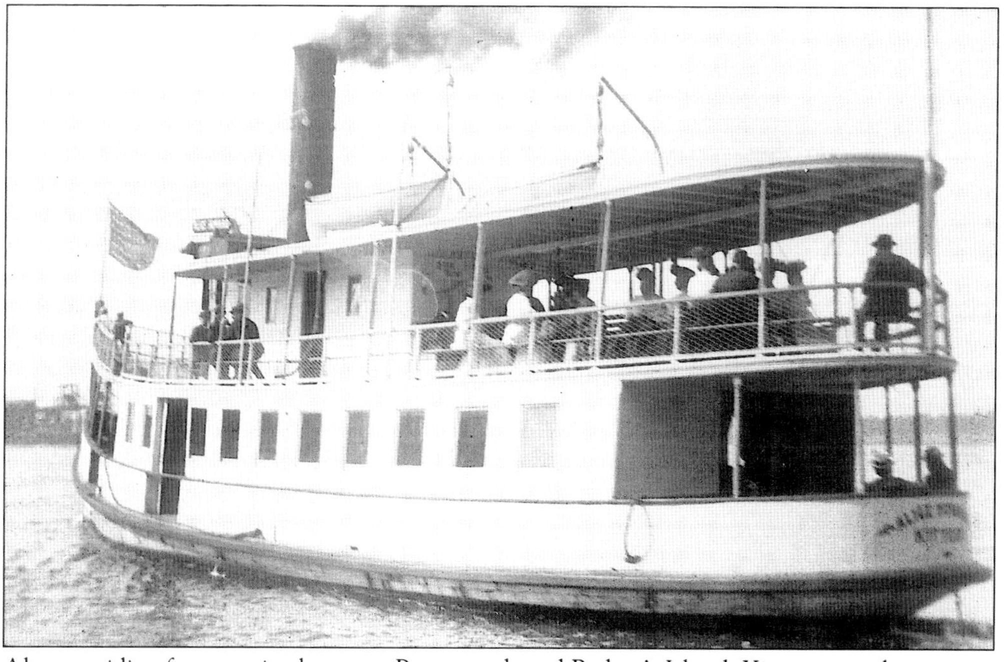

Also providing ferry service between Portsmouth and Badger's Island, Kittery, was the steamer *Alice Howard*, built at Peaks Island, Maine, in 1899 and acquired by the Portsmouth, Kittery & York Street Railway in 1901. During that summer, it was run over a circuit extending from Portsmouth to Kittery Point, Gerrish Island, and New Castle. (Similar service was given in 1902, 1903, and 1904.) After the end of trolley service over the former PD&Y on March 17, 1923, the *Alice Howard* was sold to interests in Belfast, Maine, and renamed the *Utility*.

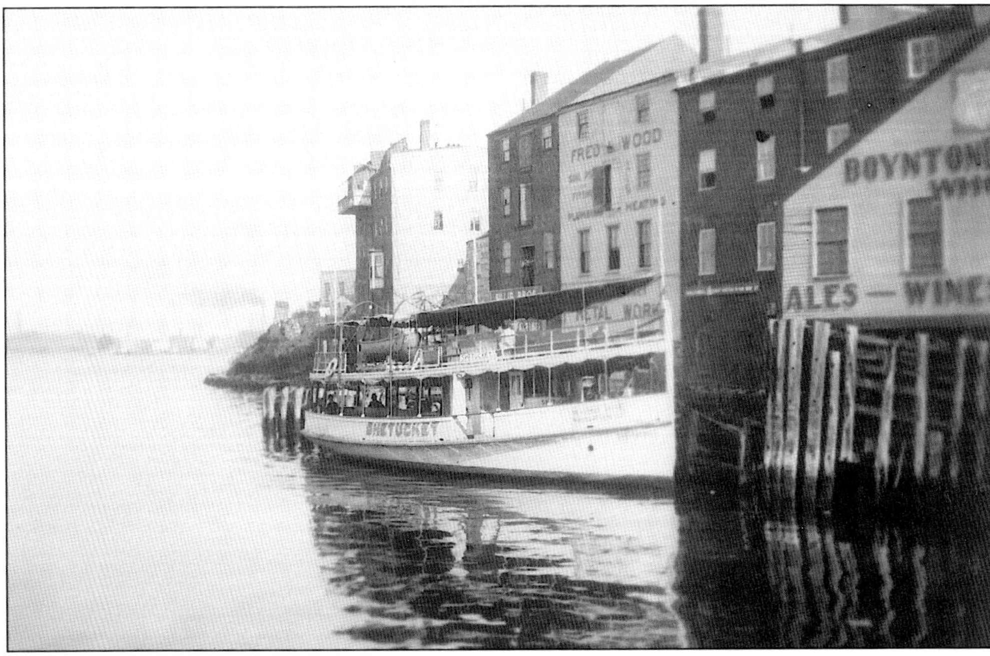

Formerly operated on the Merrimack River in Massachusetts, the motor vessel *Shetucket* was acquired for the Portsmouth-Kittery ferry service in 1917. Proving unsatisfactory because of the unreliability of its twin gasoline engines, it was sold in 1921 to the Deer Isle Granite Company of Stonington, Maine, and became the *George A. Fuller*.

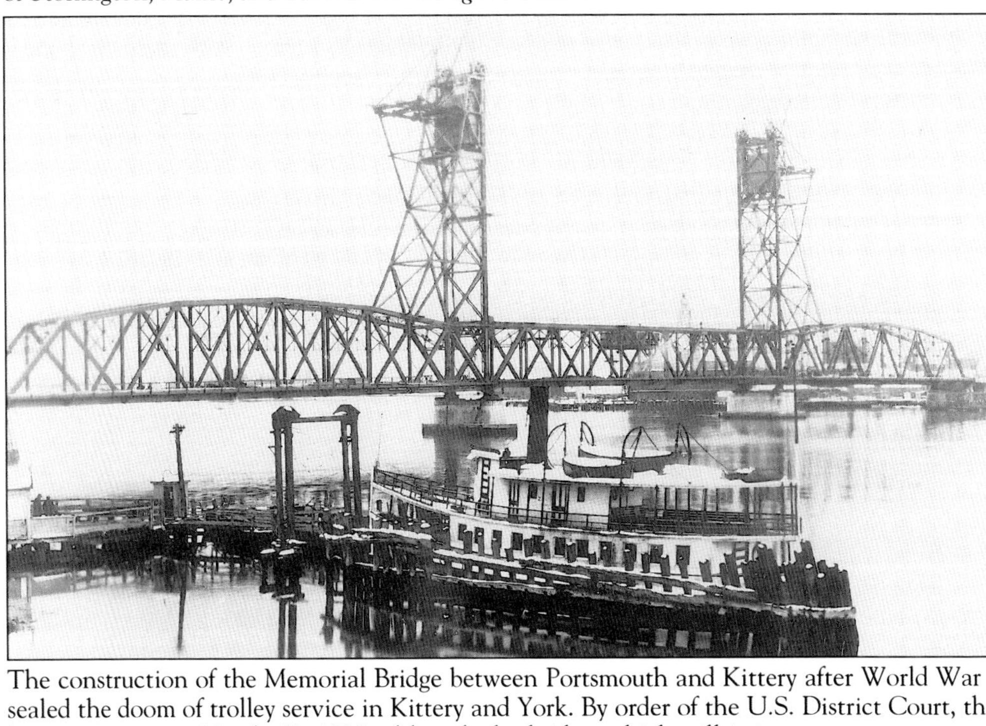

The construction of the Memorial Bridge between Portsmouth and Kittery after World War I sealed the doom of trolley service in Kittery and York. By order of the U.S. District Court, the last cars were run March 17, 1923, although the bridge, which still is in use, was not opened until August. The idle *Alice Howard* is docked at the Badger's Island ferry slip prior to its sale.

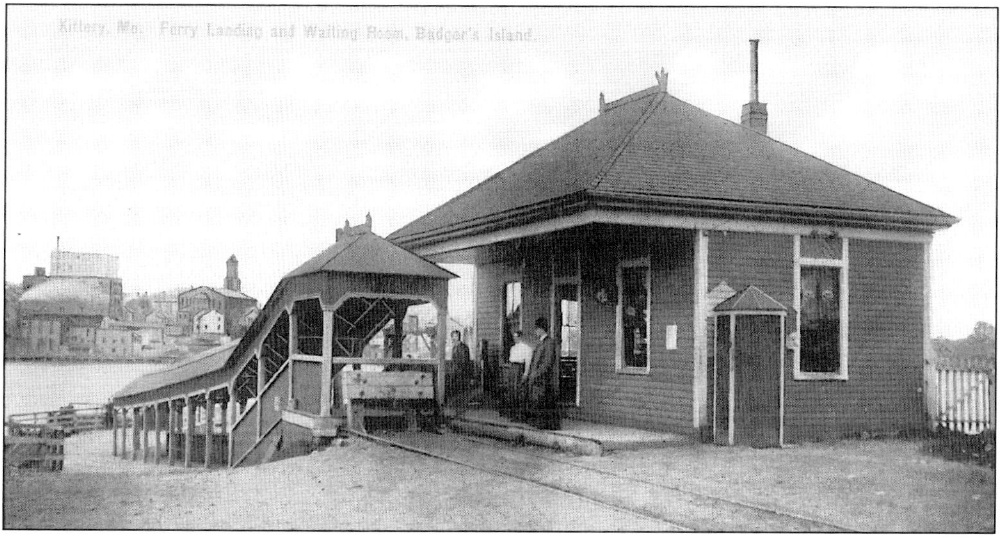

The "head house" at the Badger's Island ferry landing housed a waiting room and a refreshment, newspaper, and tobacco stand. The building still stands today as part of a dwelling. During the trolley era it was heated in winter by a large "pot belly" coal stove similar to those provided in suburban railroad stations of the Boston & Maine Railroad.

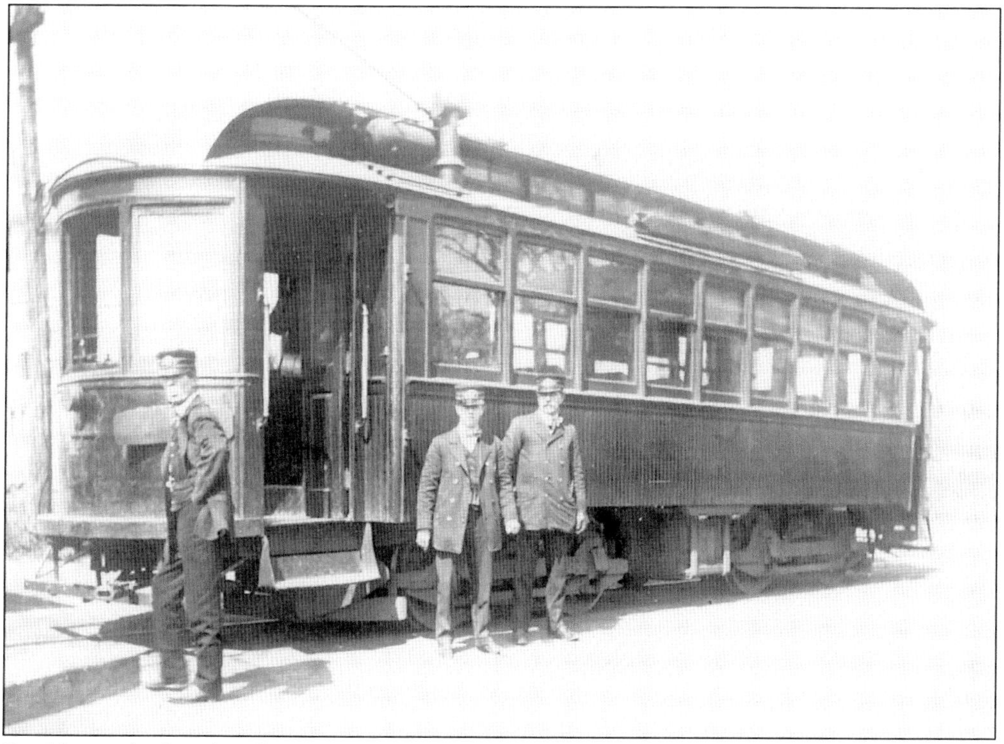

Double-truck closed trolleys of the Atlantic Shore Line and Atlantic Shore Railway had hot water heating systems. The stack of the coal-burning boiler shows in this c. 1920 view at Badger's Island. It was the responsibility of conductors to see that an adequate supply of coal was available in the car before they began their day's run but, if needed, hods of additional fuel could be picked up at a railway carhouse.

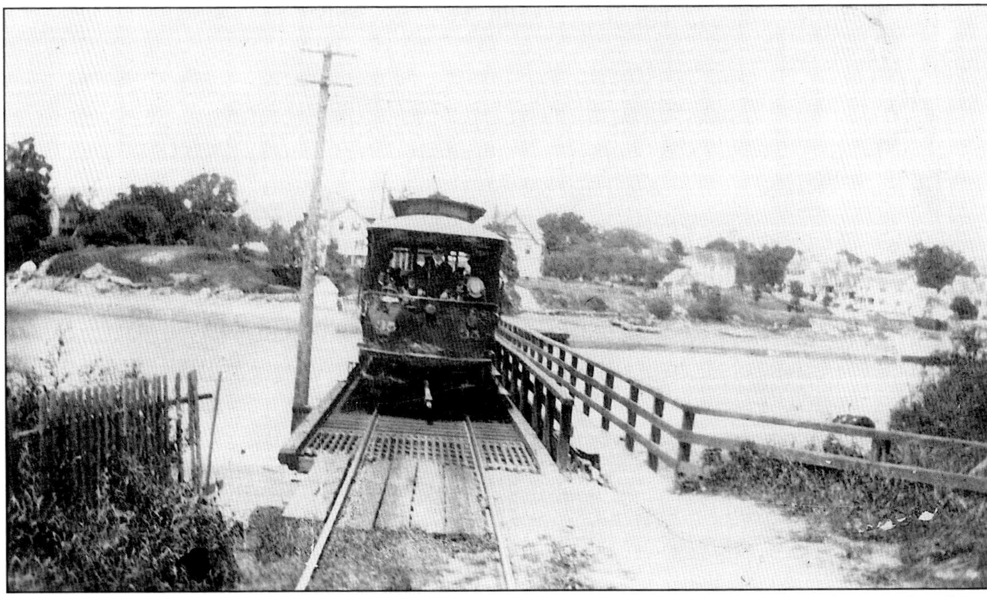

A 580-foot pile trestle spanned the back channel of the Piscataqua between Badger's Island and the foot of New March Street, Kittery. The open trolley is headed for the ferry landing. There originally was a carriageway but this was eliminated when the trestle was rebuilt after 1907. After trolley service ended in 1923, the rails on the trestle were removed but some of the piles remained for many years thereafter.

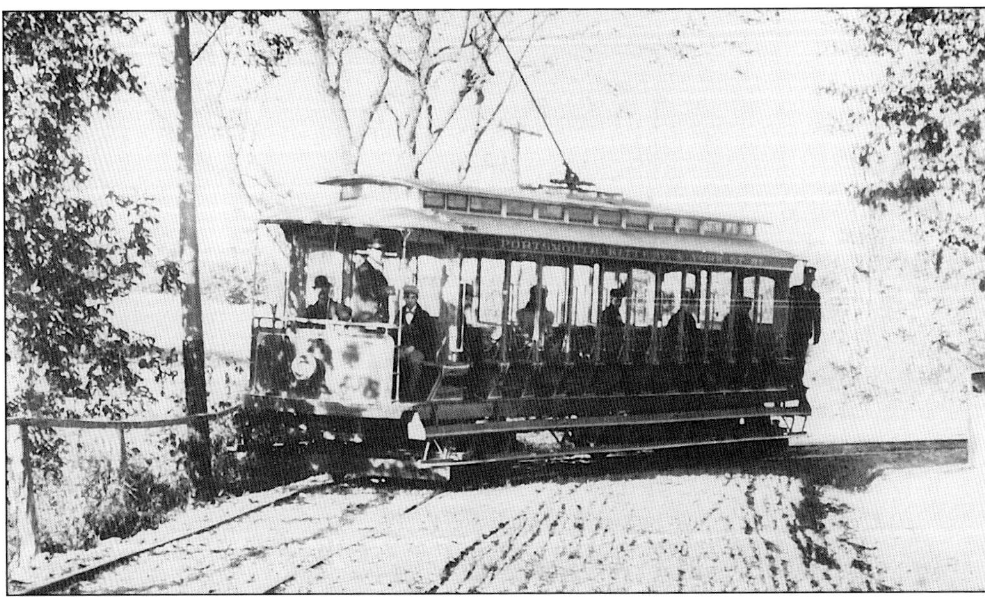

An open "breezer" of the Portsmouth, Kittery & York Street Railway turns from New March Street onto Government Street, Kittery, about 1900. The PK&Y owned seven of these 14-bench cars and all but one survived until 1923. Each had a seating capacity of 70 and conductors walked along the double running boards on the sides to collect fares. Their natural "air conditioning" gave passengers a cool refreshing ride even on the hottest days of summer.

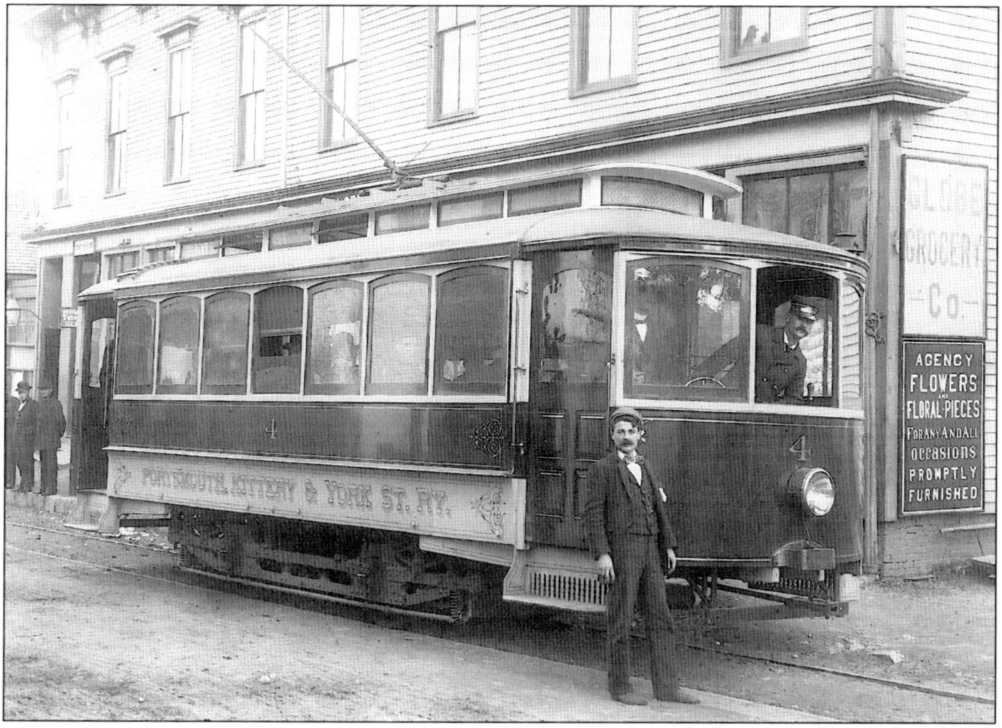

En route to the Badger's Island ferry landing, PK&Y No. 4 stops for the photographer in front of Wentworth Hall on Government Street, Kittery. Like three identical cars, Nos. 2, 6, and 12, No. 4 had plush-upholstered seats of the walkover type and was nicely warmed in the winter by electric heaters. Wentworth Hall was destroyed by fire in 1925, two years after trolley service in the town ended.

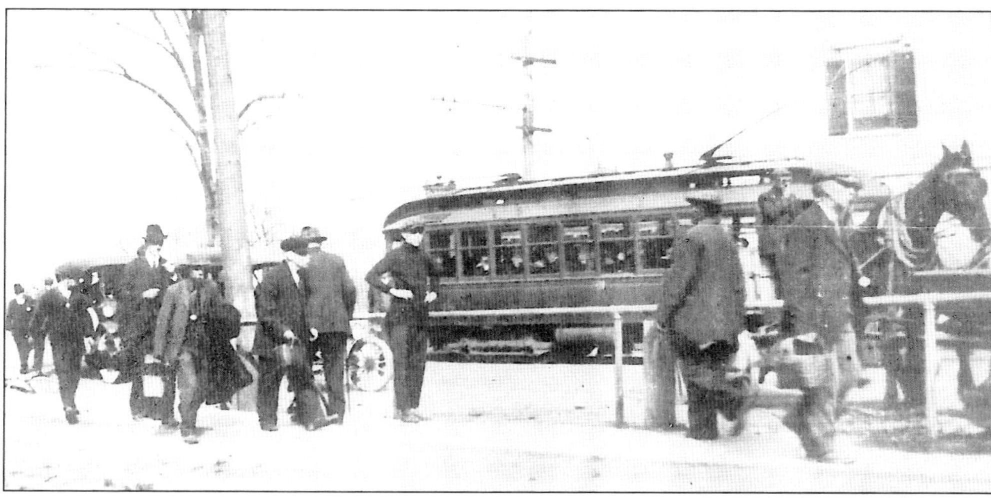

Some special event apparently is in progress as Atlantic Shore Railway No. 26 pauses on Wentworth Street near Wallingford Square, during the World War I years. This car was built for the Portsmouth, Dover & York Street Railway by the Laconia (New Hampshire) Car Company Works in 1905 and was regularly assigned to the Western Division of the Atlantic Shore Line and Atlantic Shore Railway from 1906 through 1916. It was scrapped at the Kittery Point carhouse in 1925.

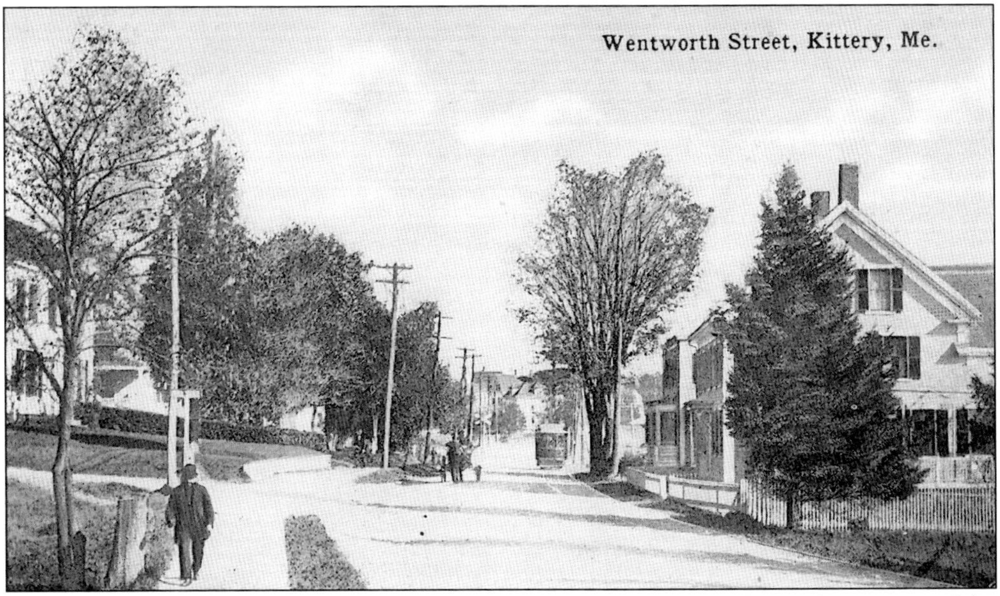

This postcard view shows a closed trolley on Wentworth Street near the grade crossing of the York Harbor & Beach Railroad's Navy Yard branch, constructed in 1901 to connect with newly laid tracks within the Portsmouth Naval Shipyard. Both passenger and freight trains were operated to and from the shipyard for many years and the rails across Wentworth Street remain in place today, although they are seldom used.

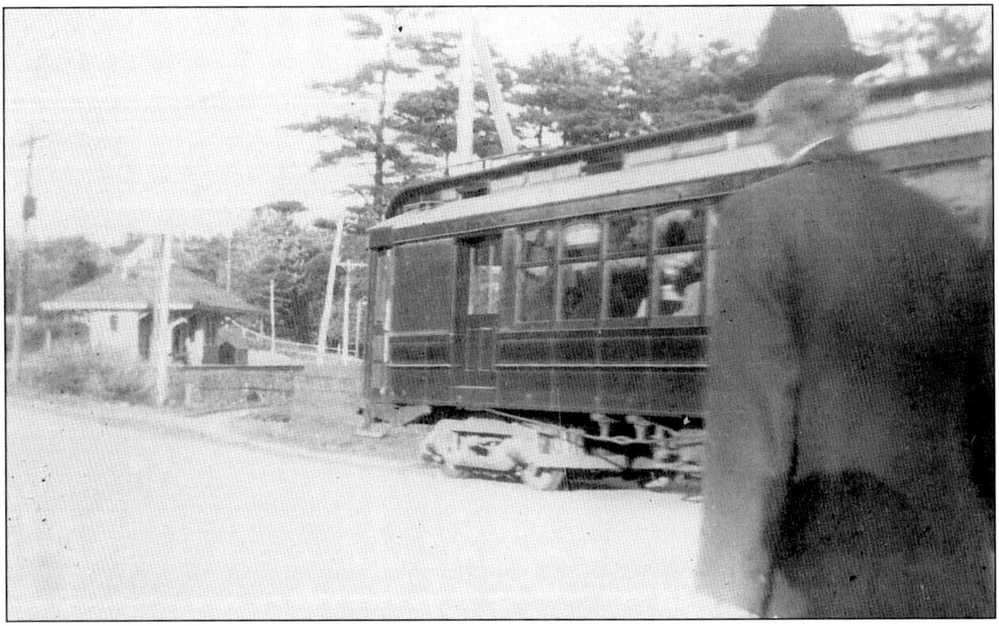

Approaching the Navy Yard depot of the York Harbor & Beach Railroad is a combination passenger-baggage car of the Atlantic Shore Line Railway about 1908. This is one of two identical cars, Nos. 52 and 54, purchased by the ASLR in 1907. Shipments of the Tarbox Express Company and its successors, the Hoyt-Tarbox Express Company and the Atlantic Express Company, frequently were carried in the baggage compartments, which, reportedly, once had one or more short benches for smokers.

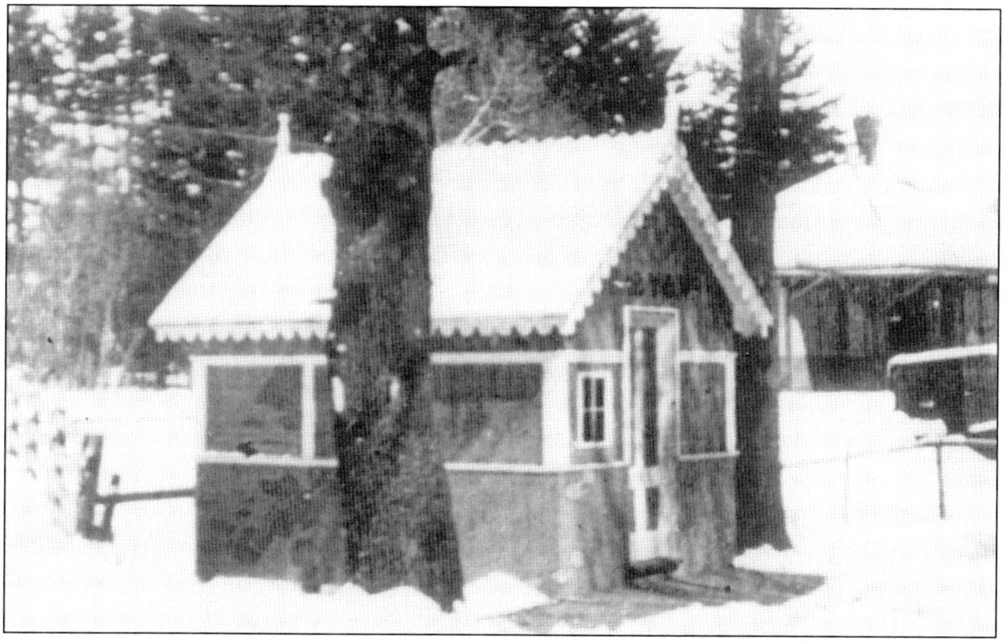

Typical of the 10 gazebo-like waiting stations erected by the Portsmouth, Kittery & York Street Railway in 1897 is this one near the Navy Yard depot of the York Harbor & Beach Railroad, which was operated by the Boston & Maine. In summer the shutters were removed to provide natural air conditioning. These stations were located trackside at points where sizable numbers of passengers were expected to board the trolleys.

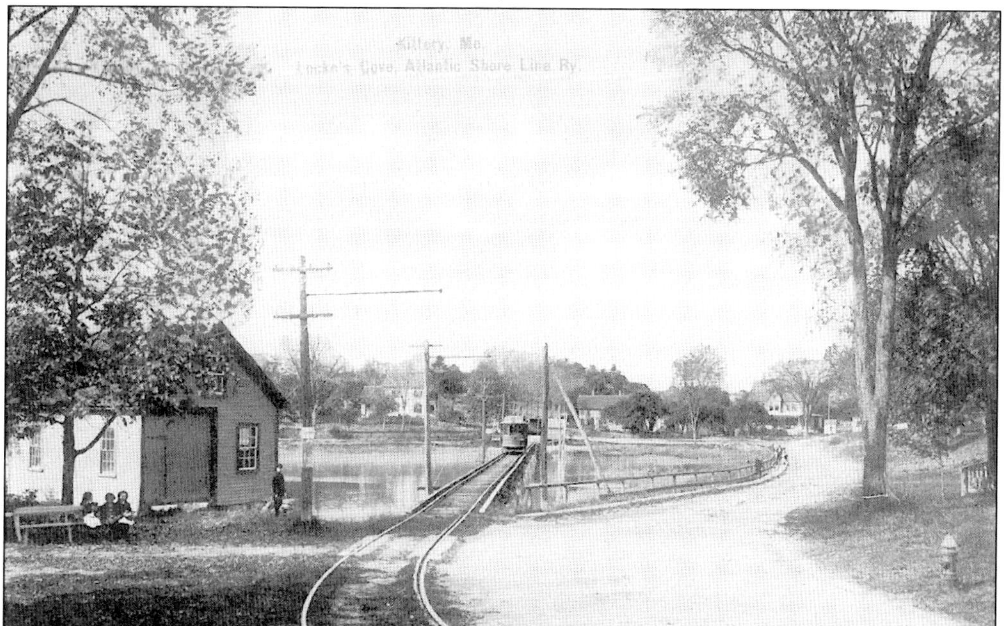

A 530-foot long pile trestle carried the street railway track across Locke's Cove, Kittery, near the present Gate 2 of the Portsmouth Naval Shipyard. It was rebuilt in 1912 when the approach track at each end was relocated to improve the curvature and was active until March 1923. No traces of it remain today.

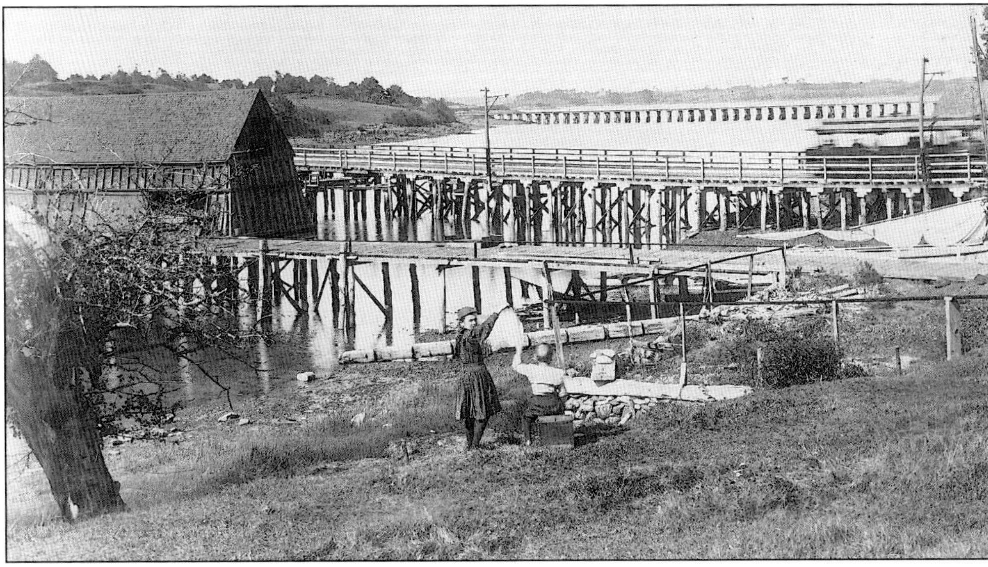

The highway-trolley bridge and the York Harbor & Beach Railroad's trestle (in the background) across Spruce Creek between Kittery and Kittery Point appear in this *c.* 1897 view. The Portsmouth, Kittery & York was required to construct a 700-foot trestle along the south side of the former and provide a new draw sufficiently wide to accommodate the roadway and the trolley track. Planking was laid on the trestle and the old bridge so the two structures appeared to be one. A modern steel structure spans Spruce Creek today.

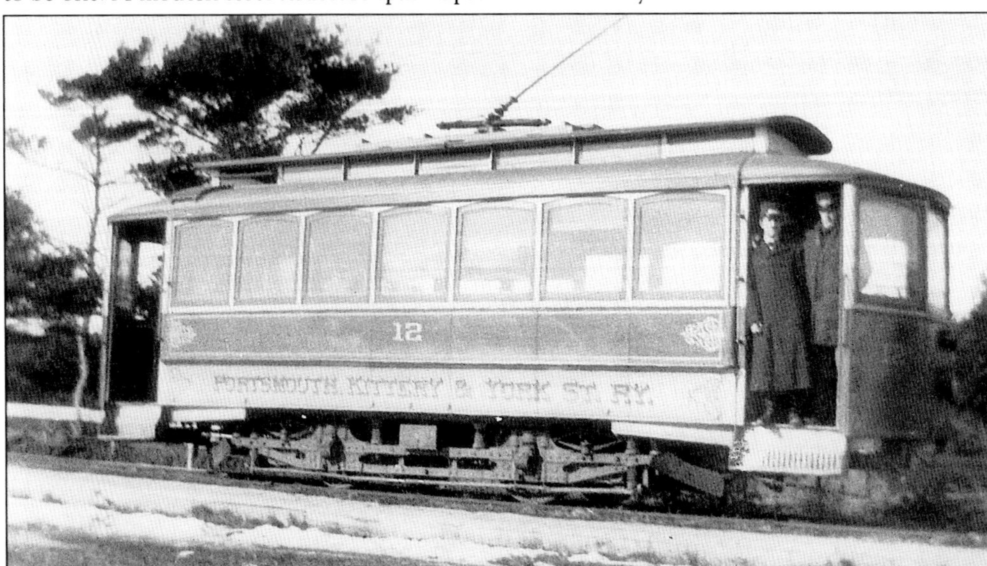

One of the four single-truck closed cars built by the Briggs Carriage Company of Amesbury, Massachusetts, for the Portsmouth, Kittery & York Street Railway in 1897, No. 12 was extensively damaged in an accident in Kittery on March 17, 1908. Repaired and renumbered 6, the car was en route from Badger's Island to Kittery Point on November 8, 1909, when it derailed as it started to cross the Spruce Creek bridge and plunged into the stream. Fortunately there were no passengers. The motorman, conductor, and another Atlantic Shore Line employee leaped to safety and all suffered painful bruises.

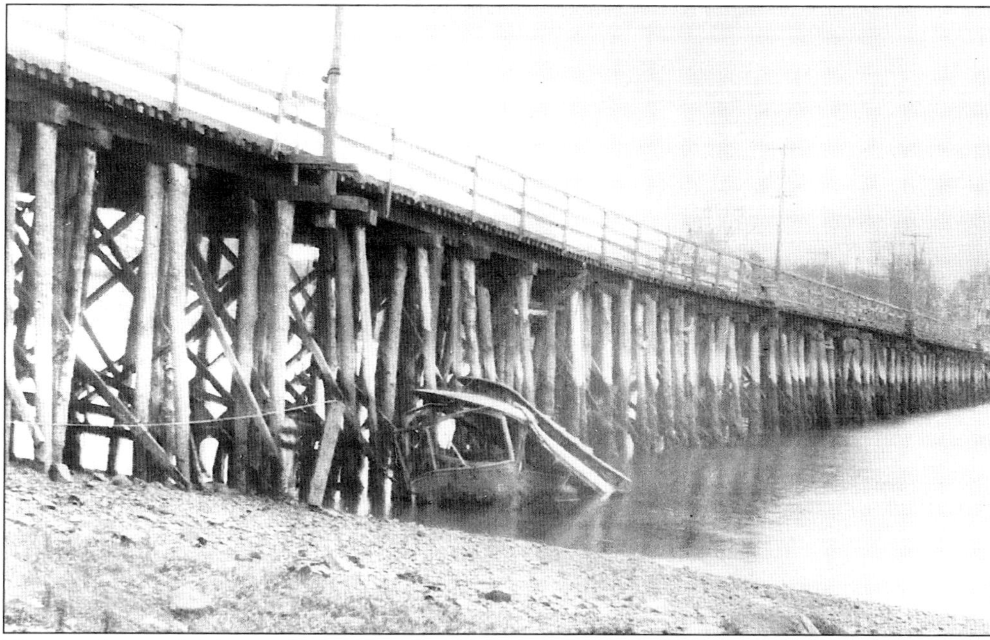

The wreckage of Atlantic Shore Line No. 6 after the derailment of November 18, 1909, was unveiled during low tide in Spruce Creek. A newspaper report said the car was broken up so badly that the creek was littered with splintered fragments for several hours after the mishap. By this time, another of the former PK&Y cars, No. 4, had been converted to a line (overhead wire repair) car and was assigned to the ASLRY's Western Division.

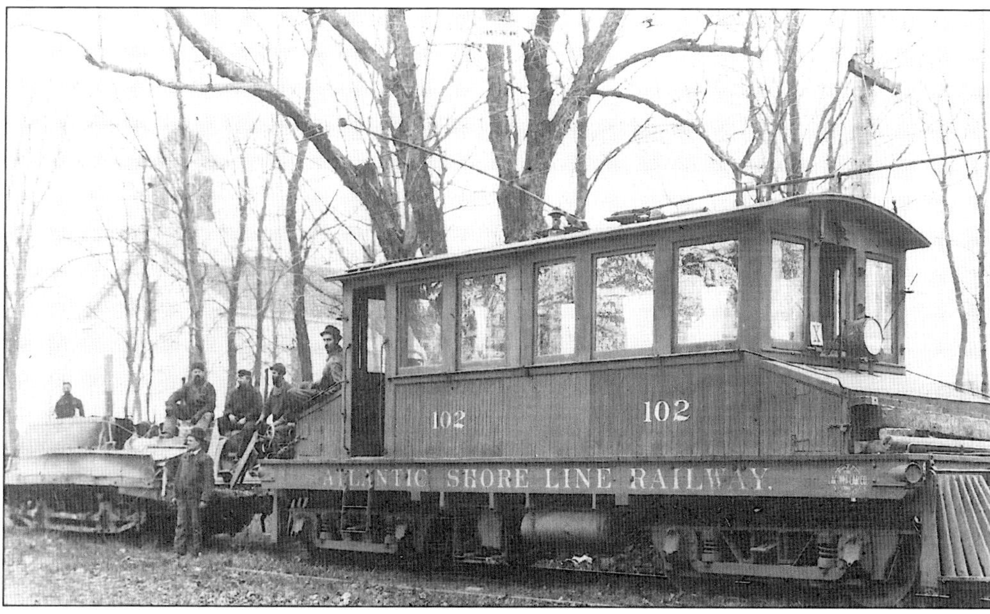

Once what remained of No. 6 was pulled from Spruce Creek, it was towed to the Kittery Point carhouse by a freight locomotive, which paused for a meet with a passenger car at Champernowne turnout on Pepperell Road, Kittery Point. The single track between this turnout and Emery's on Whipple Road, Kittery, was protected by automatic signals to prevent possible head-on collisions.

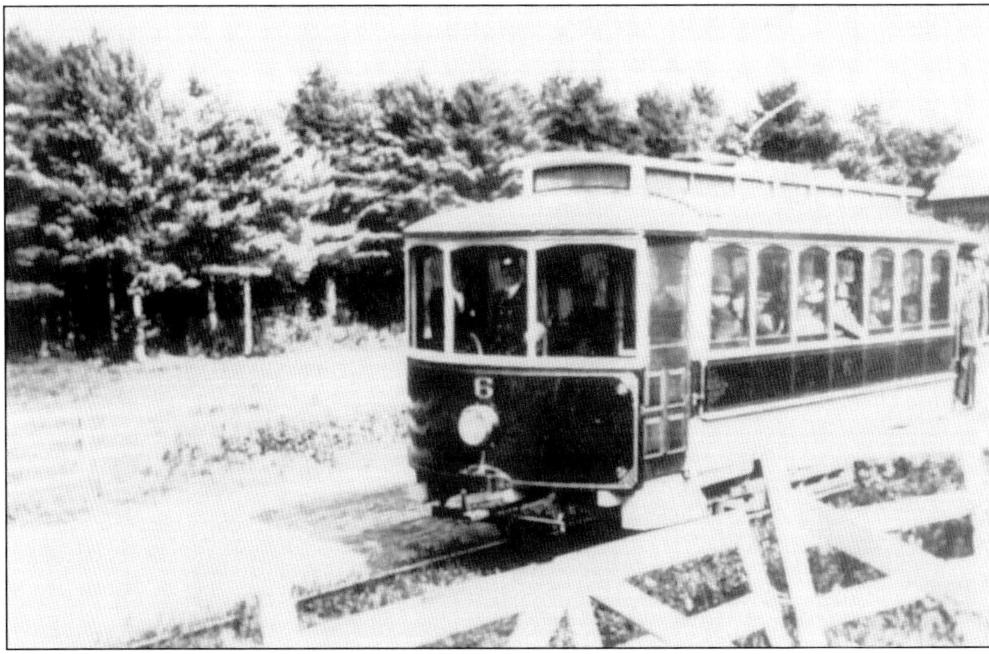

PK&Y No. 6 is on Pepperell Road near Fort McClary at Kittery Point. This car was lost when the original York Beach car barn, built in 1897, was destroyed by fire on October 9, 1904. A double- truck closed car and a snow plow also were destroyed in the blaze. Situated on the same site, a replacement carhouse was opened in 1905. Used primarily for storage, it remained active until 1923.

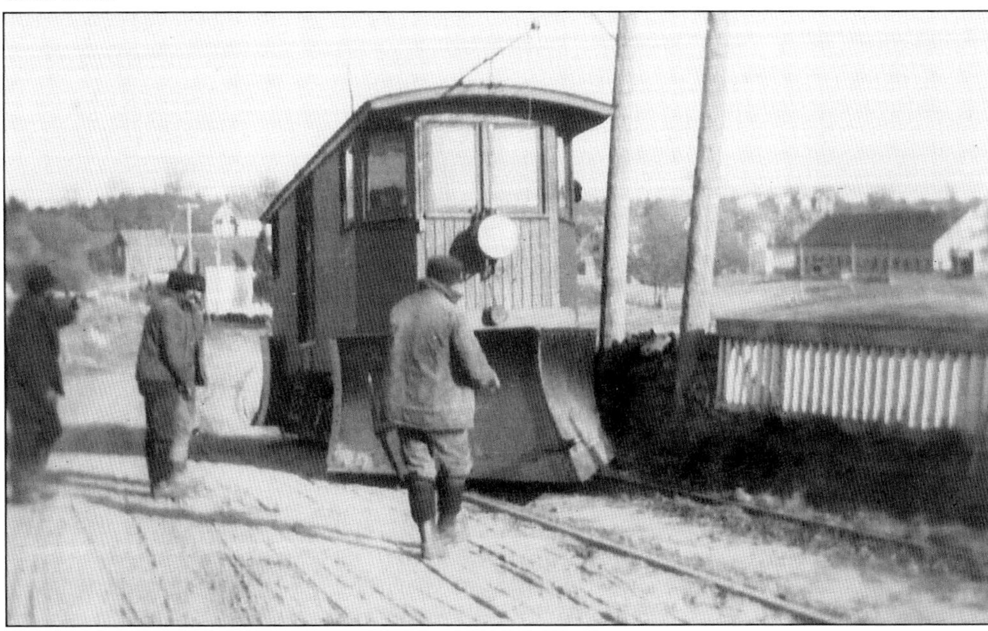

Winter was fast approaching when this snow plow of the Atlantic Shore Line was taken out for a trial run on Pepperell Road near the Kittery Point carhouse. Plows like this were dispatched to clear the tracks after severe winter snowstorms so that trolley service could be maintained without serious or lengthy disruption.

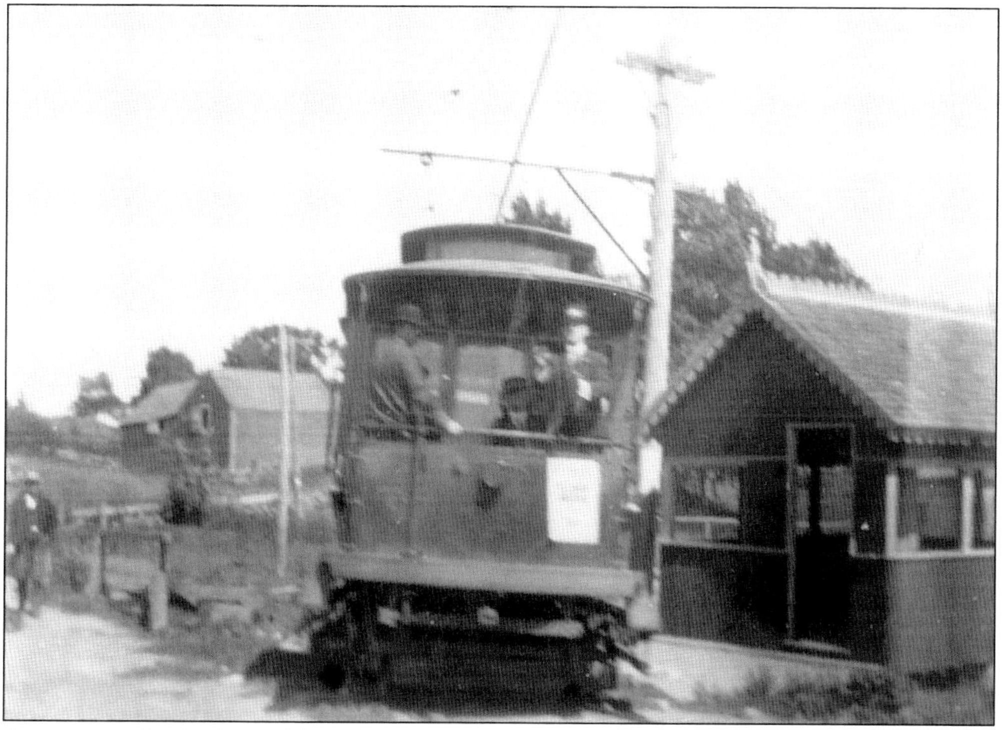

An open trolley is pictured here leaving the waiting station at Hutchins' Corner (now Lewis Square) at Kittery Point. The "breezer" probably was headed for York Beach, the major development of which as a middle-class summer resort did not really begin until August 1887 with the opening of the York Harbor & Beach Railroad, which also served Kittery Point and York Harbor. Through trains were run between Portsmouth and the beach and carried throngs of people in the summer months until the opening of the competing Portsmouth, Kittery & York Street Railway in 1897.

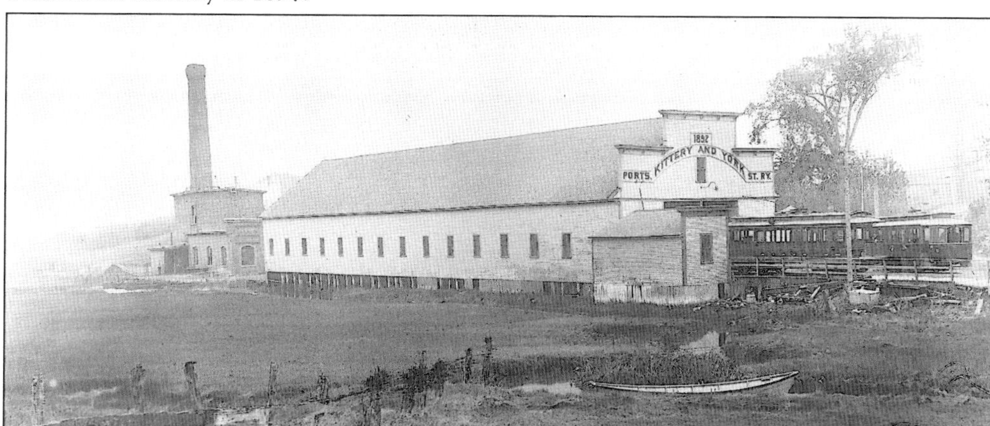

The Kittery Point carhouse is shown here shortly after the opening of the Portsmouth, Kittery & York Street Railway in 1897. The building was an active operating center until trolley service in Kittery and Kittery Point ended; it was then razed. As early as 1909 fears were expressed that the wood-frame structure would be blown down in any severe windstorm but such a calamity did not occur. An attempt to burn the building on August 16, 1908, did not succeed, either.

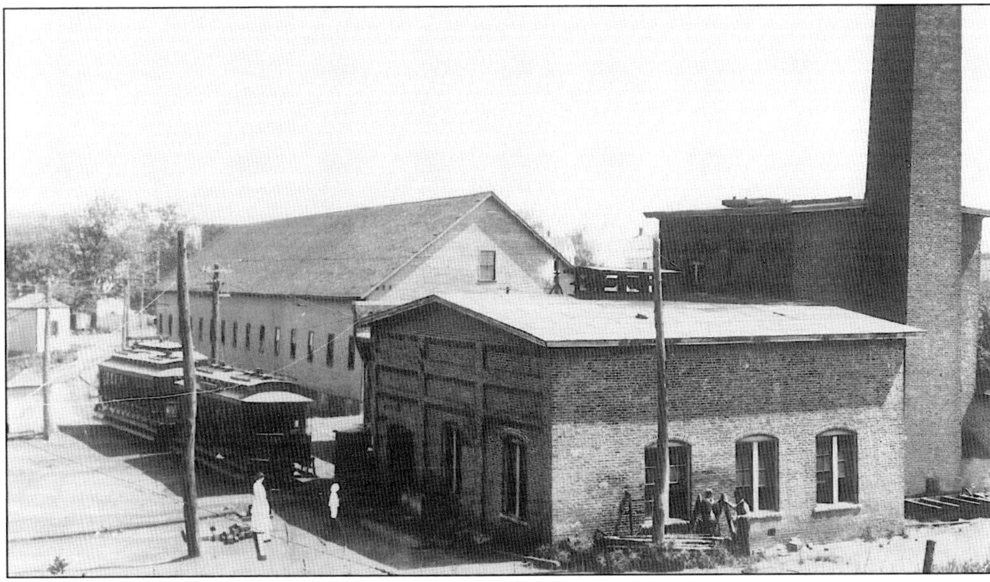

The Kittery Point power station of the Portsmouth, Kittery & York was situated directly behind the carhouse. Coal for the boilers was hauled from Cutts Wharf near the Kittery Point bridge. Original equipment of the plant in 1897 included three boilers, two engines, and two generators; two more boilers, another engine, and a third generator were added in 1900. The by-then-obsolete station was placed on reserve status in 1918 after arrangements were made to purchase power from the Rockingham County Light & Power Company of Portsmouth.

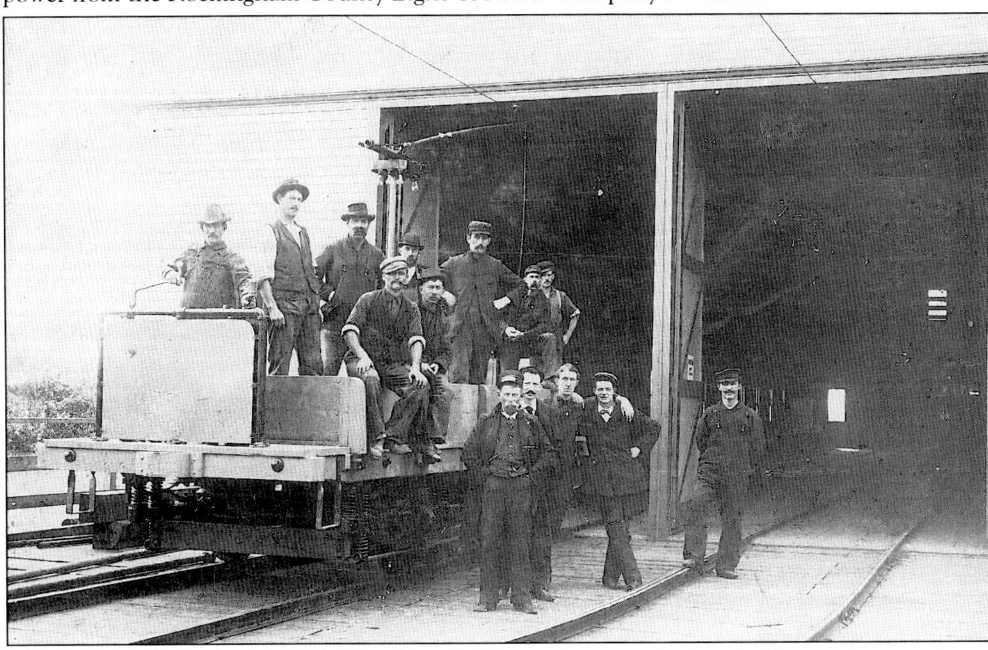

Work car "B" of the Portsmouth, Kittery & York was photographed at the Kittery Point carhouse c. 1897. It's believed to have been sold or scrapped about 1904 after being replaced by "E," a double-truck motor, flat car. The underframe of the latter collapsed under an excessively heavy load a few years later and eventually the trucks and electrical equipment were installed on another car.

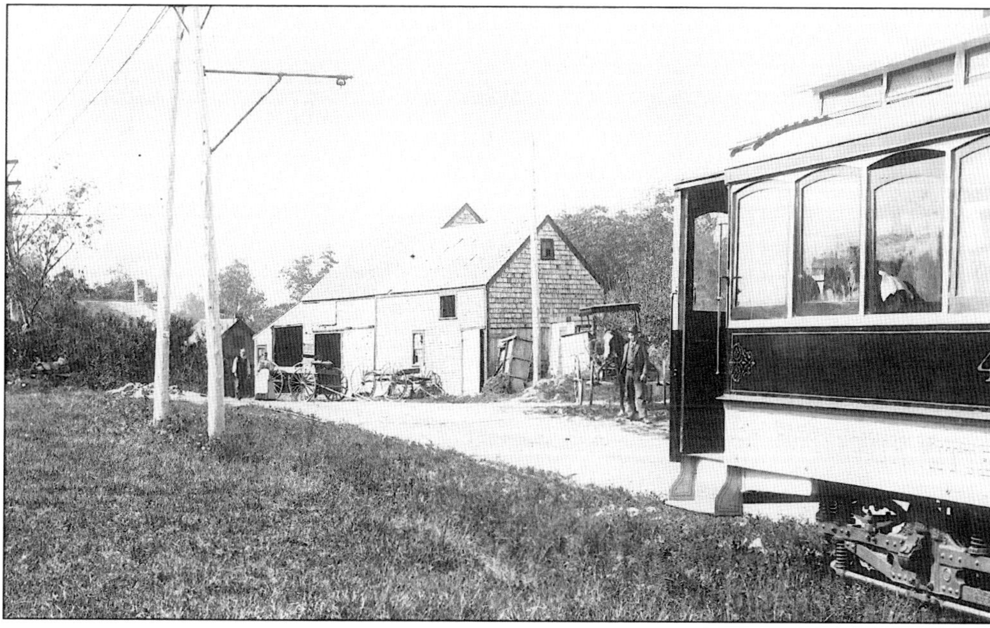

This closed trolley was brand new when it was photographed on Chauncey Creek Road, near Tenny Hill Road, Kittery Point, in 1897. Numerous identical cars were built by the Briggs Carriage Company for other New England street railways in the late 1890s, and while many had side seats, others had a combination of reversible transverse and longitudinal corner seats. The seating capacity was 28.

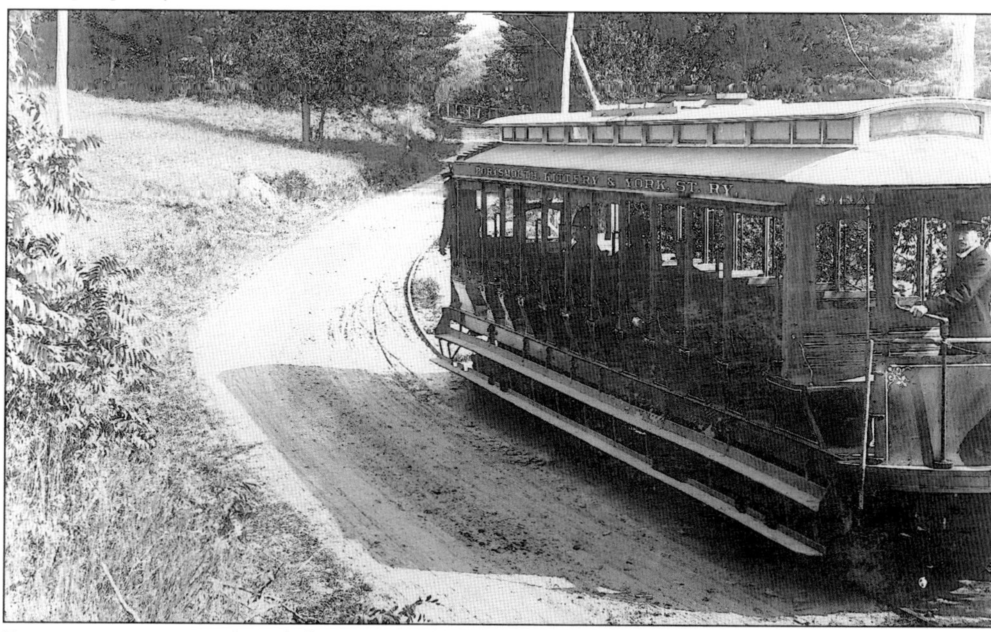

Few passengers were aboard this open trolley on Chauncey Creek Road in 1897. At the time it had only hand brakes, which were applied by turning a brass "gooseneck" handle. All "breezers" of the Portsmouth, Kittery & York Street Railway carried two-man crews, a motorman and a conductor, with the latter being in overall charge in addition to being responsible for collecting and registering cash and ticket fares.

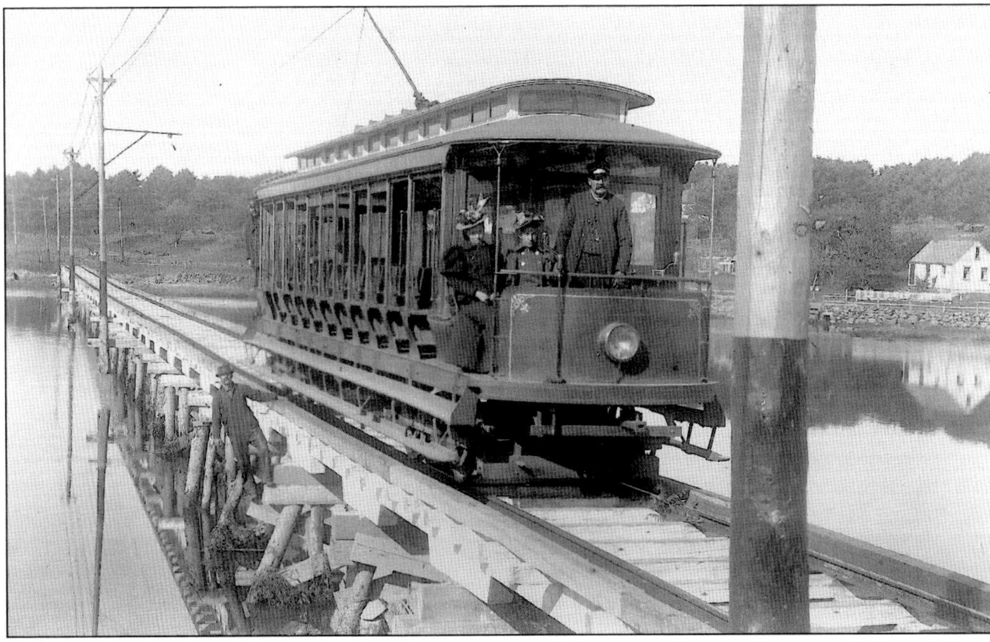

Call's Trestle, 512 feet long, crossed Chauncey Creek between Kittery Point and Cutts Island. When first placed in service, the Portsmouth, Kittery & York's 14-bench opens carried no numbers, these not being applied until 1898. Sea Point Beach on Cutts Island was a popular destination for PK&Y passengers in summer and while there appear to have been no public facilities, a refreshment stand served those who did not bring picnic lunches.

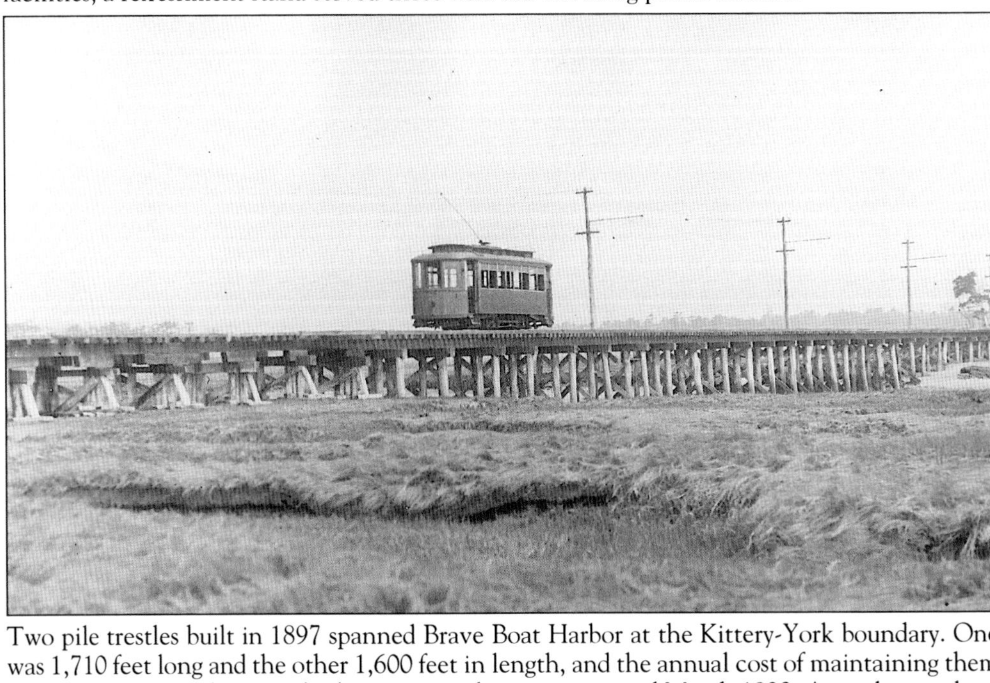

Two pile trestles built in 1897 spanned Brave Boat Harbor at the Kittery-York boundary. One was 1,710 feet long and the other 1,600 feet in length, and the annual cost of maintaining them was substantial. Both were rebuilt in 1914 and were in use until March 1923. A similar trestle to the west of the harbor was built by the York Harbor & Beach Railroad in 1887 and until recent years piles of all three still were visible.

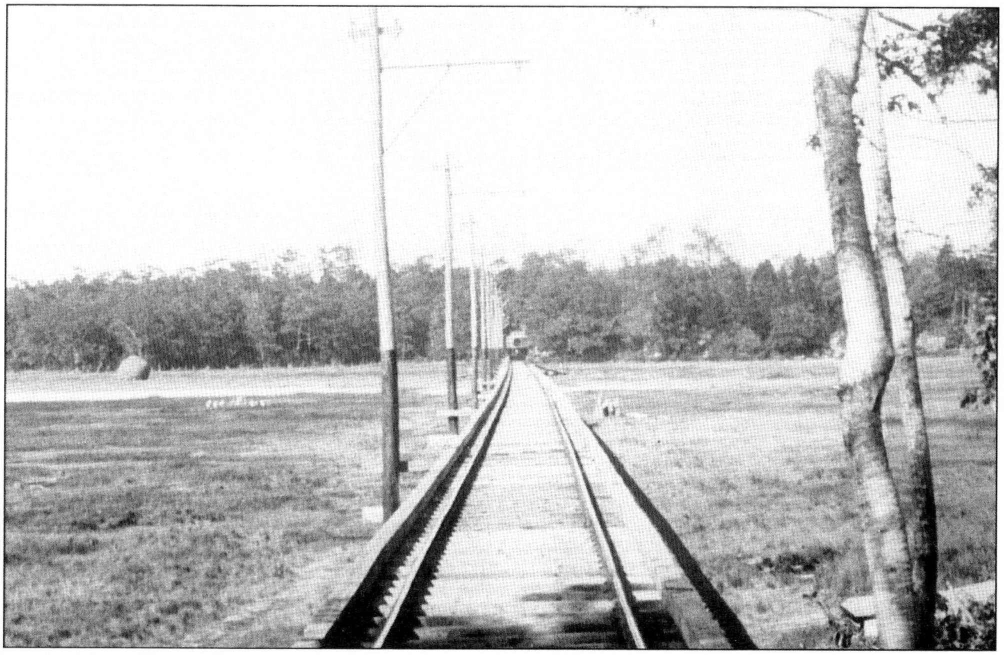

A closed trolley can be seen in the distance in this 1897 view of the southerly trestle across Brave Boat Harbor, which sometimes froze over whenever the winter weather was bitterly cold. Altogether, 10 pile trestles were constructed by the Portsmouth, Kittery & York Street Railway in 1897 and identified as the builder of many of them was George E. Macomber of Augusta.

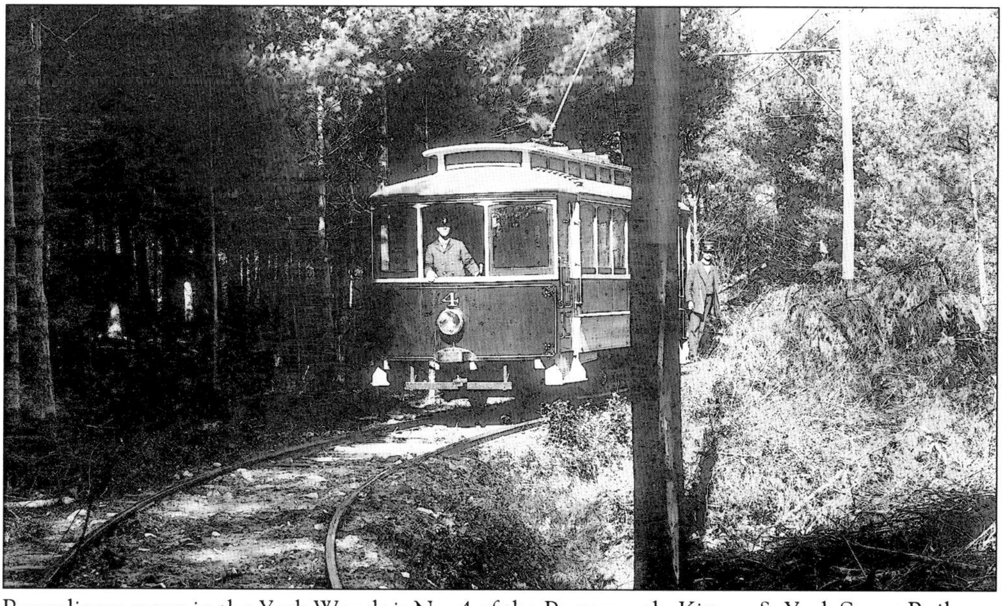

Rounding a curve in the York Woods is No. 4 of the Portsmouth, Kittery & York Street Railway. Few stops ever were made in this area because of the sparse and scattered population but some of the dwellings had children who had to be carried to and from York Village schools Monday through Friday from early September until mid-June. Special reduced-rate tickets were available for the youngsters, who had to arise at the crack of dawn and did not get home until late in the afternoon in winter because of the trolley schedule.

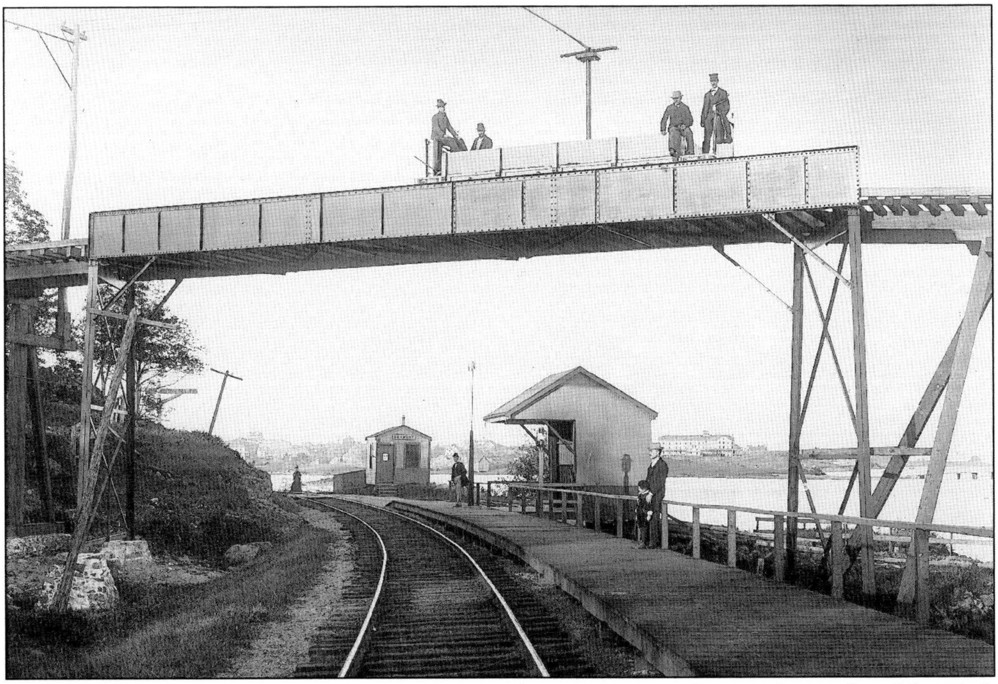

This 215-foot steel viaduct carried the Portsmouth, Kittery & York over the tracks of the York Harbor & Beach Railroad (YH&B) at Seabury in York. Flat car "B" is crossing the structure in 1897. Below are the YH&B waiting shelter and so-called station. Some year after the YH&B was abandoned, its former roadbed in York was taken over by the state for highway purposes and is now part of Route 103.

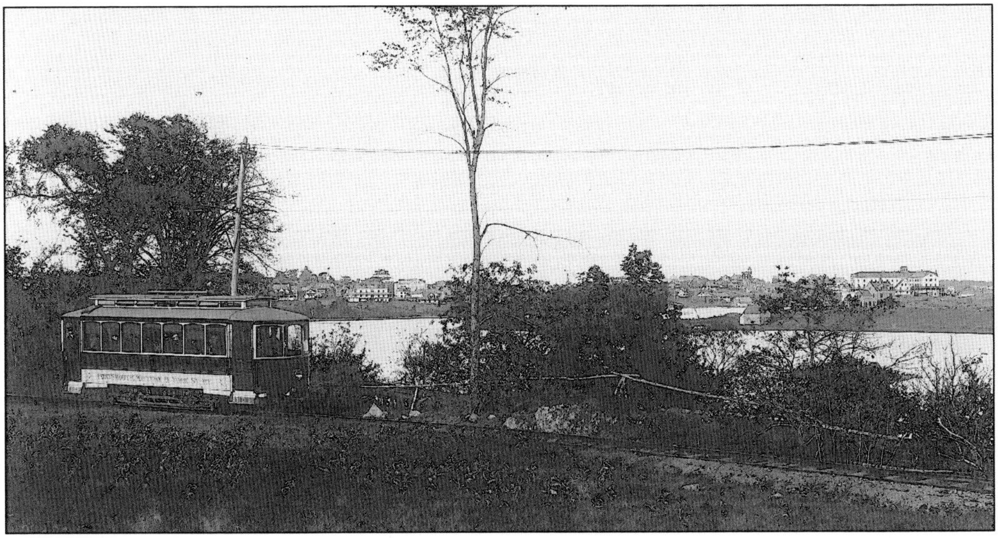

PK&Y No. 4 on the private right of way extending from Seabury to Sewall's bridge in York. The York River is in the background as also are several York Harbor hotels. While half-hourly service was maintained between Portsmouth and York Beach by open cars in summer, cars run every 90 minutes or two-hourly in other seasons when closed cars like this carried the people. The running time between Badger's Island and York Beach Square, 15.4 miles, was 1hour 25 minutes.

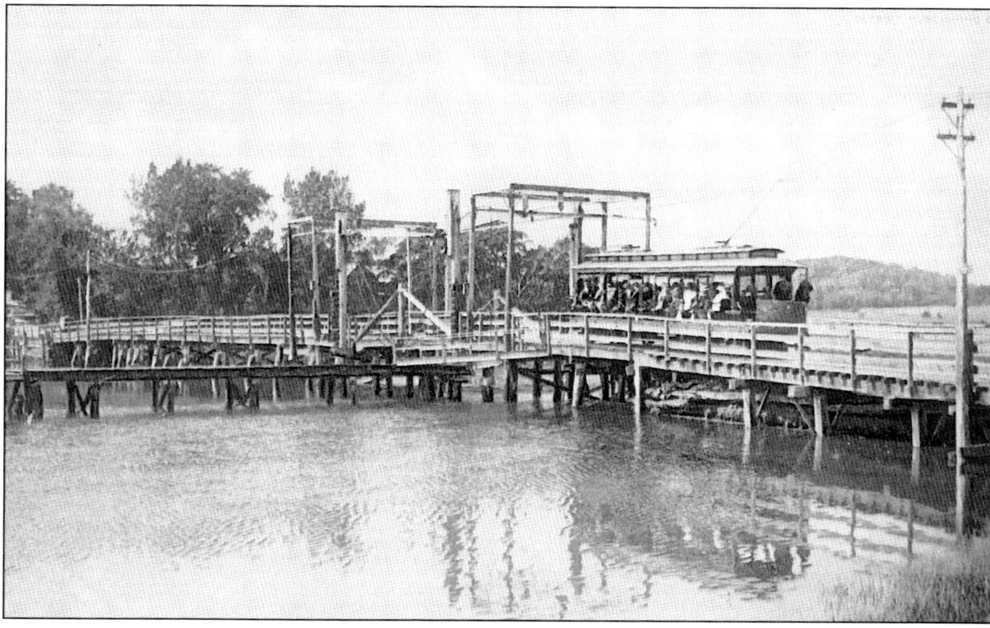

Sewall's bridge across the York River had to be strengthened extensively and widened before the Portsmouth, Kittery & York Street Railway could lay rails on the 150-foot structure in 1897. This was the first pile drawbridge in America when it was opened in 1761 and it carried trolley cars for more than a quarter century.

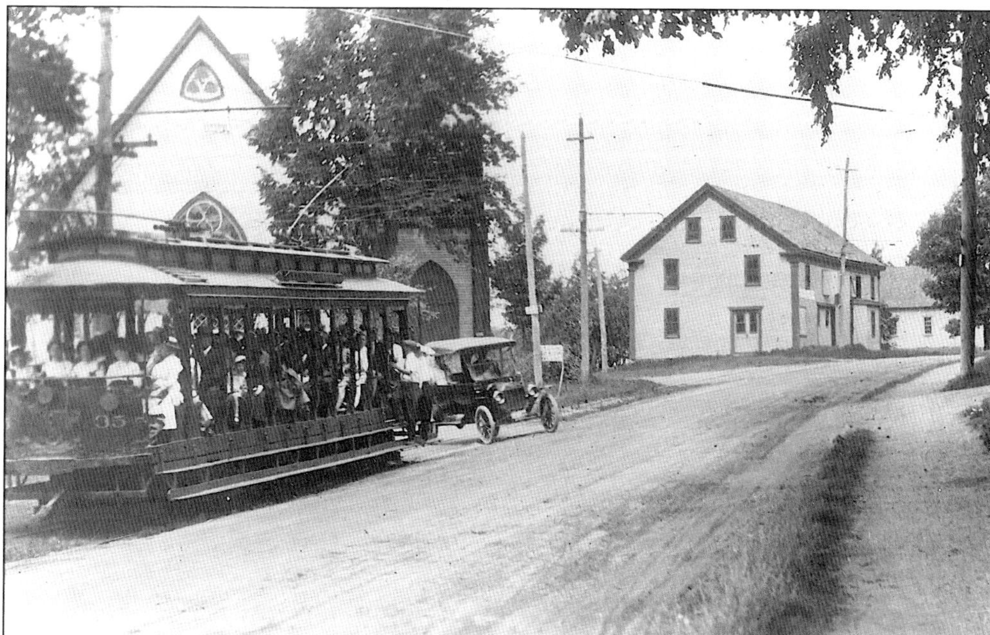

An Atlantic Shore 13-bench open car, seating 65 passengers, at York Corner Junction near York Village about 1914. The trolley lines from Badger's Island and from Dover connected at this point, where a small wood frame building, which still exists as a dwelling, housed a waiting room and a power substation. In the right background is the present York Street Baptist Church.

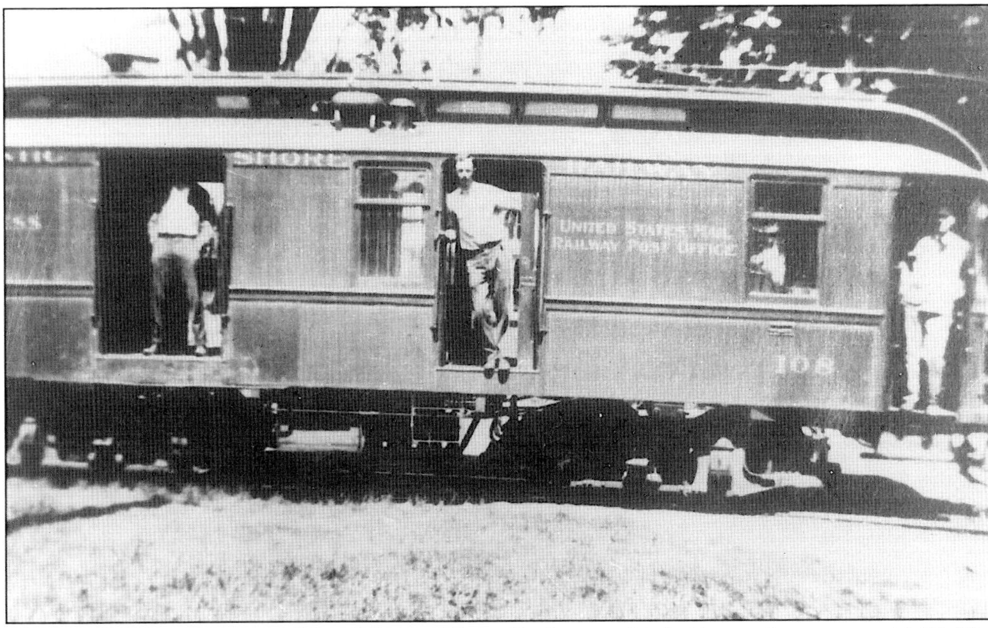

Mail and Express Car 108 of the Atlantic Shore Railway at York Corner Junction c. 1915. The York Beach & Portsmouth RPO schedule for many years called for four round trips daily except Sunday during the summer and two round trips in other seasons. A clerk of the Railway Mail Service handled the postal matter and the mail compartment had slots on each side for the posting of letters by those living along the trolley line.

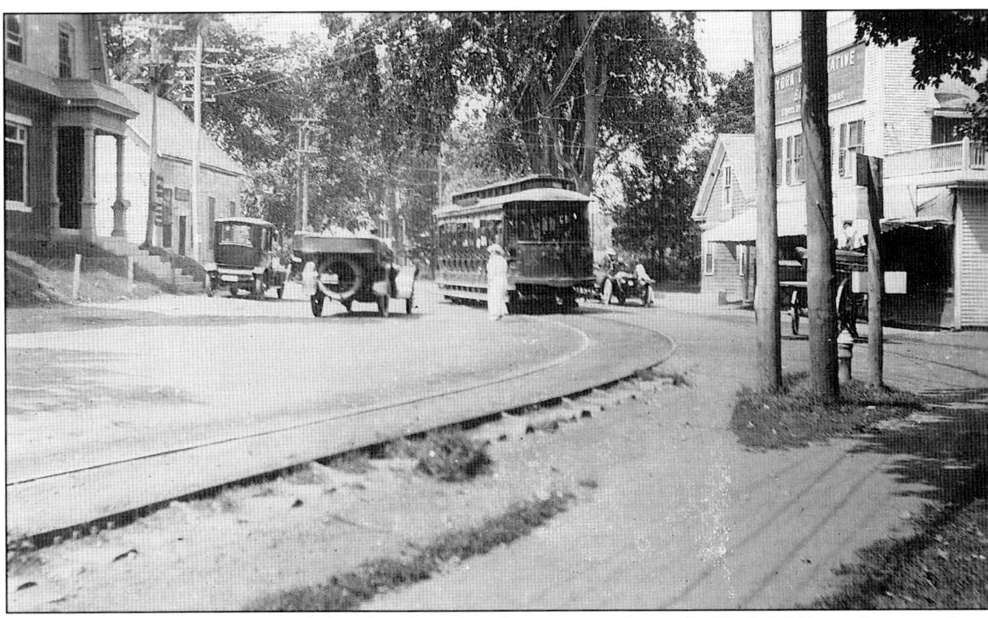

An open car, No. 25, bound for the ferry landing passes through York Village Square about 1917. It was about 10 miles from the square to Badger's Island and the running time was a little more than one hour. Only a few automobiles are in sight in this view taken by the late Myron Cox, who owned and operated the Cox Store in the square for many years.

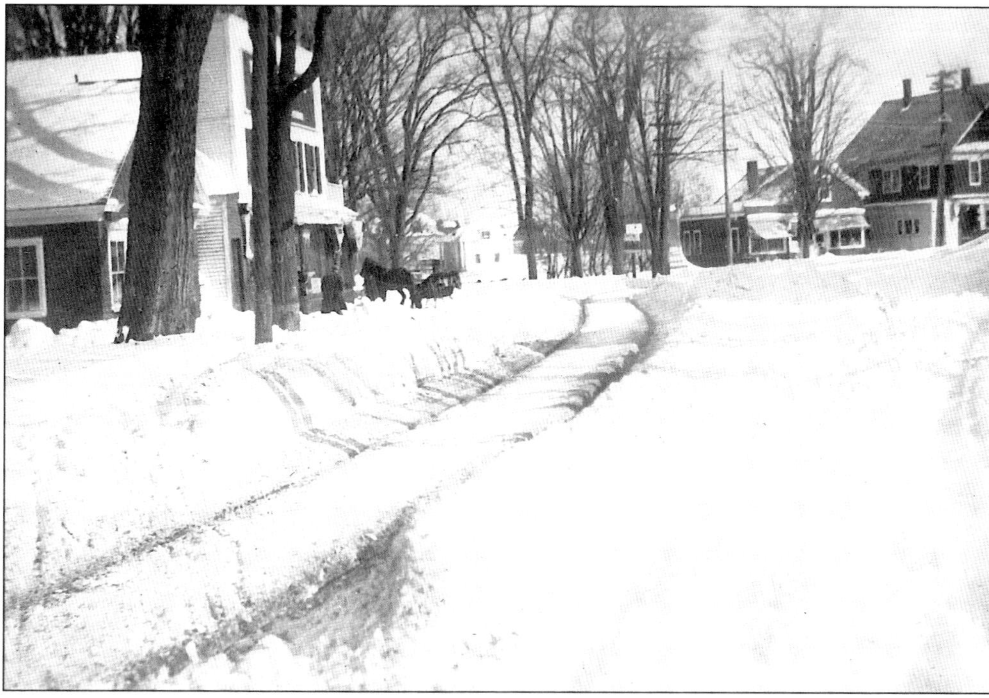

Only the trolley tracks in York Village Square were open after a winter snowstorm about 1906. York Street through the square had not been cleared and only horse-drawn sleighs and sleds could move through the great white cold. Some communities used huge horse-drawn rollers to pack the snow and improve sleighing conditions in the pre-automobile era but whether York did so is not known.

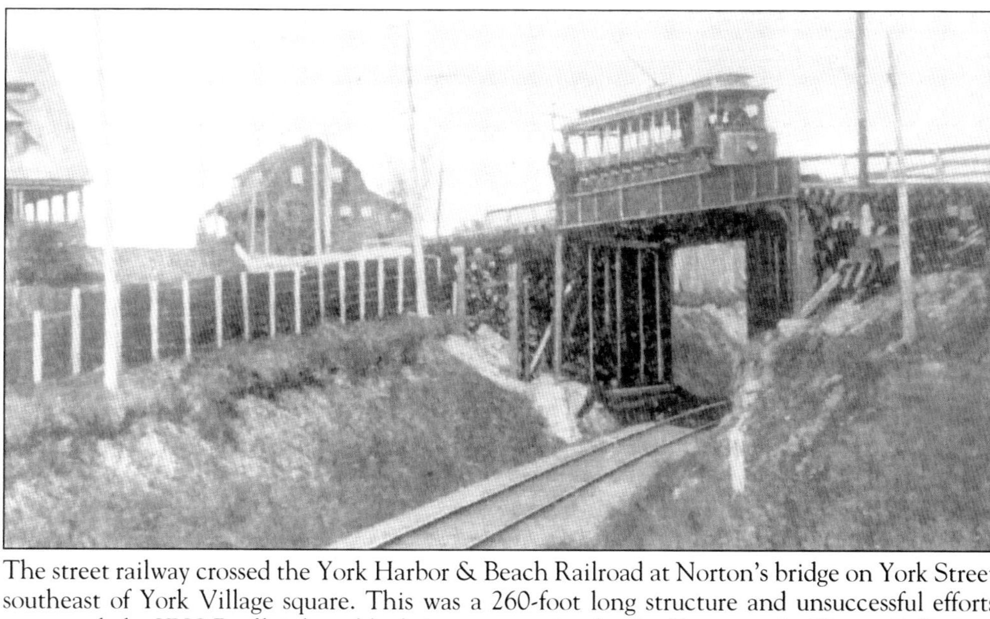

The street railway crossed the York Harbor & Beach Railroad at Norton's bridge on York Street southeast of York Village square. This was a 260-foot long structure and unsuccessful efforts were made by YH&B officials to block its construction by the Portsmouth, Kittery & York in 1897. Both the railroad and the bridge are long gone and there's no evidence today that either existed.

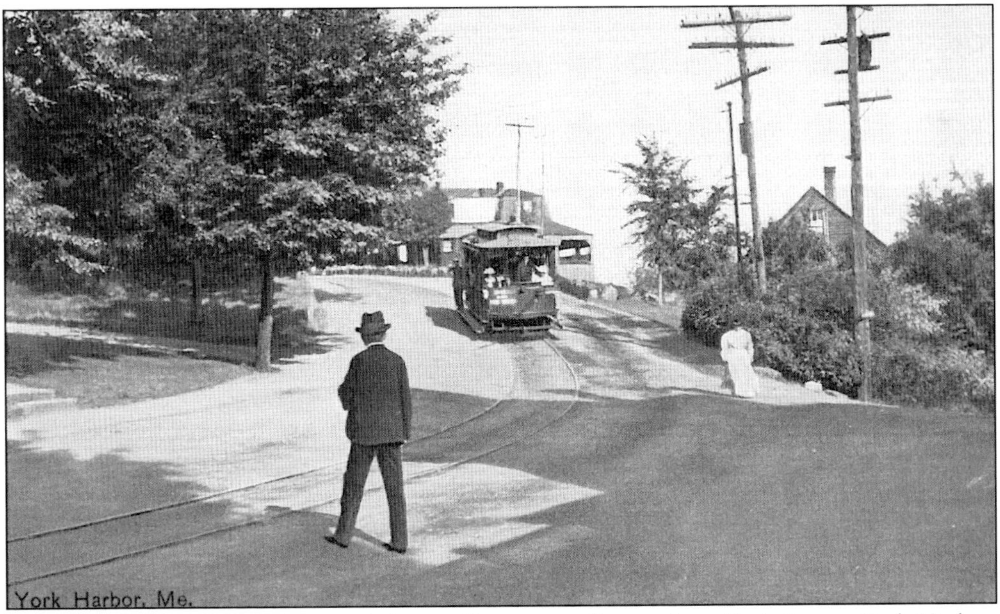

Returning from York Beach is an Atlantic Shore open "breezer" on York Street, York Harbor. Residents of the harbor strongly opposed the building of the Portsmouth, Kittery & York through the area in 1897 but their bid for an injunction was rejected by the York County Court. They charged that "cars of great width, size and cumbersome" were to be operated by the street railway and asserted that its construction "would utterly change and destroy the character of York Harbor as a place of quiet summer resort and retreat from the hustle and bustle of city life."

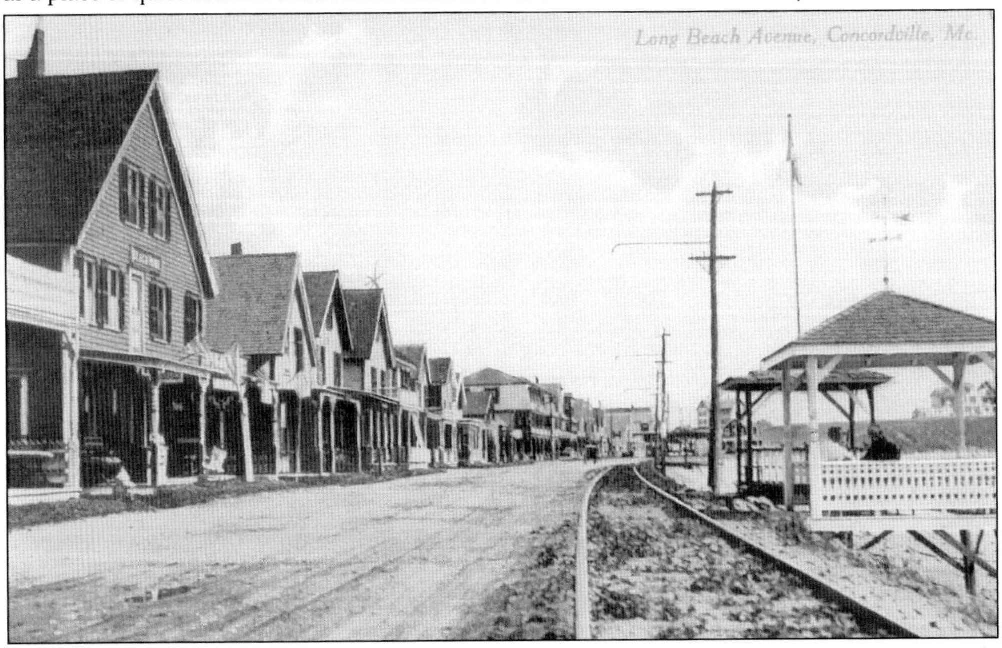

The trolley line ran along the east side of Long Beach Avenue at York Beach, the trackside shelters being provided by proprietors of hotels on the west side of the avenue for the convenience of their guests waiting to board a streetcar. Coastal storms sometimes extensively damaged or destroyed the shelters, which were quickly repaired or rebuilt.

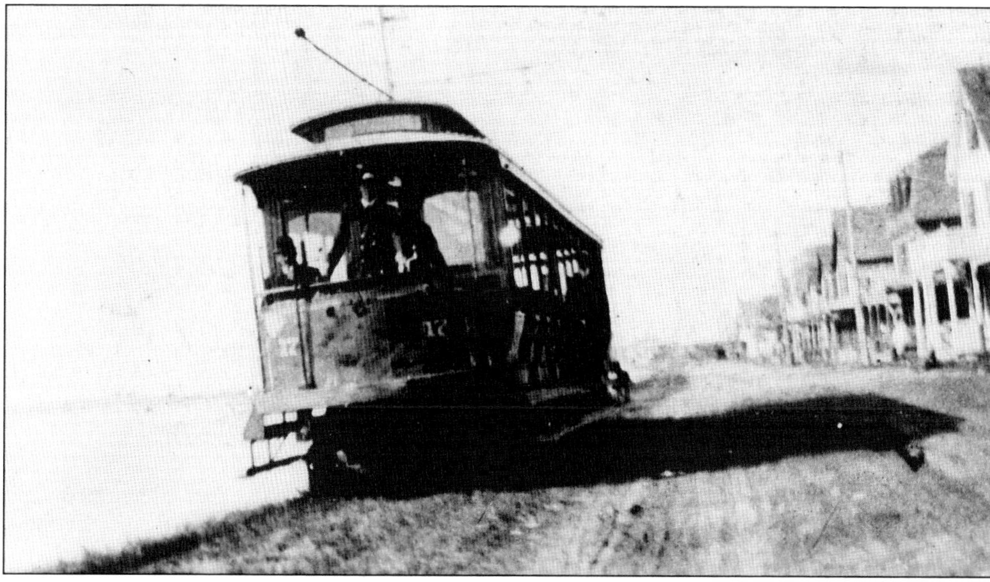

Open Car 35 runs along Long Beach Avenue on its way to York Beach Square during the summer of 1922. Coastal storms and high tides sometimes washed out trolley tracks at Long Sands and caused suspension of service for a few hours or even several days, and every spring crews leveled and aligned the rails, replaced worn ties and applied gravel ballast when necessary so everything would be ready for the heavy summer traffic.

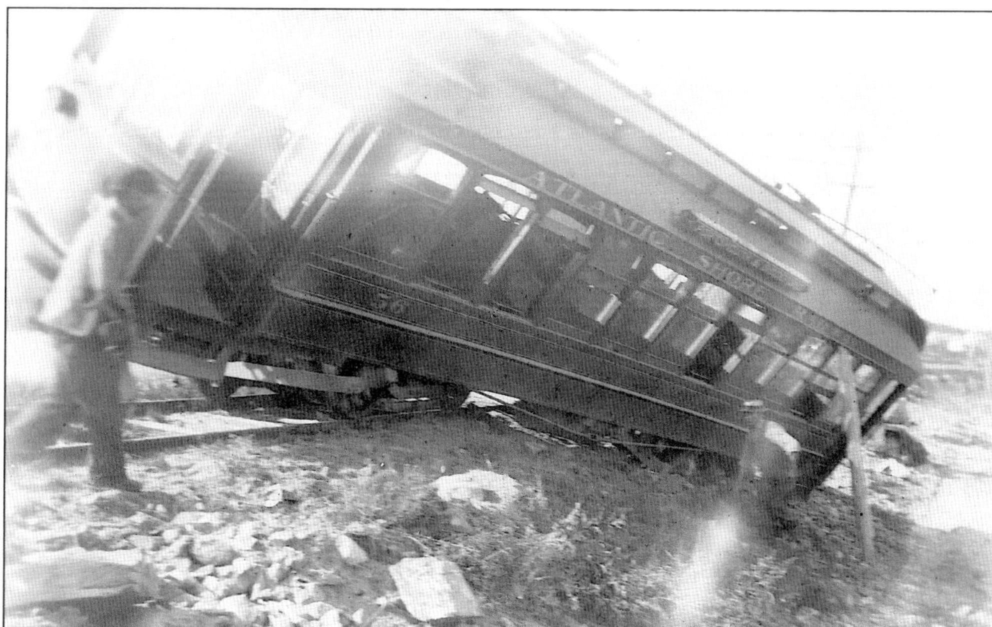

Ten passengers escaped serious injury when Atlantic Shore Railway car 56 derailed on Long Beach Avenue on Sept. 18, 1915. A broken rail was the cause of the mishap. A lot of blocking and numerous jacks had to be assembled before the car could be rerailed and once this was accomplished, No. 56 was towed to the Kittery Point carhouse for repairs. The car continued in service on the Atlantic Shore Railway and the successor York Utilities Company for many years after 1915.

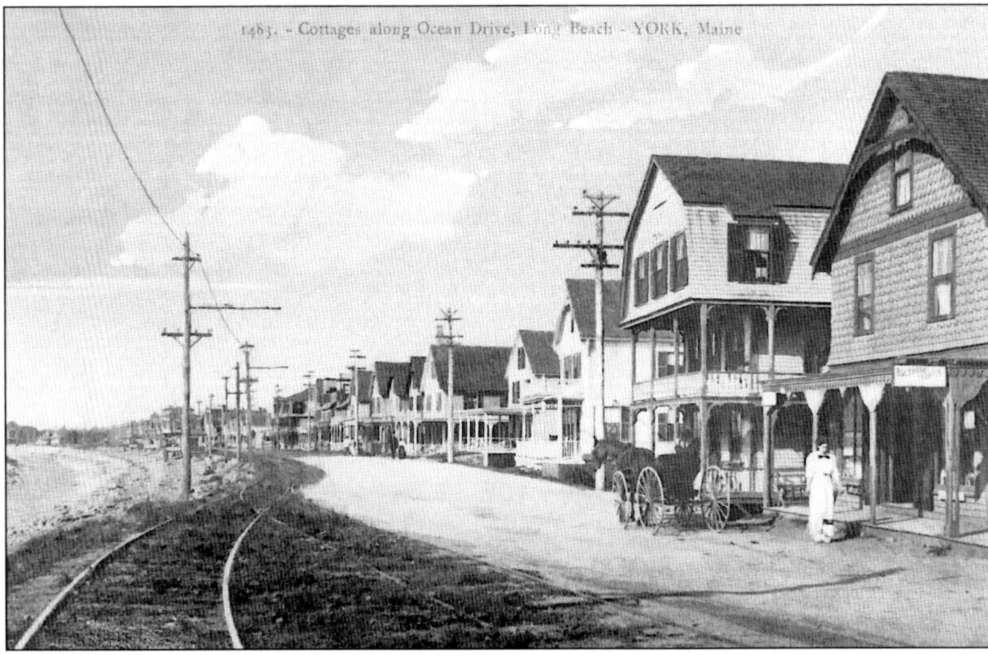

Breakers turnout, a regular meeting point for trolleys at York Beach, was situated at the north end of Long Beach Avenue near its intersection with Nubble Road. The turnout was named after The Breakers cottage nearby and from this point it was a long walk to the Cape Neddick Nubble and its famous lighthouse, erected in 1879.

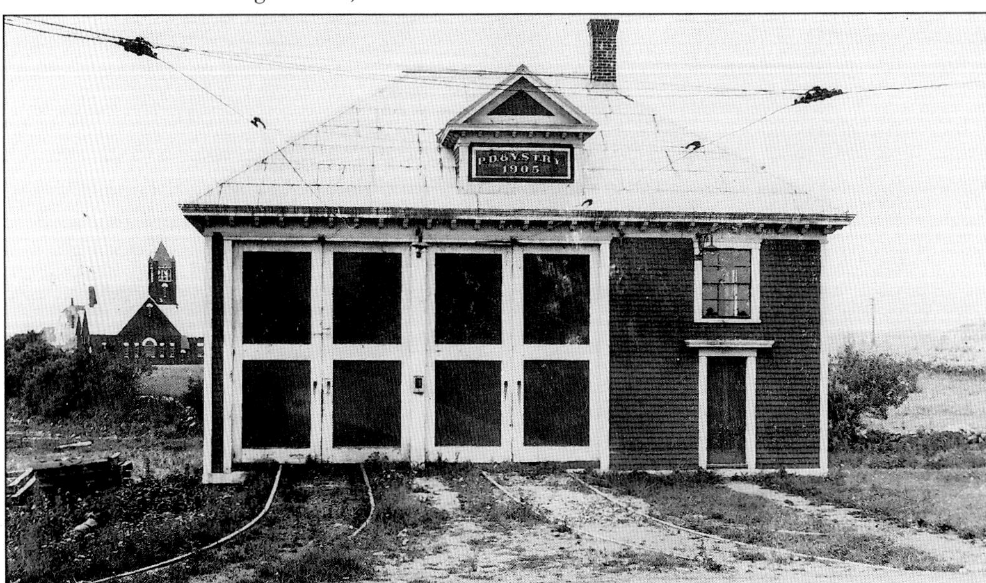

After the original York Beach carhouse was destroyed by fire in 1904, a replacement was erected by the Portsmouth, Dover & York Street Railway in 1905 on the same site on the west side of Long Beach Avenue between Nubble Road and Church Street. There were two tracks inside the building, which also housed a 220-cell storage battery required to ensure adequate voltage at the resort. After trolley service ended in 1923, the building was sold and eventually became the York Beach Casino, a popular dance hall, which was destroyed by fire on May 6, 1976.

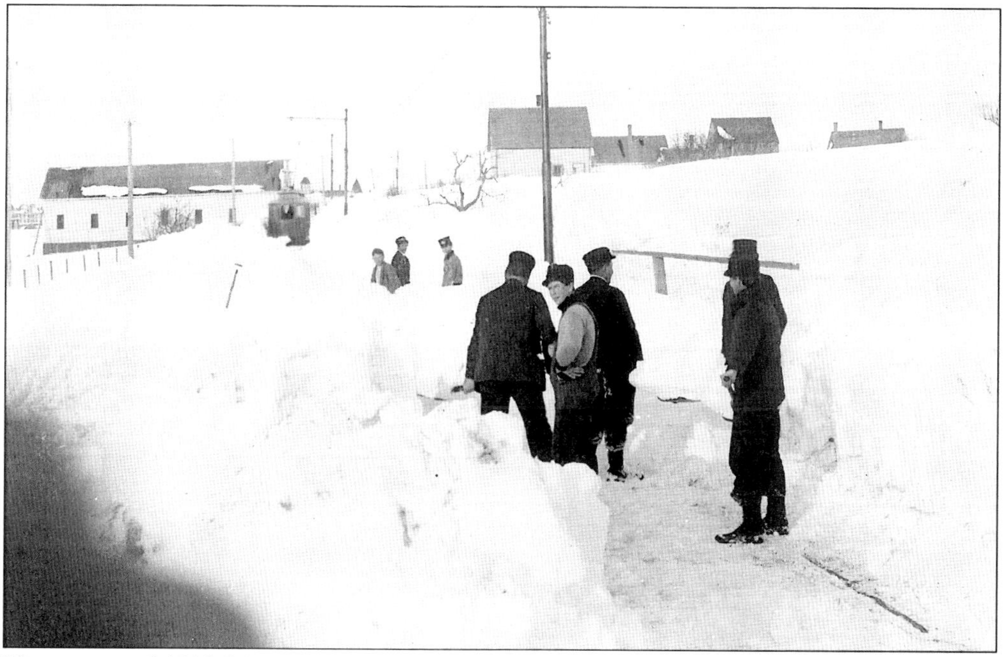

The winter of 1903-04 was a severe one, and at times the snow was so deep that the street railway's plows simply could not clear the tracks. Shovelers had to be hired by the Portsmouth, Dover & York and some of them are shown at work on Long Beach Avenue near the carhouse. Probably the closed car in the distance was used to give the men a place to warm up occasionally as they dug through the drifts.

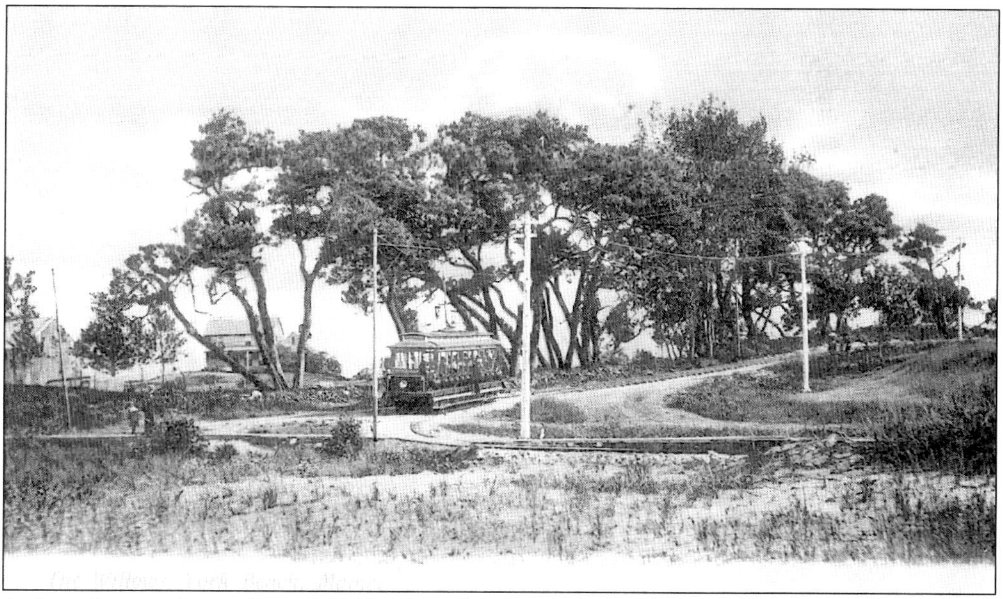

A short distance beyond the York Beach car barn was The Willows at the base of Cape Neddick. Here the trolleys turned onto the present Ocean Avenue and passed the Ocean House and the Rockaway Hotel before arriving at The Goldenrod in York Beach Square. Established in 1896 by E.A. Talpey, who served as Portsmouth, Kittery & York ticket agent for a time, The Goldenrod is still in business as a restaurant and confectionery store.

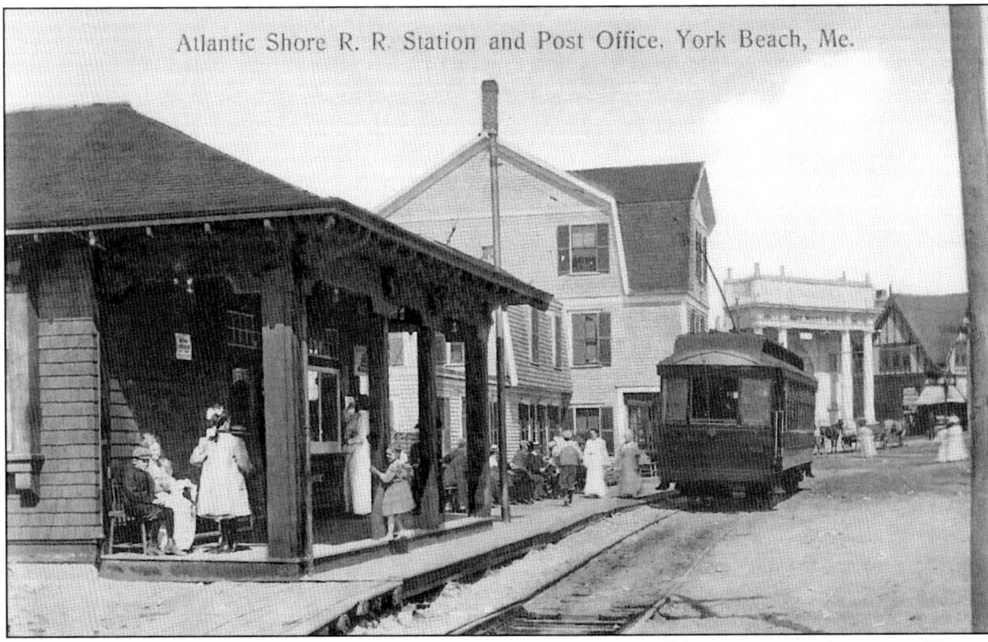

The Atlantic Shore waiting station at York Beach was situated for a time in the post office at the rear of The Goldenrod. The closed car, No. 62, was purchased by the Atlantic Shore Line Railway in 1909 and had 20 cross and 3 longitudinal corner seats accommodating 46 passengers. A Baker hot water heater and coal bin occupied the fourth corner. Possibly the car continued on from York Beach to Ogunquit, Wells, and Kennebunk.

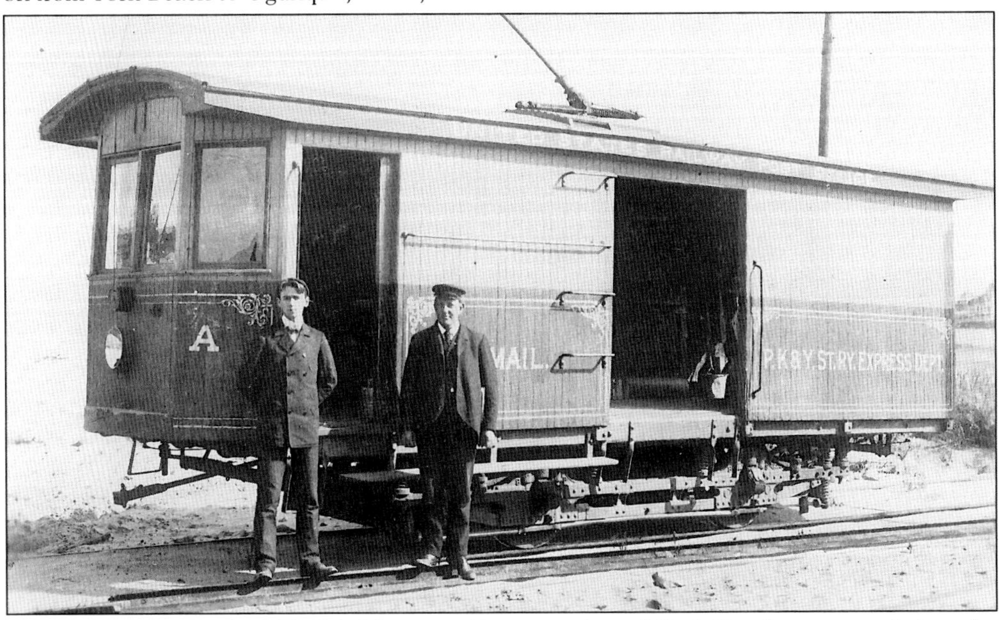

A contract to carry the U.S. Mail between Portsmouth and York Beach was awarded to the Portsmouth, Kittery & York Street Railway in April 1898 and Car A was acquired to maintain the schedule of the York Beach & Portsmouth RPO. It had two compartments, one eight feet long for mail and one ten feet long for baggage and express. "A", which is shown at York Beach about 1899, was retired in mid-1904 and replaced by a double truck car early in 1905.

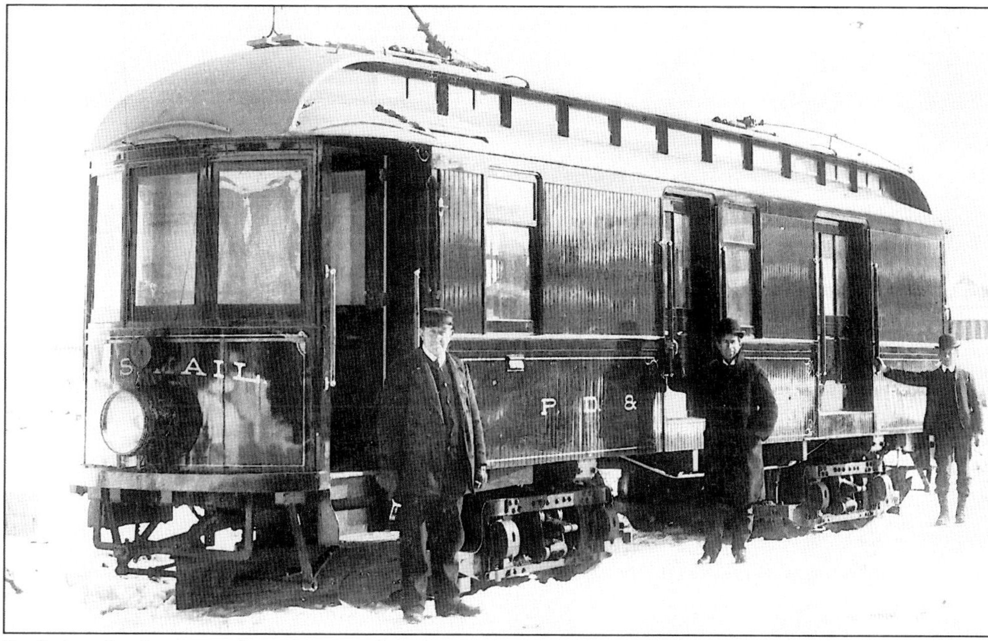

Built by the Laconia (New Hampshire) Car Company Works for the Portsmouth, Dover & York Street Railway this double truck mail and express car, which replaced "A", is at York Beach in 1905. The car subsequently became No. 108 of the Atlantic Shore Line Railway. Its mail compartment was 15 feet long inside and postal equipment included a bag rack, a slotted shelf above, sorting cases and a work table. Regular stops were made at the Kittery Foreside, Kittery Point, York Village, and York Harbor post offices, and that at York Corner was also served.

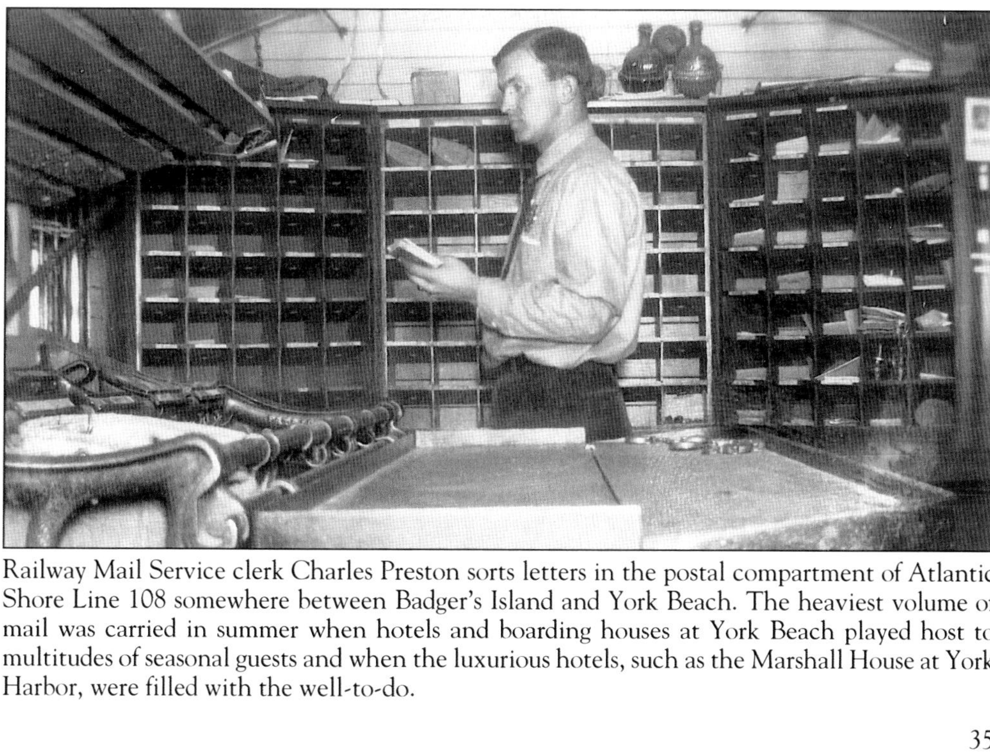

Railway Mail Service clerk Charles Preston sorts letters in the postal compartment of Atlantic Shore Line 108 somewhere between Badger's Island and York Beach. The heaviest volume of mail was carried in summer when hotels and boarding houses at York Beach played host to multitudes of seasonal guests and when the luxurious hotels, such as the Marshall House at York Harbor, were filled with the well-to-do.

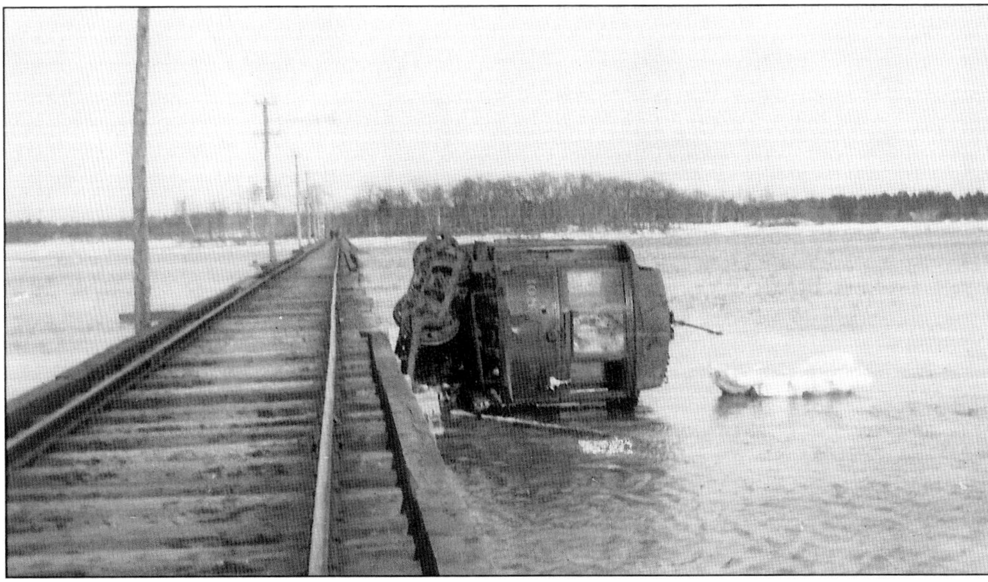

Mail Car 108 toppled off the longer of the Brave Boat harbor trestles on January 12, 1918 after the track on the span was thrown out of line by a large cake of ice. Two days later, operation of the York Beach & Portsmouth RPO was taken over by the York Harbor & Beach Railroad. After the car was righted, it was towed over a temporary track to Cutts Island and thence to the Kittery Point carhouse. About a year later, it was converted to a line car and was used as such until 1923. It was sold in 1925 to the York Utilities Company, which attached knuckle couplers to No. 108 so it could double in brass as a locomotive if necessary.

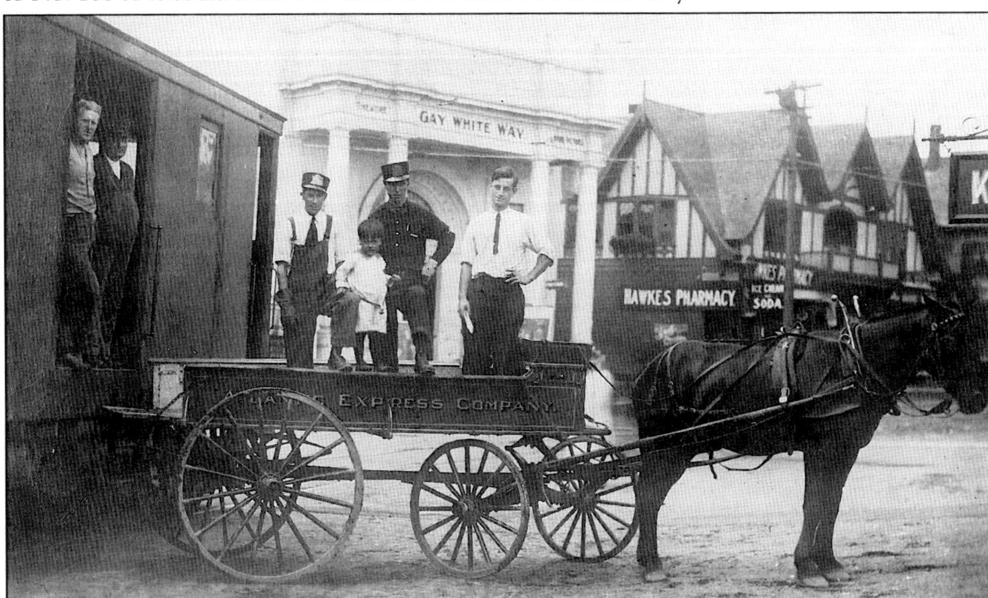

The Atlantic Express Company maintained express service over the Atlantic Shore Railway system for a number of years after 1912. Here merchandise is being transferred at York Beach Square to an express company delivery wagon. In the background is the Gay White Way, opened about 1910 by one Frank Ellis and featuring a dance hall and other attractions. A York Beach landmark for many years, it was torched by an arsonist on March 21, 1951.

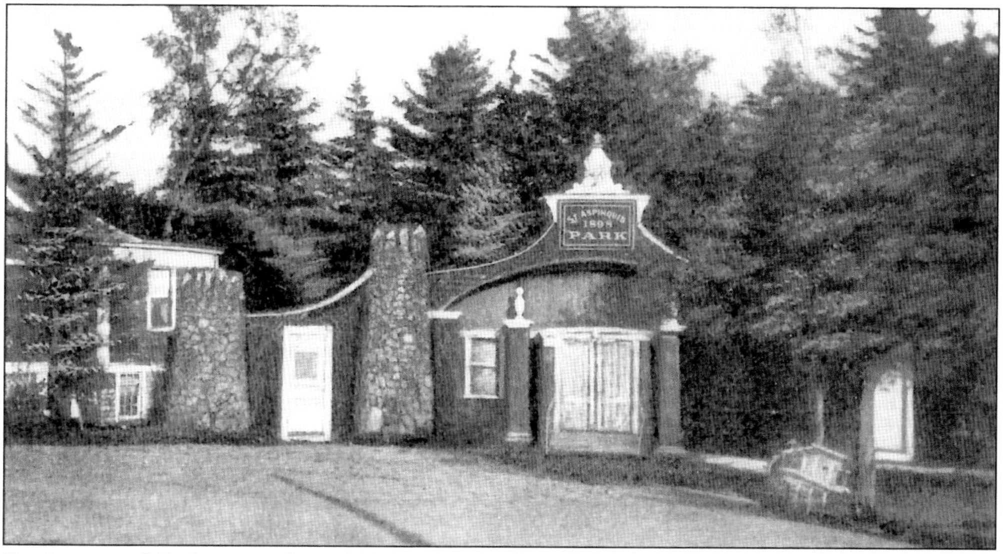

St. Aspinquid Park, opened in 1898, was situated on the east side of Main Street, York Beach, about a half mile north of The Goldenrod. Trolleys began running to the resort on June 28, 1900 and continued to do so every summer for the next three years. Created by Henry E. Evans, the park covered about 14 acres of woodland, and among its attractions were a tea house, a large casino complete with dance hall and a large stage, a cafeteria, and a small menagerie. The casino was moved to York Beach Square in 1909 to become the nucleus of the Gay White Way.

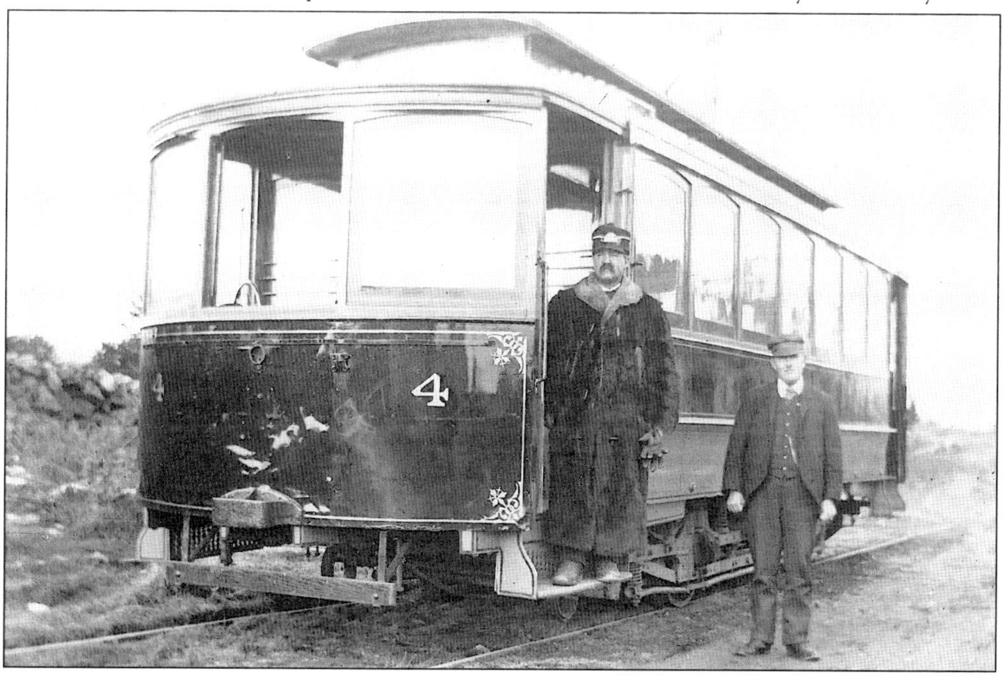

The crew of Portsmouth, Kittery & York No. 4 poses for the photographer outside St. Aspinquid Park about 1903. Cars ran regularly to the park only in summer but occasional trips were made in other seasons. The motorman and conductor are unidentified but the former is wearing a heavy coat with fur collar while the latter is clad in the regulation uniform. While the interior of the car was heated, the vestibules, which was the domain of the motorman, were not.

Stmr. Alice Howard.

Daily Time Table. Summer, 1901.

Connecting Portsmouth, New Castle, Kittery Point, Gerrish Island and Hotels Champernowne, Pepperrell, Park Field and Pocahontas.

DOWN

Leave P. K. & Y. Landing, Portsm'th	Leave New Castle.	Leave Kittery Point*	Due at Hotel Pocahontas, Gerr. Isl'd
7.35 a. m.	8.05 a. m.		
8.30 "	8.50 "	8.55 a. m.	9.15 a. m.
10.30 "	10.50 "	10.55 "	11.15 "
12.15 p. m.	12.35 p. m.	12.40 p. m.	1.00 p. m.
3.00 "	3.20 "	3.25 "	3.45 "
†5.30 "	5.45 "	5.50 "	6.10 "

UP

L've Hotel Pocahontas, Gerrish Island	Leave Kittery Point*	Leave New Castle	Due at Portsm'th
		8.05 a. m.	8.25 a. m.
9.30 a. m.	9.45 a. m.	9.55 "	10.15 "
11.30 "	11.45 "	11.55 "	12.15 p. m.
2.15 p. m.	2.30 p. m.	2.35 p. m.	3.00 "
4.00 "	4.15 "	4.20 "	4.40 "
6.15 "	6.30 "	6.35 "	6.55 "

Tides may cause slight variations from this schedule. Subject to change and unavoidable delay.

*Tide permitting.

†Special Excursion rate 25 cents round trip.

TELEPHONE CONNECTIONS:

Ferry Landing, Portsmouth.
General Manager's Residence, Kittery.
Car House, Kittery.

OFFICIAL TIME TABLE.

PORTSMOUTH, KITTERY AND YORK STREET RAILWAY.

SUMMER ARRANGEMENT, 1901.

Subject to changes and unavoidable delays

W. G. MELOON, Gen'l Mgr.

Collection of a five-cent fare will be made between the following limits:

Portsmouth and Ferry Lane, Kittery;
Ferry Lane and Sea Point;
Sea Point and Seabury Station;
Seabury Station and York Harbor;
York Harbor and St. Aspinquid Park.

Have your Trunks and Packages sent by the P. K. & Y. Express.

SPECIAL CARS ON SHORT NOTICE

The 1901 summer timetable of the Portsmouth, Kittery & York Street Railway. During this season the *Kittery* was making the Portsmouth-Badger's Island ferry trips while the steamer *Alice Howard* was being run on the so-called River Route to New Castle, New Hampshire, Kittery Point, and Gerrish Island. Similar service was given during the summers of 1902, 1903, and 1904 but was not resumed in 1905 because of the closing of the Hotel Pocahontas on the Gerrish Island after a poor 1904 season.

Two

Eliot and South Berwick

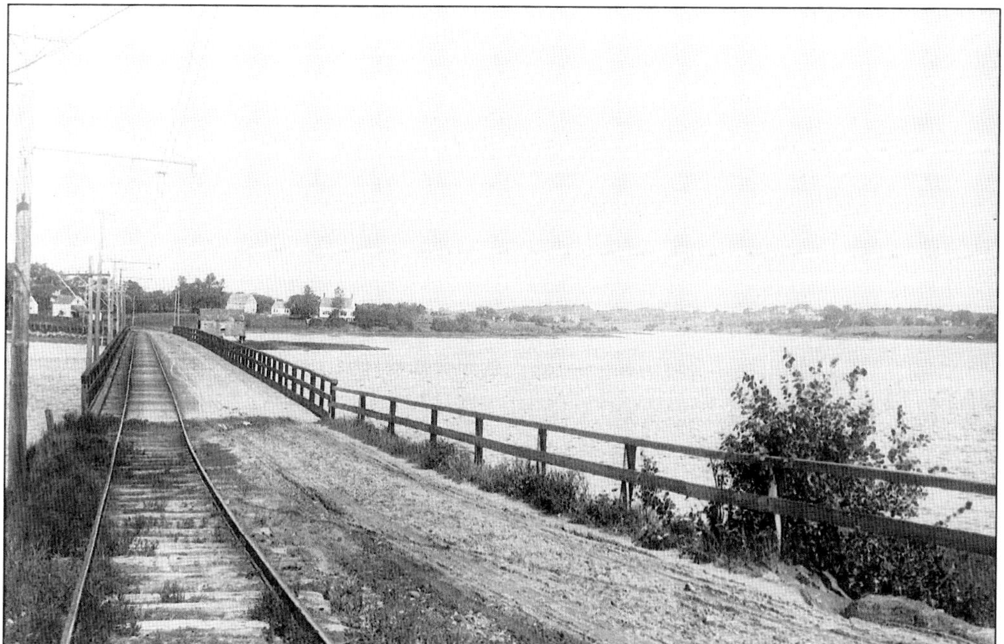

The Kittery & Eliot Street Railway was opened July 26, 1902 between Government and New March Streets, Kittery and the Green Acre Hotel in South Eliot, 3.4 miles, and crossed the Spinney Creek bridge between Kittery and Eliot Neck. The company was required to reinforce the 521-foot span before laying rails. Built by the railway itself was a 409-foot pile trestle across Weir Creek in Kittery.

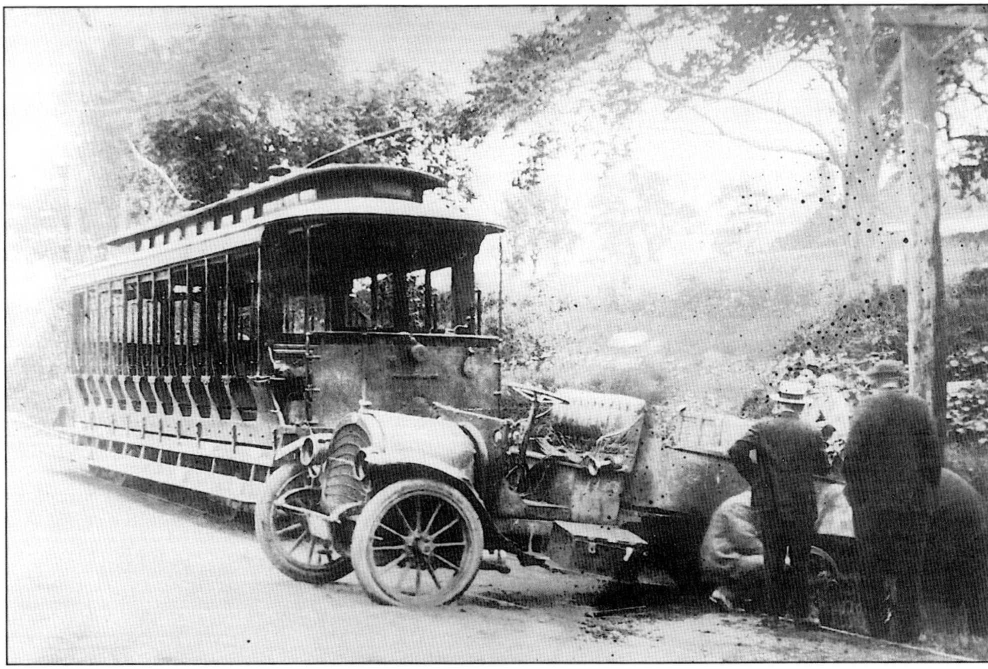

What appears to have been a trolley-truck collision at Rice's Hollow on Government Street, Kittery, in 1916. Actually, the motor vehicle skidded into the ditch before the electric car, headed for South Eliot, Eliot, and Dover, came along. There are no passengers on the trolley, and the crew is nowhere in evidence. How long the track was blocked is anybody's guess.

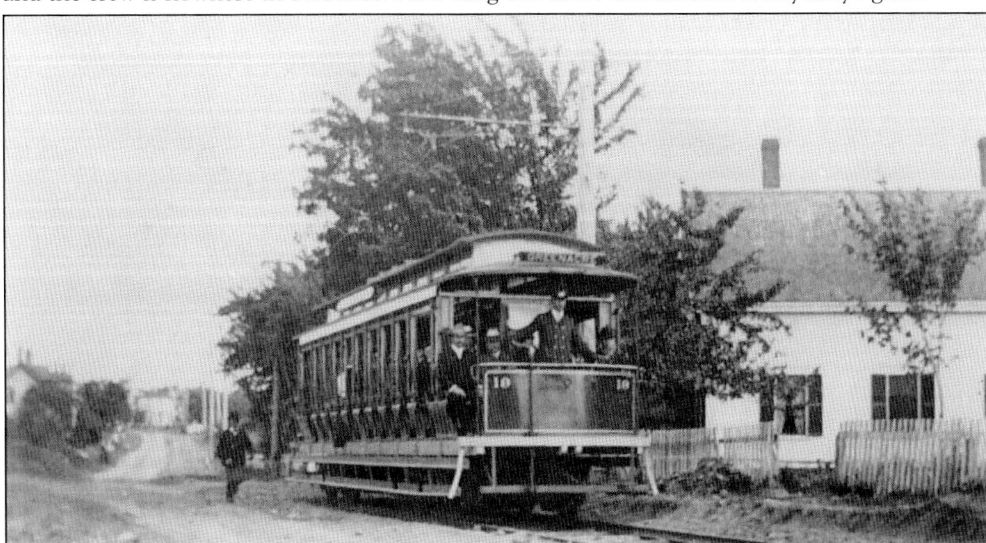

Bound for the Green Acre Hotel is 13-bench open No. 19, of the Portsmouth, Kittery & York, which provided cars, crews and power for the Kittery & Eliot (K&E) under a contract which called for the former to receive 60 percent of the K&E's revenues as compensation. The Kittery & Eliot was merged on July 1, 1903 with the Portsmouth, Dover & York Street Railway, which opened an extension from the hotel to Rosemary Junction in Eliot on July 13, 1903. Through cars were placed in operation between Badger's Island and Dover via South Eliot, Eliot, and a corner of South Berwick shortly thereafter.

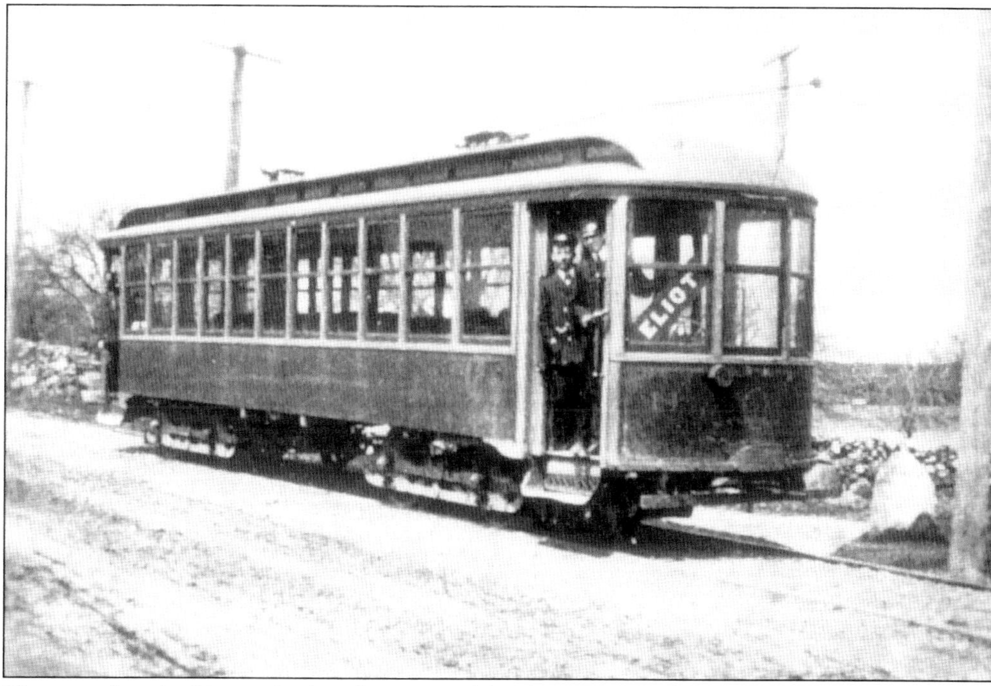

The very first double-truck closed car owned by the Portsmouth, Kittery & York was No. 14, acquired in 1900. It was photographed near Cross Street, South Eliot. It originally had only two motors and hand brakes but two more motors were added in January 1903 and by 1908 it had been equipped with General Electric air brakes. Regularly assigned to the Atlantic Shore Line's Western Division, it was destroyed in a carhouse fire on February 7, 1909.

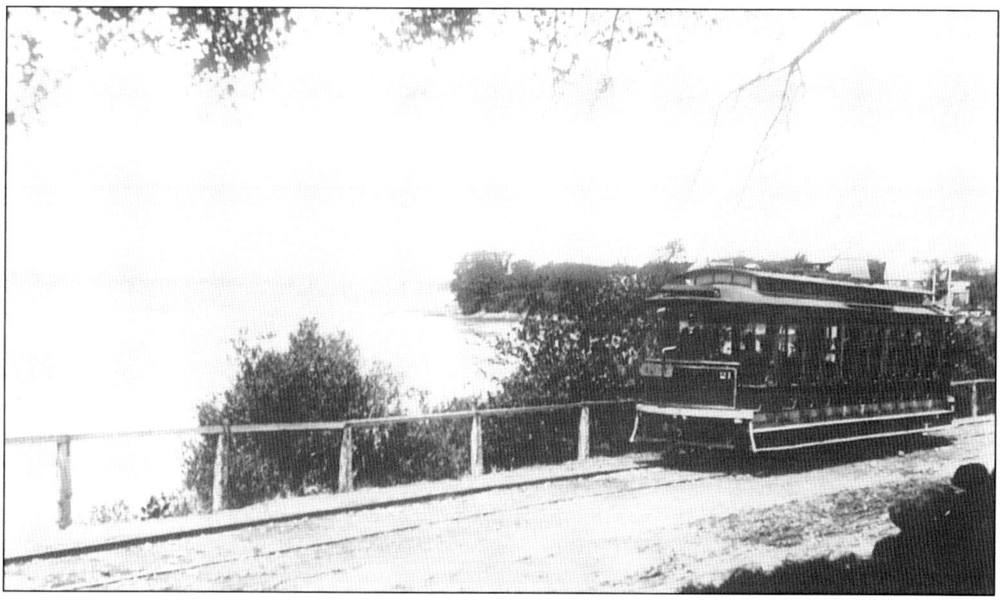

PK&Y 13-bench open 21 runs along the present Maine Route 103 in South Eliot on its way to the Green Acre Hotel about 1902. Spinney Creek is at the left. The hotel was originally known as the Sarah Farmer Inn, built in 1889, and among its early guests was the noted poet John Greenleaf Whittier. The Green Acre Baha'i School now occupies the hotel site.

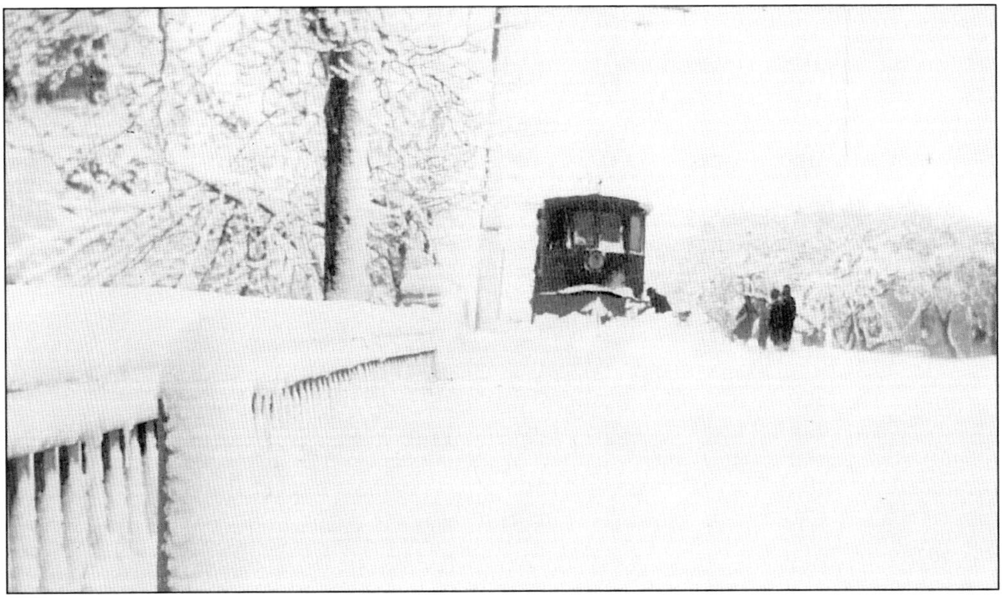

A snow plow bucks the drifts near Cross Street in South Eliot. Sometimes the drifts was so high that plows had to make two or three attempts before they could break through, and there were occasions when a passenger car had to be used as a pusher. Several men usually rode on a plow, the interior of which was warmed by a coal stove, and all except the motorman used shovels to clear switches at turnouts .

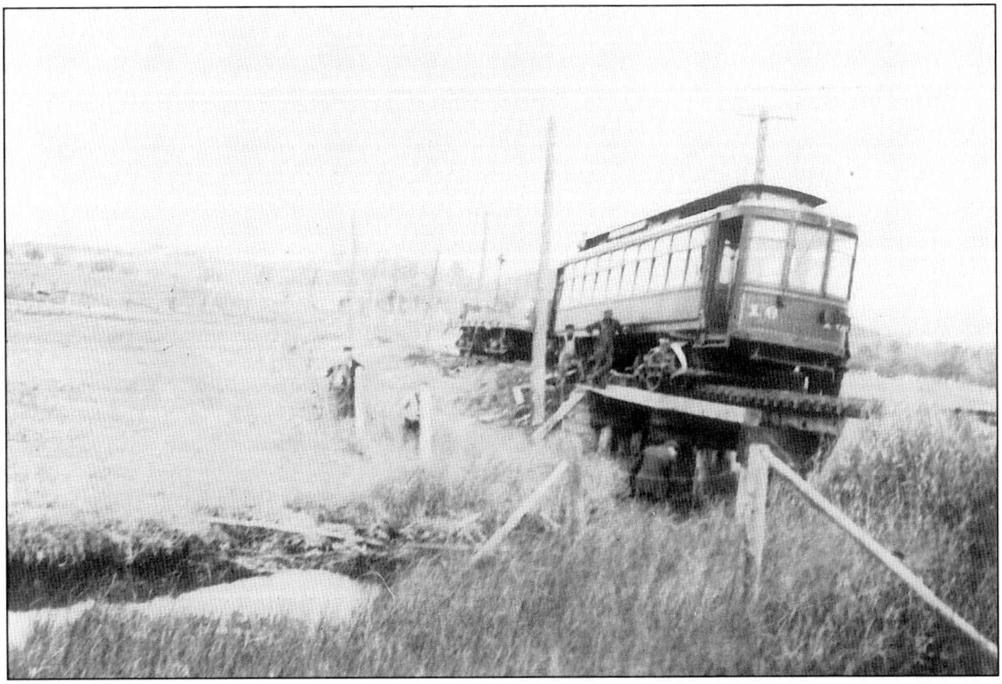

A crew works to rerail Atlantic Shore Line No. 16 on the Sturgeon Creek bridge, a short distance south of Rosemary Junction, in Eliot. The car originally was owned by the Metropolitan Street Railway of New York City and came to Maine in 1902. It still was active when trolley service in Eliot ended in 1923 and appears to have been scrapped in 1925.

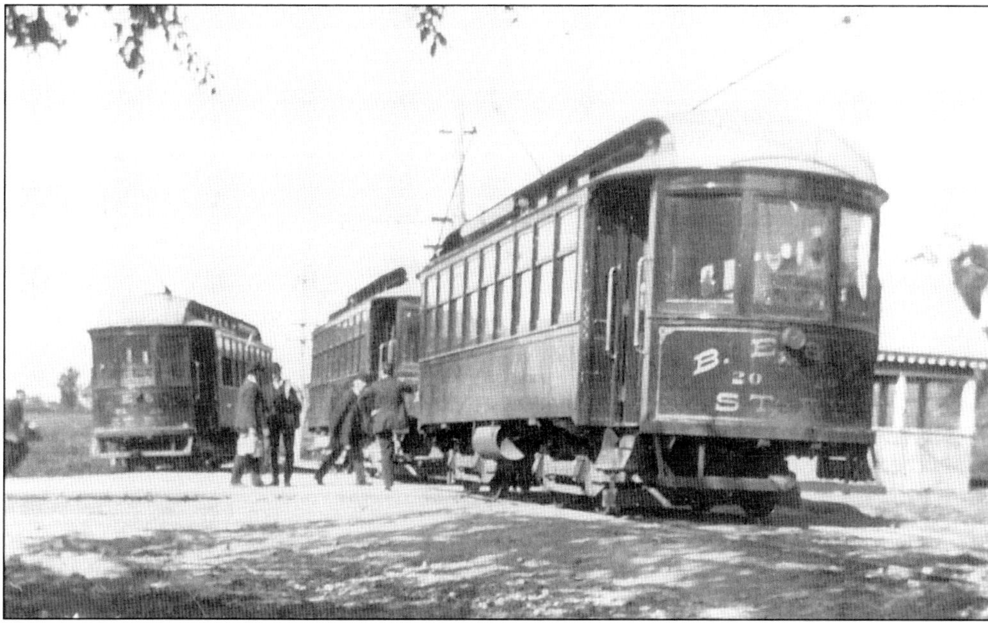

This is a view of the Rosemary Junction, Eliot, about 1903. The car at the left has just arrived from Badger's Island while No. 20, at right, is headed for York Beach over what was popularly known as "The Air Line" between Rosemary and York Corner Junction. Through cars were run hourly between Dover and the resort in summer, shuttle trips being operated on a two-hour headway between Rosemary and The Goldenrod in other seasons.

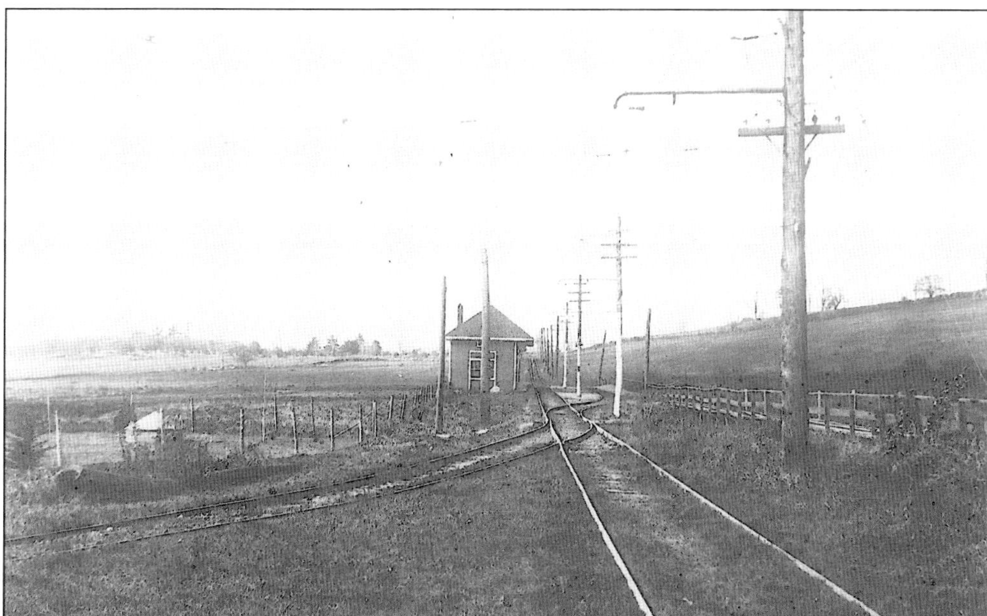

A later view of Rosemary Junction after the erection of an enclosed waiting station there. The refreshment stand inside was managed for a number of years by one W.C. Willey, who became famous for the high quality of his hand-made candy kisses. This building burned on December 5, 1922, just a few months before trolley service through the junction ended.

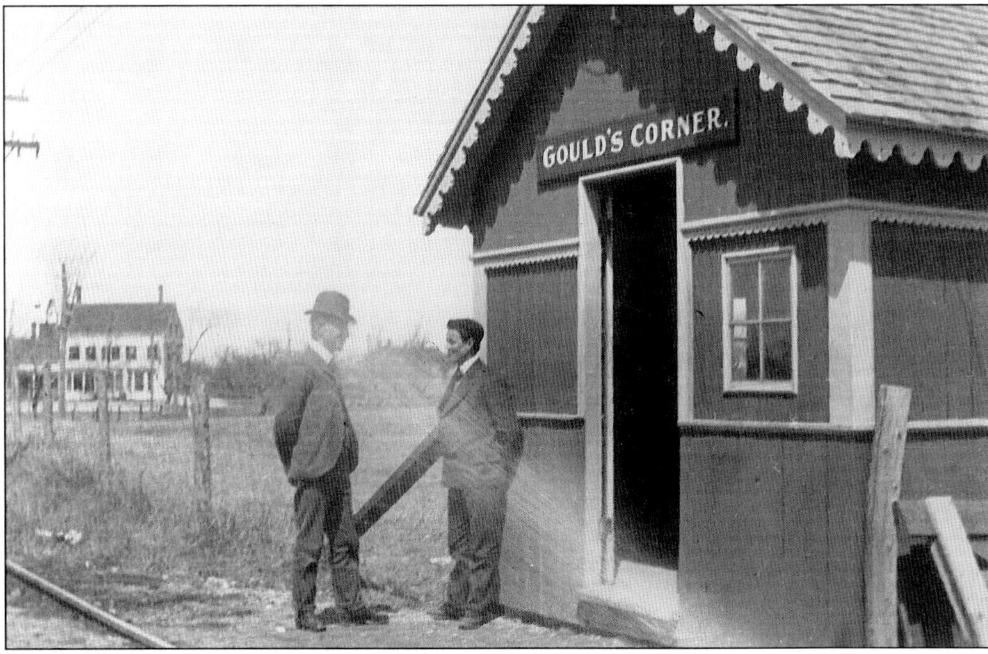

The Gould Corner, Eliot waiting station reveals itself in "winter dress" about 1903. This point was on the present Maine Route 103 about a mile northwest of Rosemary Junction and was a regular stopping point for trolleys running between Dover and Portsmouth and between the Garrison City and York Beach. Six women suffered bruises in a collision of two open cars here shortly before 1 p.m. on September 8, 1912. Damage to the trolleys was minor and none of the injured was hospitalized.

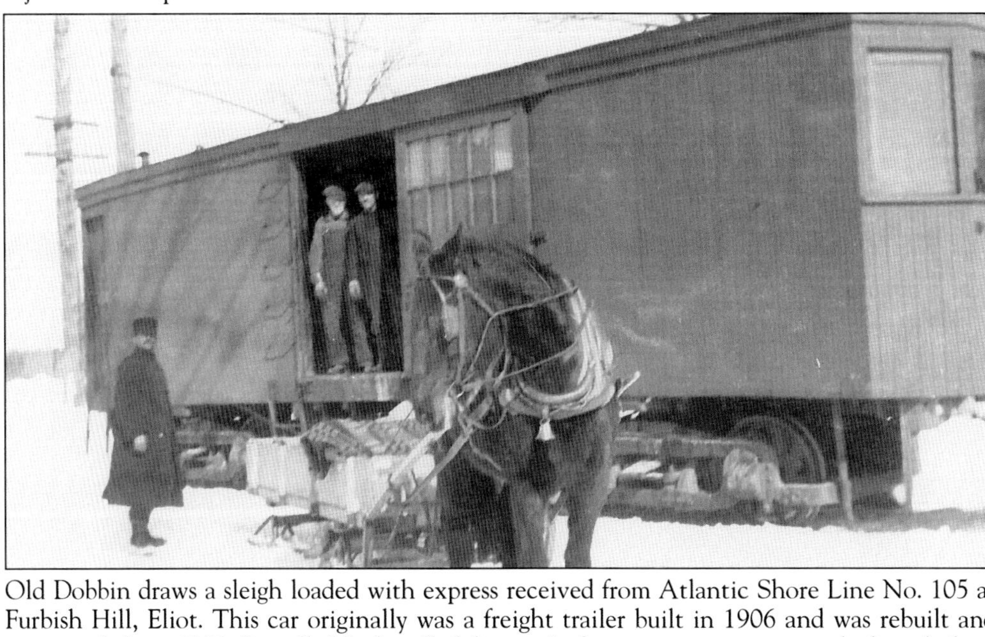

Old Dobbin draws a sleigh loaded with express received from Atlantic Shore Line No. 105 at Furbish Hill, Eliot. This car originally was a freight trailer built in 1906 and was rebuilt and motorized about 1909. So-called "sidewalk deliveries" of express matter were made directly from the car to consignees along the trolley lines on both the Western and Eastern Divisions of the railway.

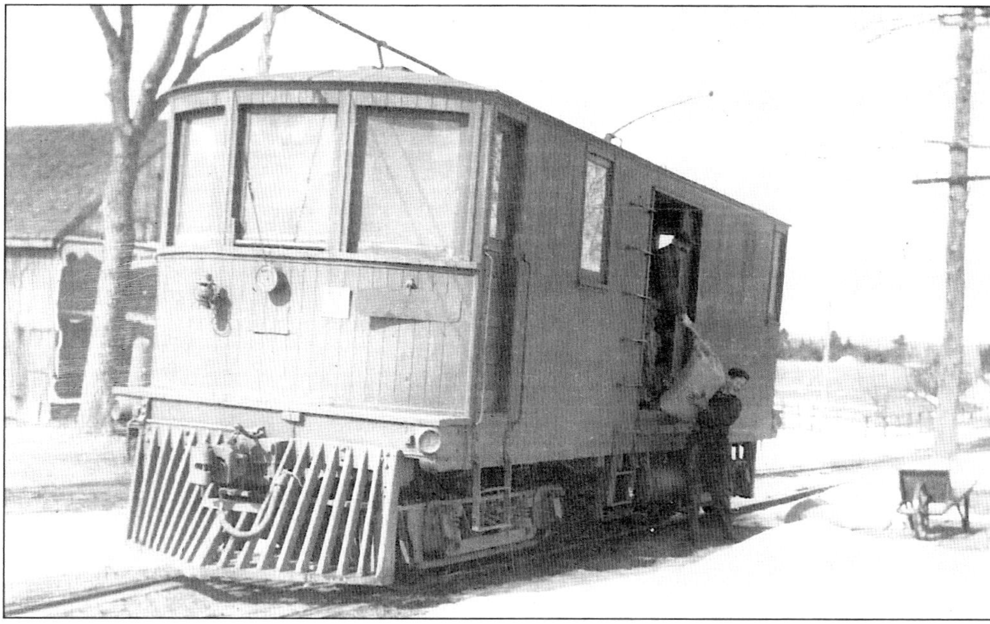

A sack of grain is unloaded from Atlantic Shore express motor 101 at Furbish Hill, Eliot, in 1915. Built as a freight locomotive in 1906, it was reconstructed in 1908 and rebuilt after being destroyed by fire at the South Berwick carhouse on December 1, 1911. All of the express matter in the car was lost in the blaze, which was thought to have been started by No. 101's coal-fired heater.

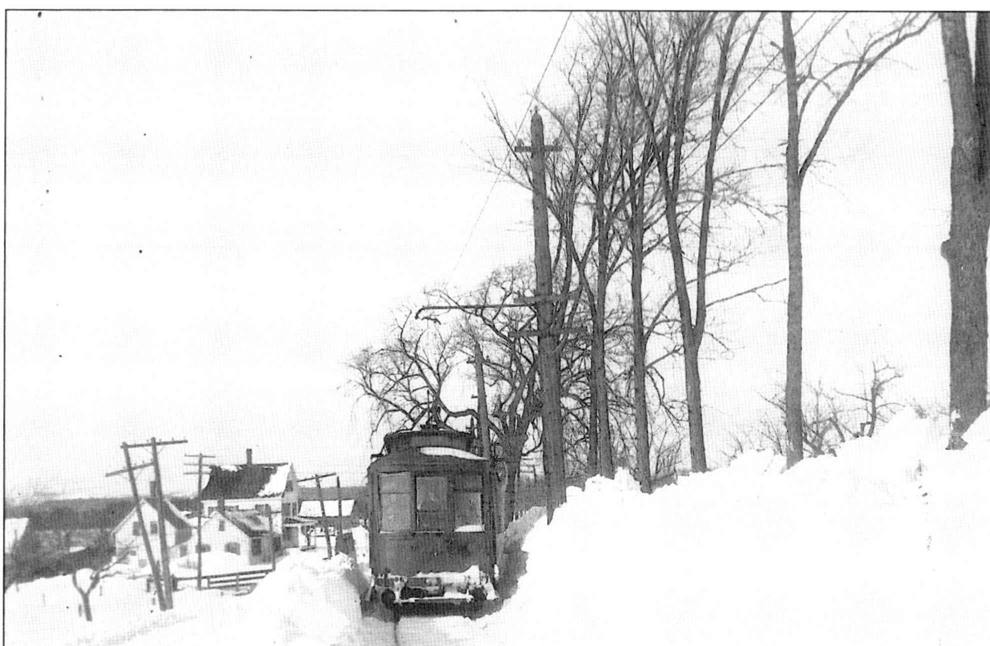

Closed car No. 16 at Furbish Hill, Eliot, about 1903. The late Philip Furbish took many snapshots of trolleys passing his home from 1903 until 1923 and bequeathed his collection of pictures and negatives to the Fogg Library in Eliot.

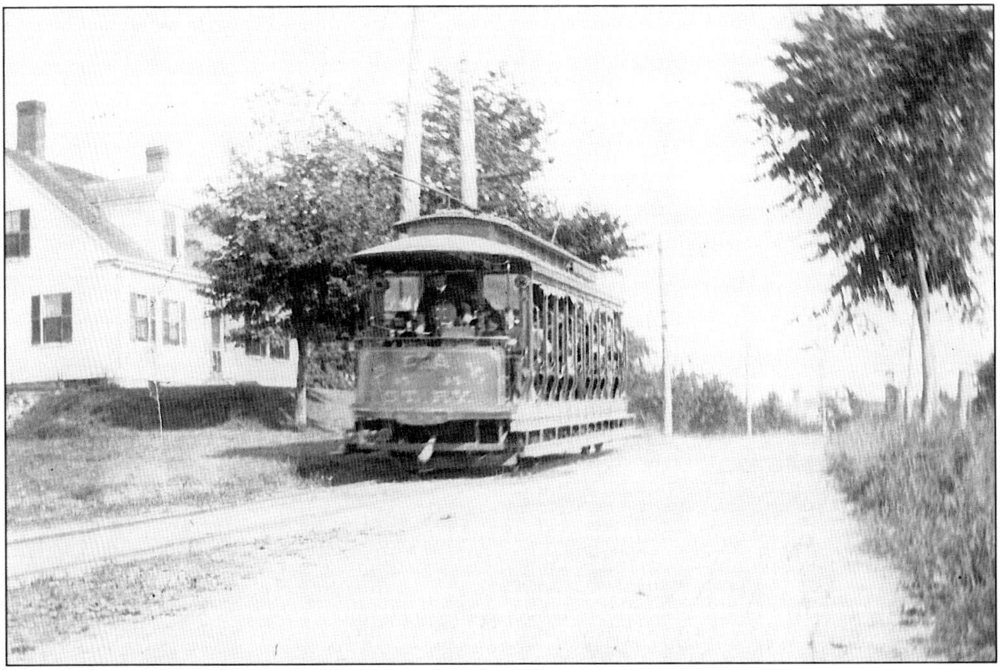

Passing the Philip Furbish home in Eliot is a 13-bench open headed for Dover. The Atlantic Shore tracks in Dover ended in Franklin Square on Central Avenue where they almost-but-not-quite connected physically with those of the Dover, Somersworth & Rochester Street Railway's Dover-Somersworth route.

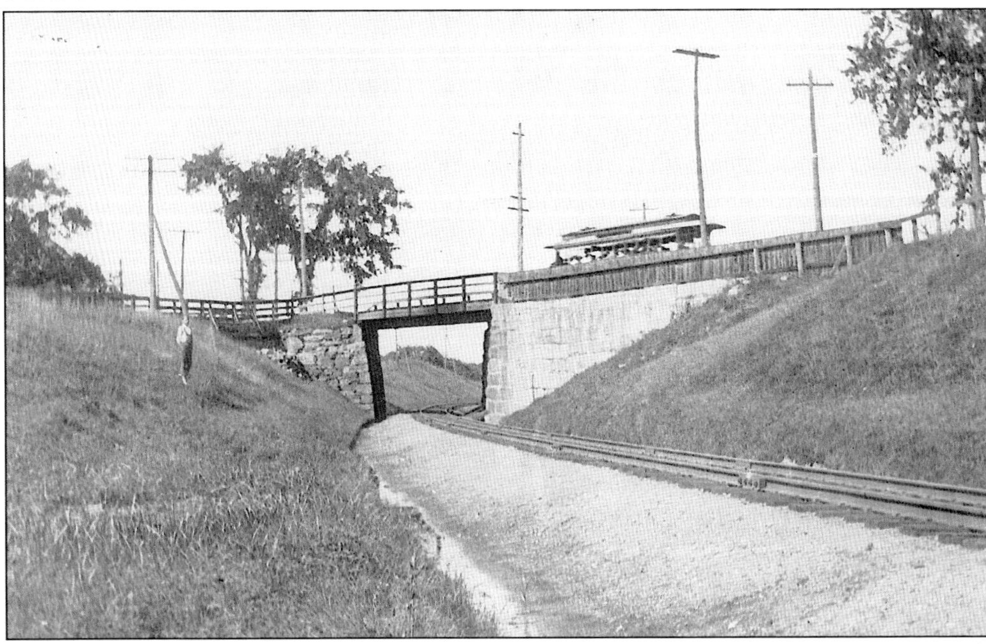

The original Shapleigh's bridge across the Eastern Division of the Boston & Maine near Gould Corner in Eliot prior to 1907. Only 37 feet long, it was strengthened by the American Bridge Company before the Portsmouth, Dover & York laid a single track across the I-beam structure in 1903.

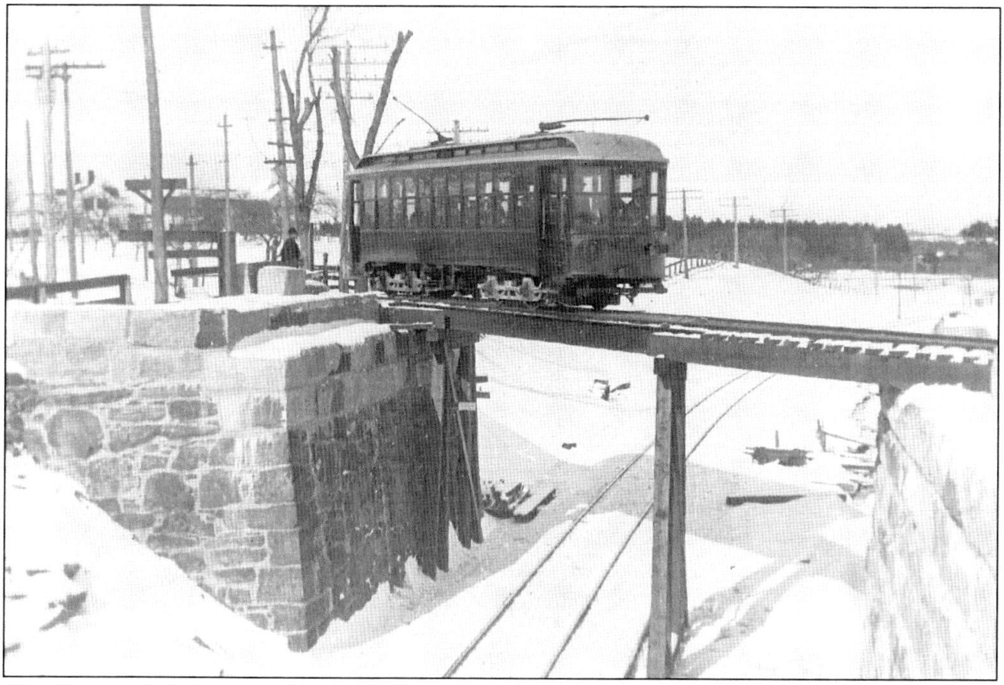

The Boston & Maine double-tracked its Eastern Division main line through Eliot in 1907-08 and Shapleigh's bridge had to be rebuilt. Car 14 crosses a temporary span between new abutments. After B&M service between North Berwick and Portsmouth ended in 1952 and the tracks were removed, the railroad right-of-way was acquired by the state of Maine for highway purposes and is now the greater part of Route 236 between Kittery and South Berwick.

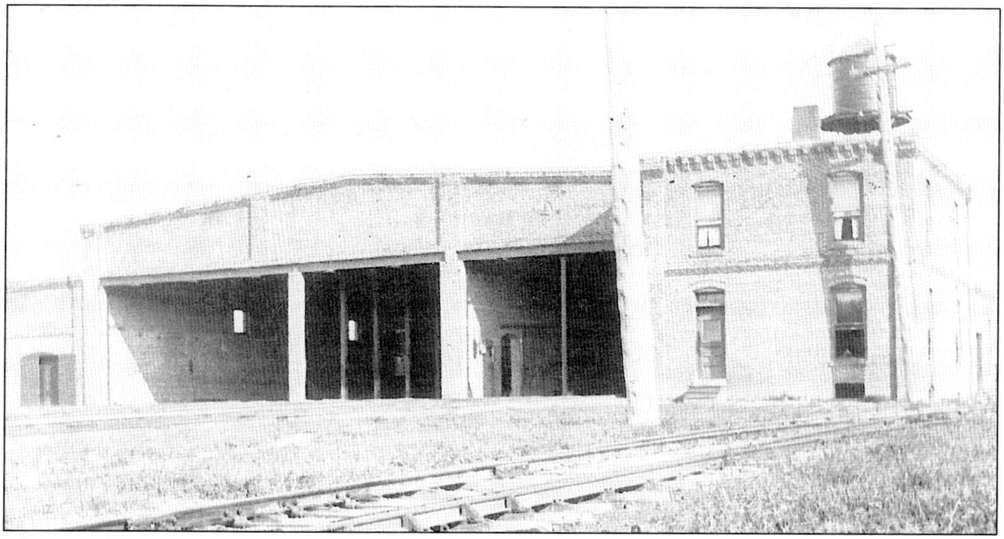

The South Berwick carhouse is shown here shortly after its completion in 1903. The elevated tank contained water for an automatic sprinkler system in the barn. There were seven tracks and two-story ell at the right contained offices, a crew's lobby, a power substation, and a second-floor dormitory. A fire on November 16, 1918 destroyed the stockroom in the ell and spread into sleeping area above. Two of eight sleeping men were found unconscious and had to be carried to safety. No trace of the carhouse remains today.

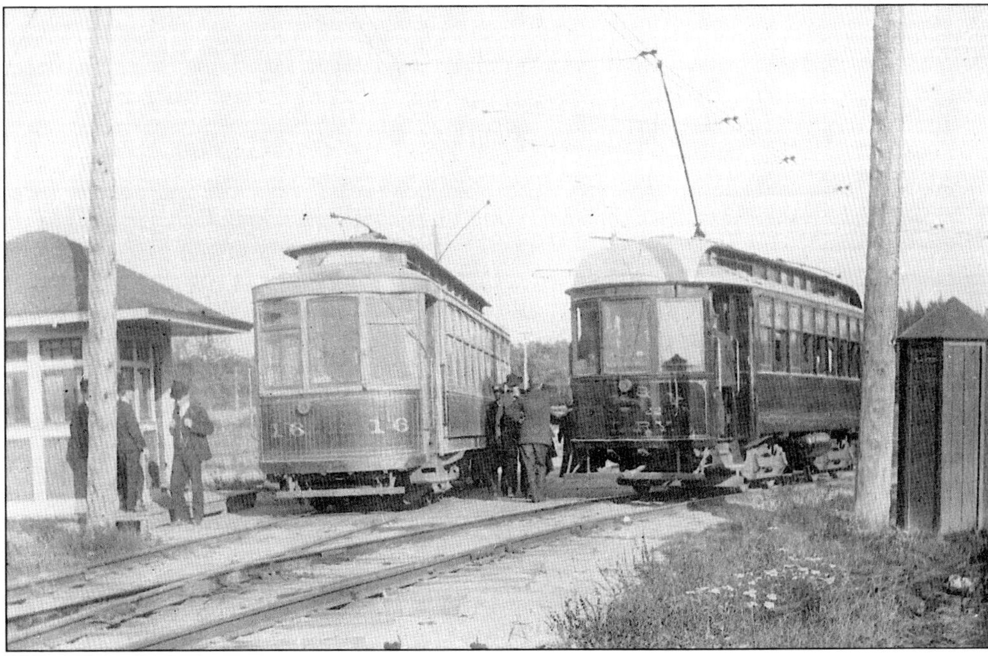

Just a short distance from the South Berwick carhouse was South Berwick Junction, where the tracks to South Berwick village branched from the main line between Dover and Rosemary Junction. Cars 16 and 22 are shown during the early days of the Portsmouth, Dover & York Street Railway. Nearby was Quamphegan Park, a privately owned resort bordering on Quamphegan Brook and the Salmon Falls River. Boating, fishing, bathing, and a dancing pavilion were among its simple attractions.

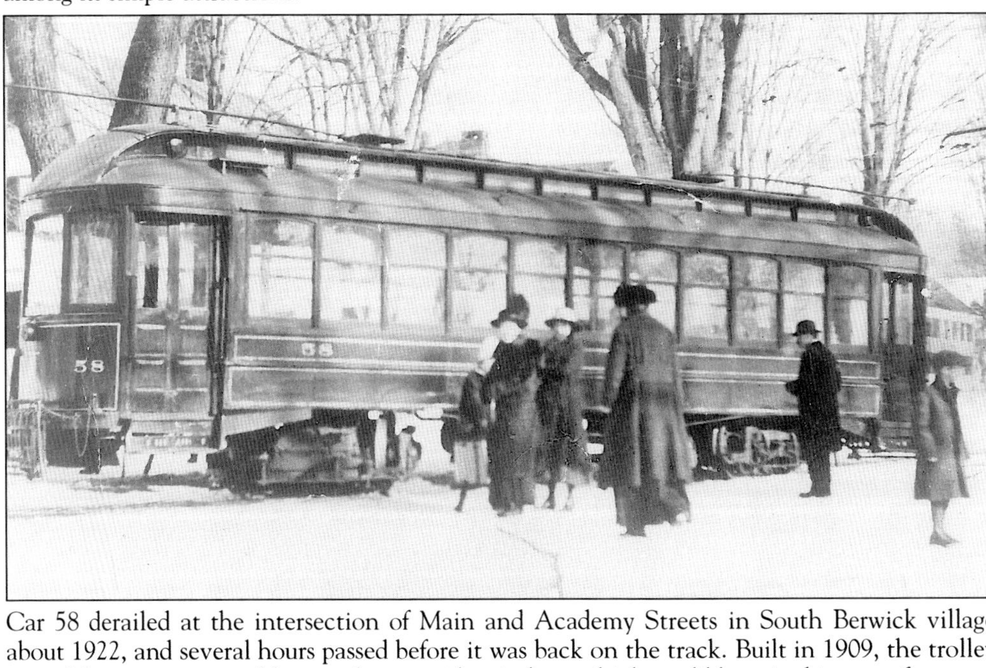

Car 58 derailed at the intersection of Main and Academy Streets in South Berwick village about 1922, and several hours passed before it was back on the track. Built in 1909, the trolley was of the semi-convertible type, having side windows which could be raised into roof recesses to create an open car effect in summer.

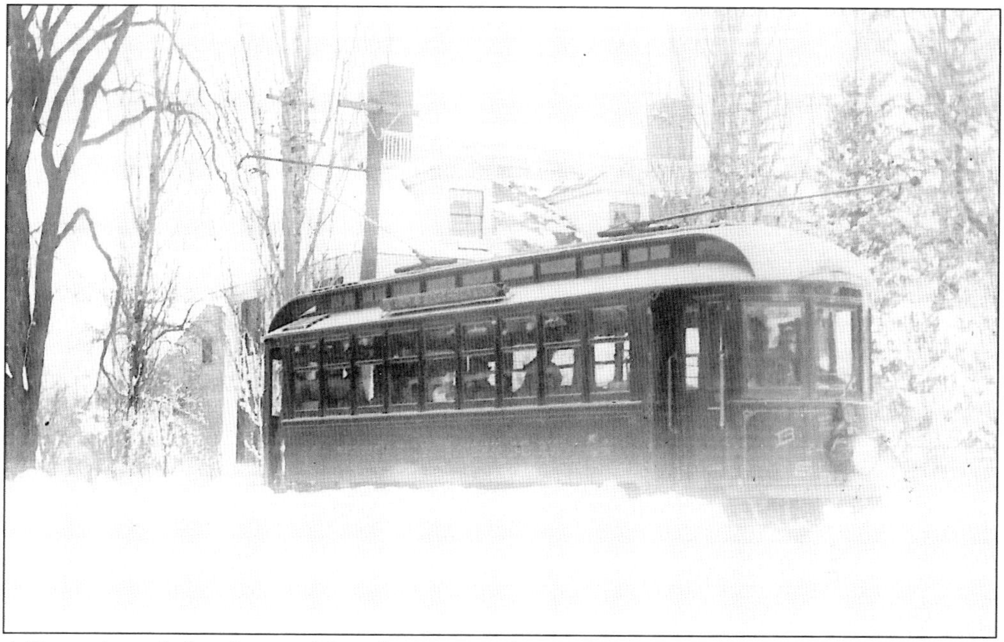

A Dover-bound closed car on Main Street, near the Sarah Orne Jewett House, in South Berwick village. Hourly service was provided between Dover and South Berwick the year round, the running time for the 7.5 mile trip being 30 minutes and a single car maintaining the schedule. The cash fare was 10 cents for many years, South Berwick Junction being the five-cent limit in either direction.

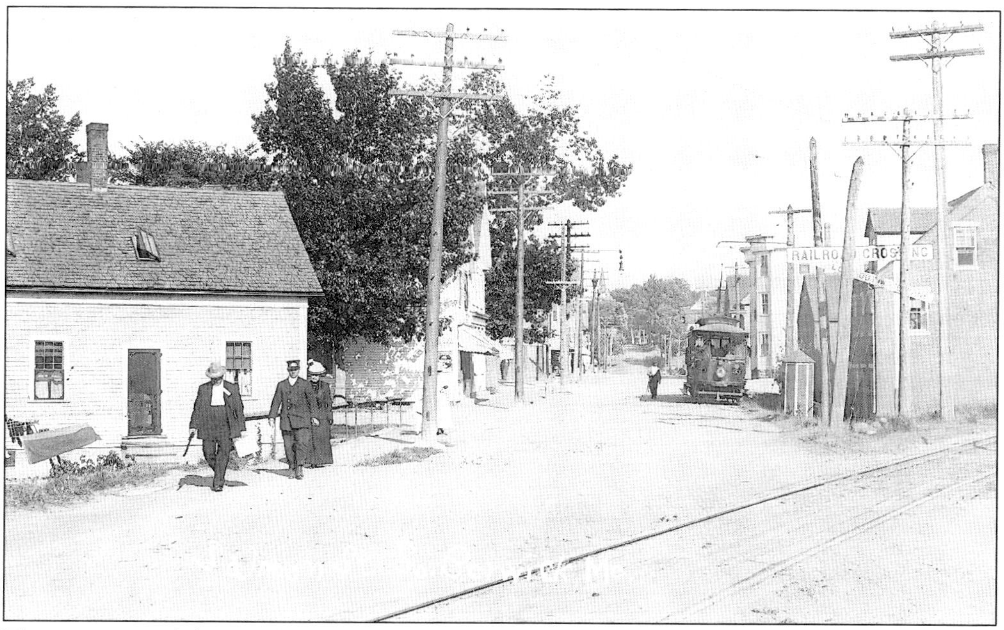

The terminus of the South Berwick village line was at a Boston & Maine Northern Division grade crossing on Salmon Street near the east end of the Salmon Falls River bridge. Just across the bridge was the village of Salmon Falls, part of Rollinsford, New Hampshire and the home of the Salmon Falls Manufacturing Company, a producer of textiles.

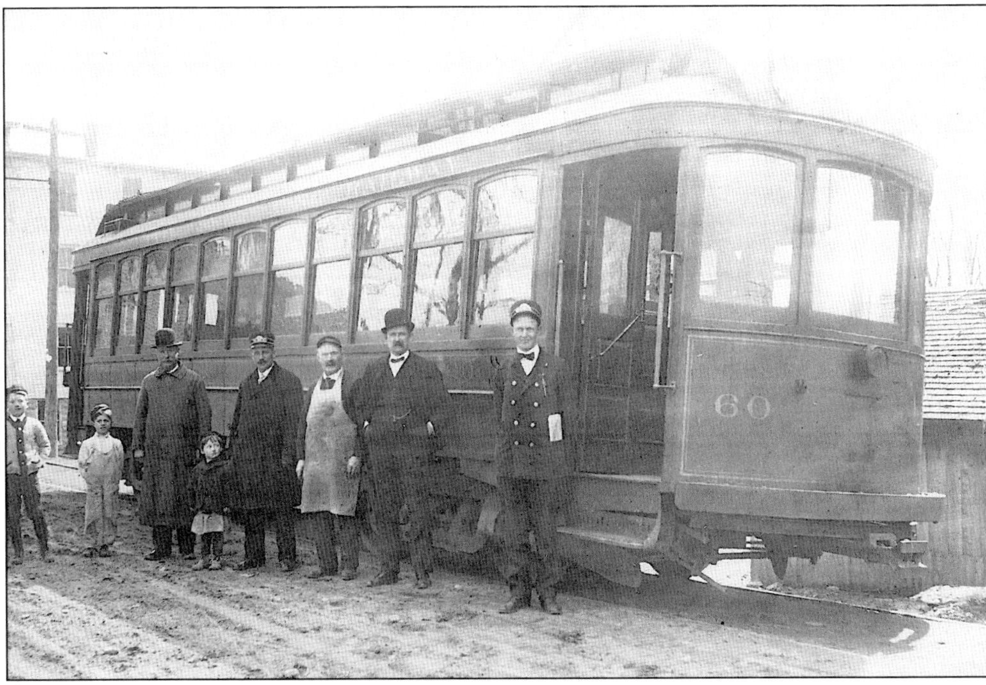

Another view at the terminus of the South Berwick line at the Boston & Maine crossing. The closed car, No. 60, carries Atlantic Shore Line Railway lettering but lacks destination signs. Three men, two small boys, and the motorman and conductor posed for the photographer before the trolley returned to South Berwick Junction and Dover.

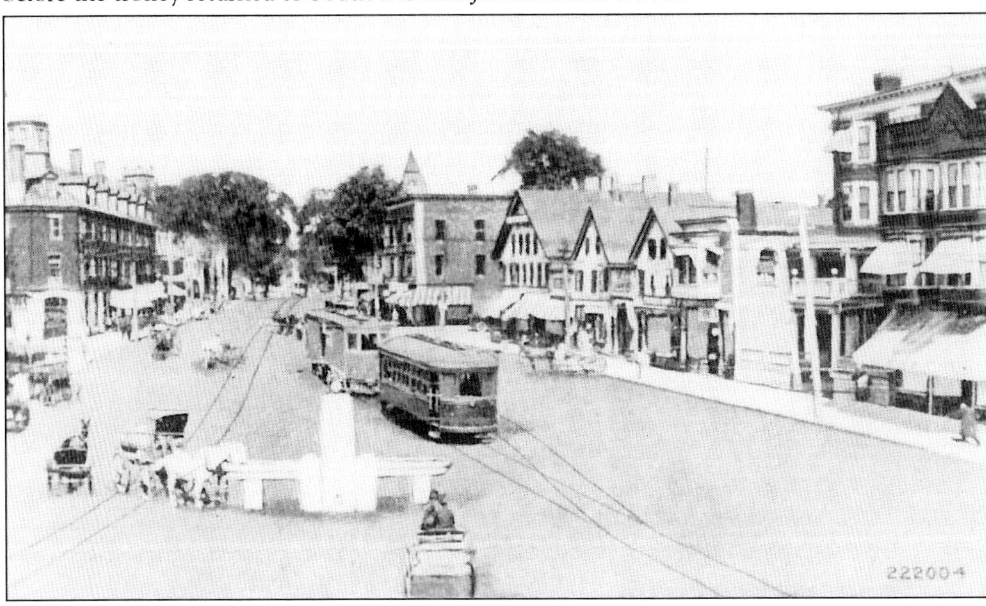

This copy of a color postcard shows an Atlantic Shore Railway passenger car and express car in Franklin Square, Dover. For a number of years, the Hoyt-Tarbox and Atlantic Express Companies maintained express service over the Dover, Somersworth & Rochester Street Railway and shipments moving between ASRY and DS&R points were transferred in the square.

Three

York Beach to Kennebunk

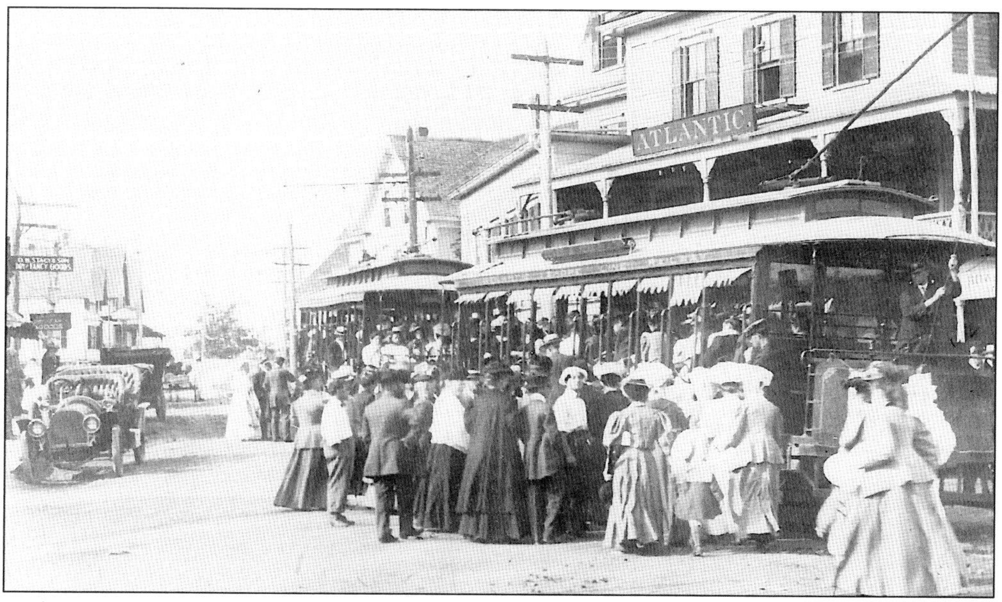

York Beach Square was a very busy place in summer after the opening of the Atlantic Shore Line Railway's Kennebunk-York Beach line in July 1907. Two open cars exchange passengers at the Atlantic House, opened in June 1888 and also known for a time as The Surf. Directly opposite was the Gay White Way.

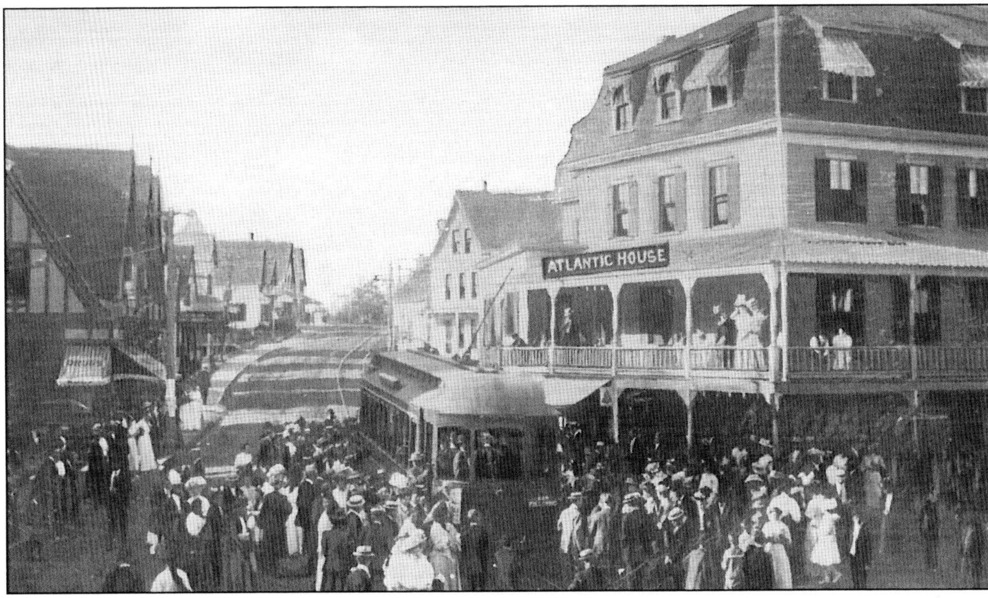

A trolley bound for Kennebunk takes on passengers in York Beach Square. For a number of years, through cars were run by the Atlantic Shore Line every two hours in winter between Rosemary Junction, Eliot, and Town House Junction, Kennebunkport, about 33.33 miles, and, of course, these passed through York Beach.

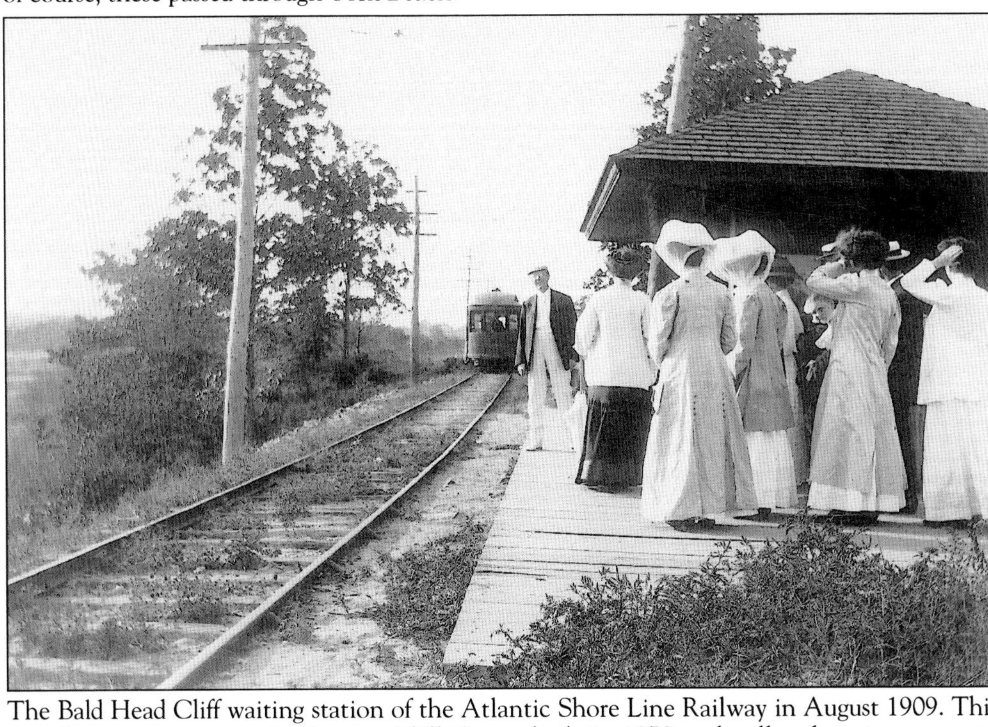

The Bald Head Cliff waiting station of the Atlantic Shore Line Railway in August 1909. This was the nearest stop to the famous Cliff House, built in 1872 and still welcoming guests in 1998. The trolley tracks ran entirely over private way between the Cape Neddick River, York, and Shore Road, Ogunquit, and there were fences on both sides, iron gates being provided at crossings.

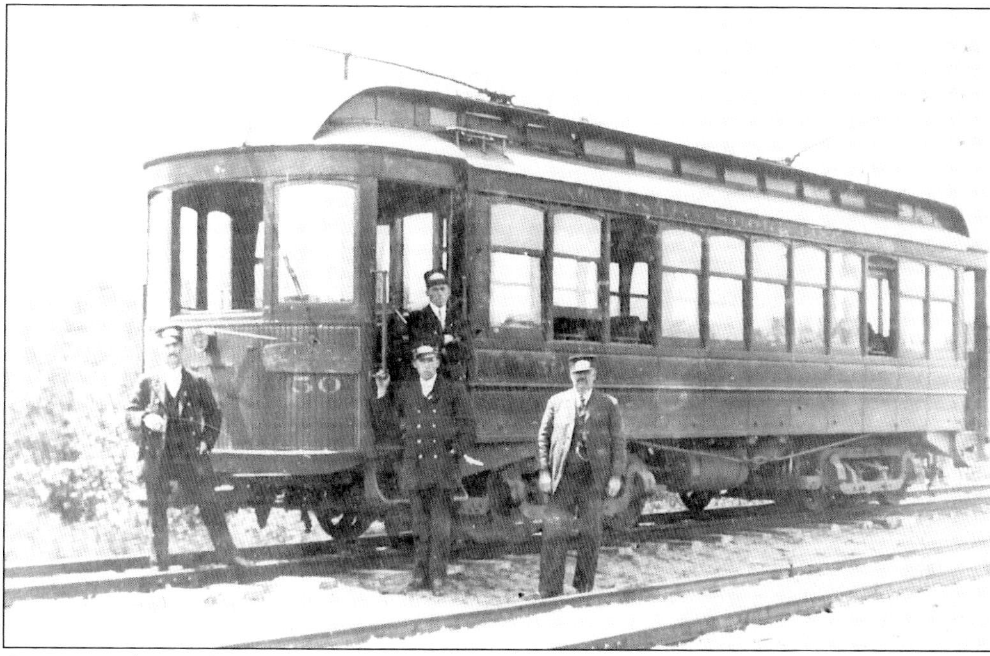

Crews were being changed at Bald Head Cliff turnout in York as Atlantic Shore Line Car 50 makes a northbound trip on the York Beach-Kennebunk line. Other turnouts between York Beach and Ogunquit were identified as Pine Hill and Summit and the latter was a short distance from the Passaconaway Inn, opened in 1893. This had accommodations for 150 guests and daily room rates in 1909 were "$4 and up."

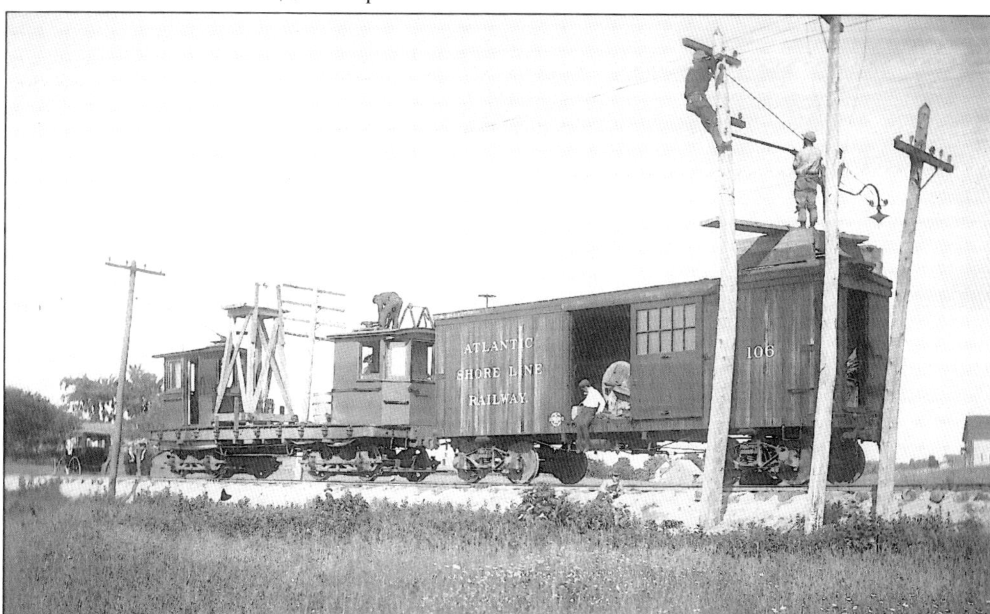

Stringing the trolley wire "alive" between York Beach and Ogunquit in the late spring of 1907. The flat car is No. 98 while the box trailer, No. 106, became a motor express car prior to 1910. There was no danger to the workmen as the tower on the flat car and the platform on the roof of No. 106 had protective insulation.

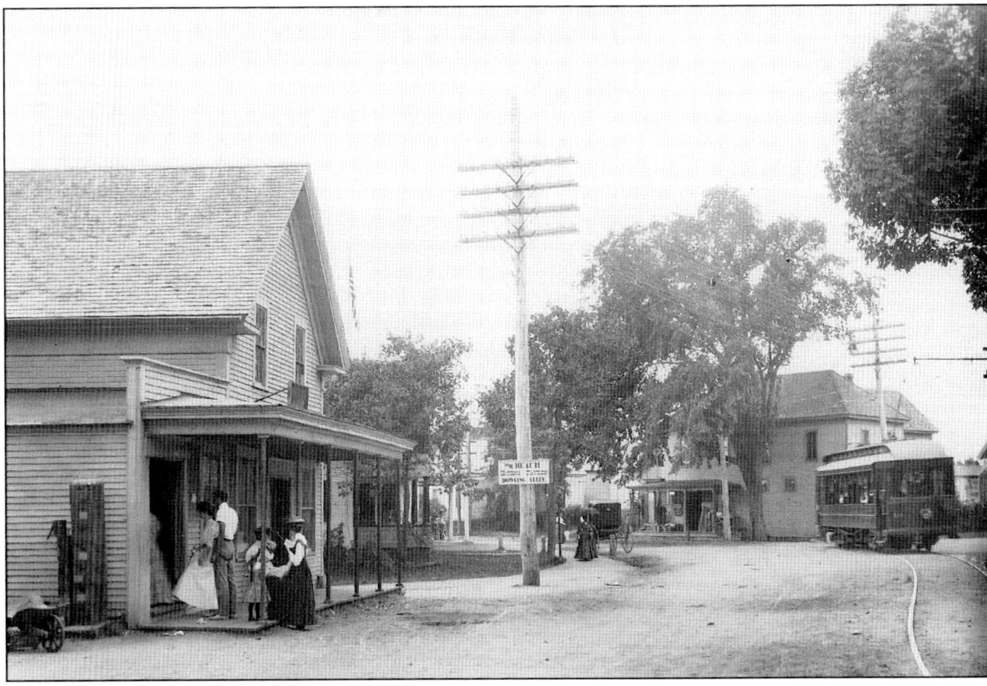

Turning from the present U.S. Route 1 into Shore Road at Ogunquit is a York Beach-bound closed car of the Atlantic Shore Line Railway. One J. H. Littlefield, who operated a general store, was the company's Ogunquit local agent for several years. He sold reduced-rate tickets in strips and books, was supplied with current timetables and was the man to see if a party wished to charter a special car.

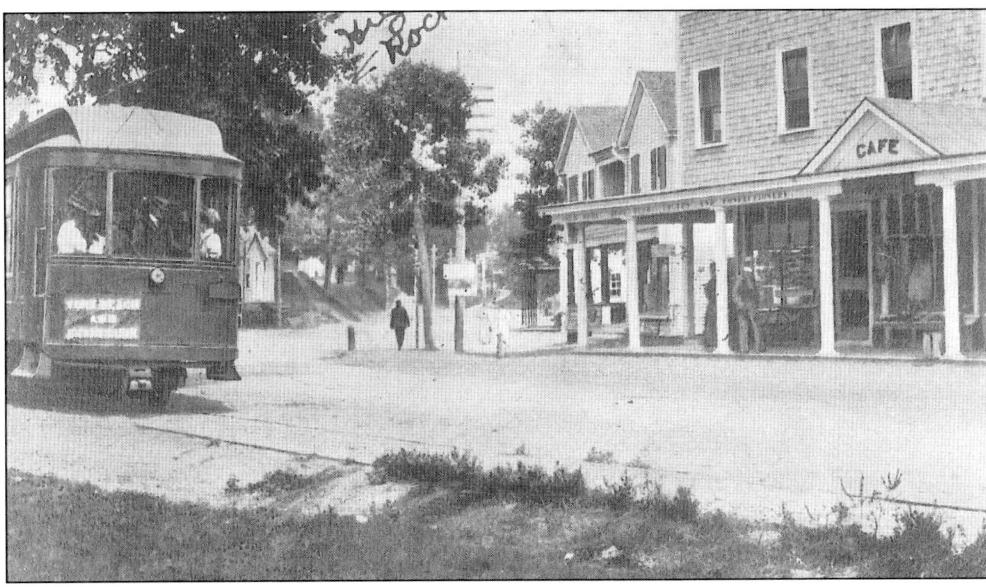

York Beach is the destination of this trolley on the present U.S. Route 1 in Ogunquit. By 1918 there was a hard surface highway all the way from Ogunquit to Kennebunk and the once heavy summer travel on the Atlantic Shore's Kennebunk-York Beach line was being lost to automobile competition.

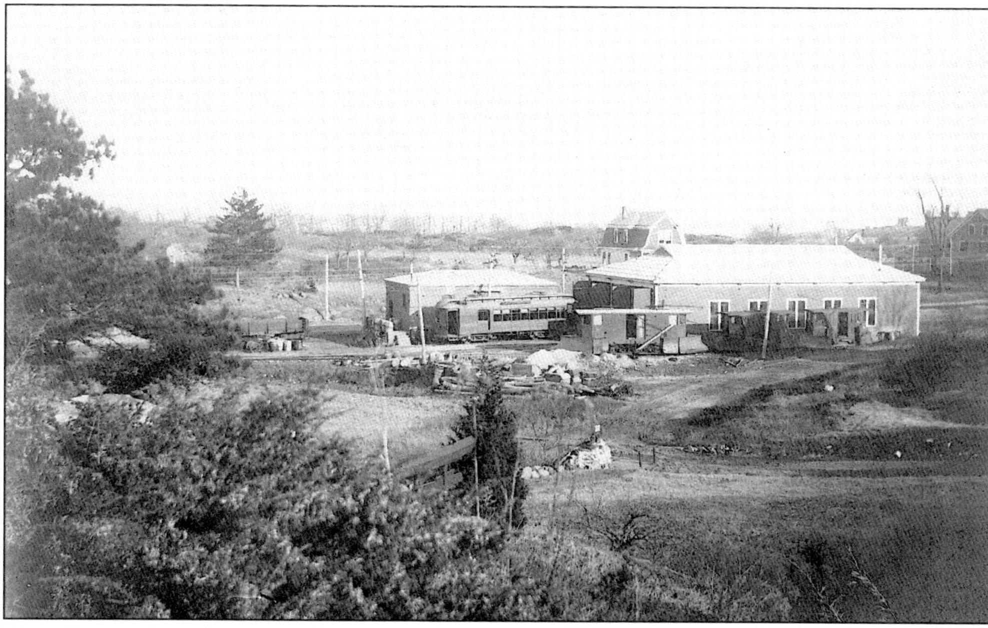

The Ogunquit carhouse and power substation is shown shortly after completion of the Kennebunk-York Beach trolley line in 1907. The carhouse, which had pits for the servicing of trolleys, was razed in 1924 but the substation was used for many years thereafter as a Central Maine Power Company storage building. The Viking restaurant now occupies the former carhouse and substation site.

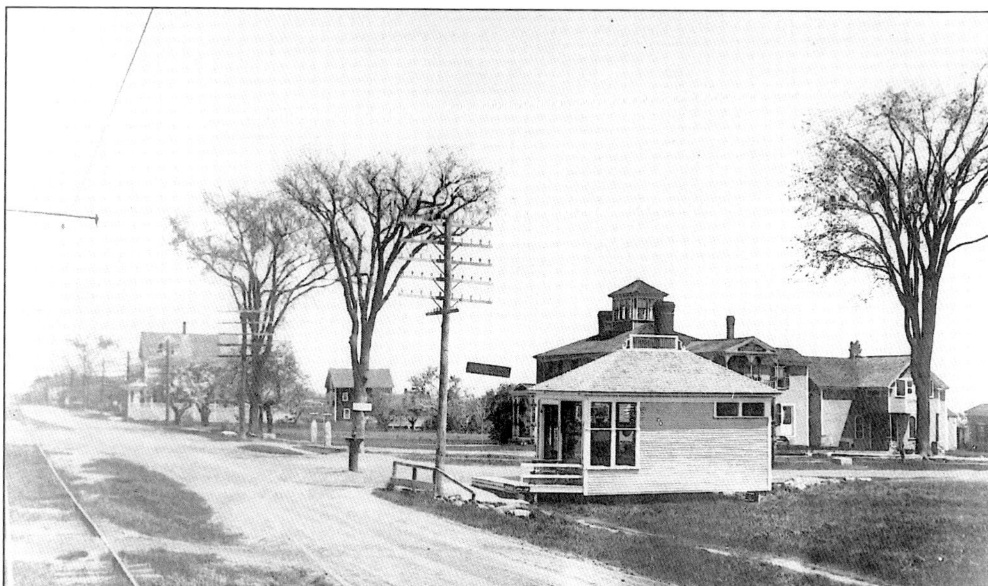

The small building at right is the waiting station of the Atlantic Shore Line Railway at the intersection of Post Road and Eldridge Road in Wells. In the background is the Eldridge Tavern, built in 1824 and still standing. Other waiting stations along Post Road in the town were at Moody, Mile Road, Wells Corner, and The Elms. Some of these housed trolley-era versions of today's minimarts.

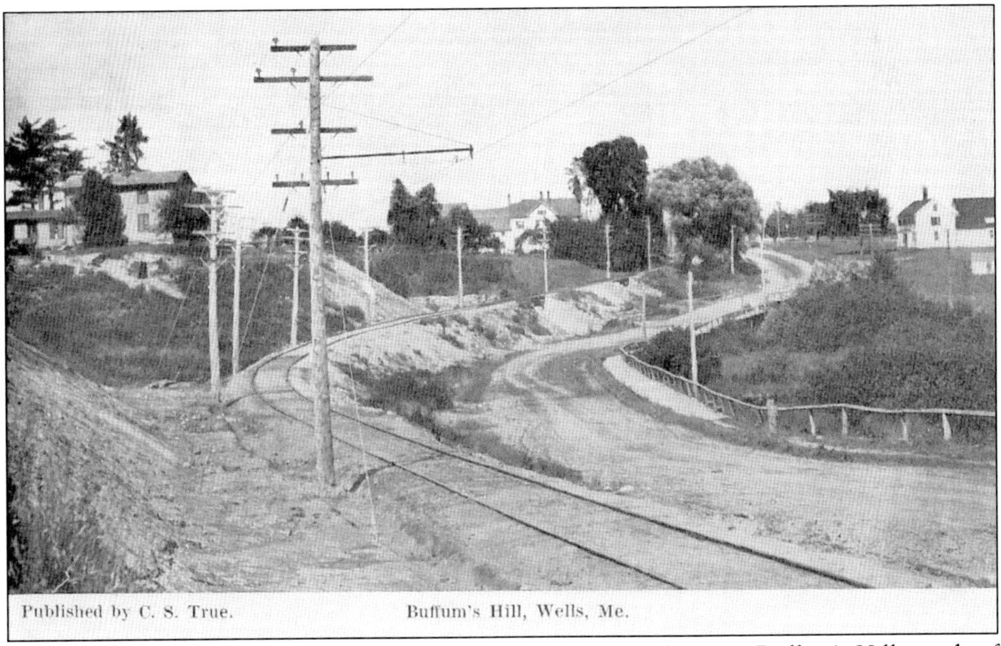

The tracks of the Atlantic Shore Line ran on private right-of-way at Buffum's Hill, south of Wells Corner. Traces of the trolley roadbed at this point and the abutments of a short bridge across the Webhannet River are still discernible 75 years after abandonment

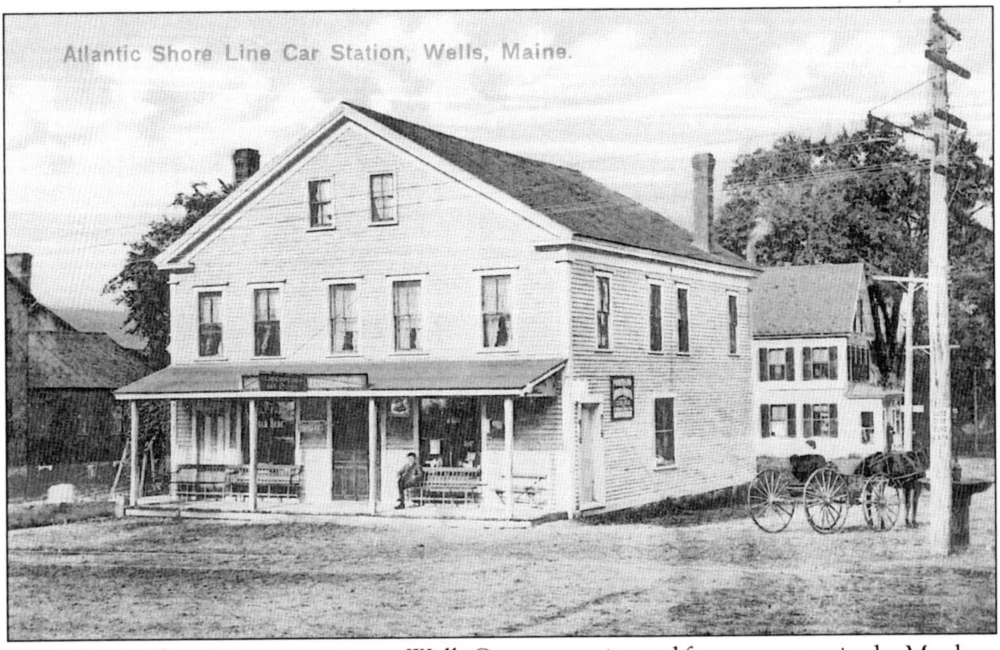

The Atlantic Shore Line car station at Wells Corner was situated for many years in the Moulton store, the proprietor of which, H.S. Moulton, served as agent for both the railway and the Atlantic Express Company. The building now is occupied by the Wells House of Pizza. The trolleys carried the closed pouch mail between the post offices at Wells Corner and Ogunquit for a number of years when they also served that at Moody.

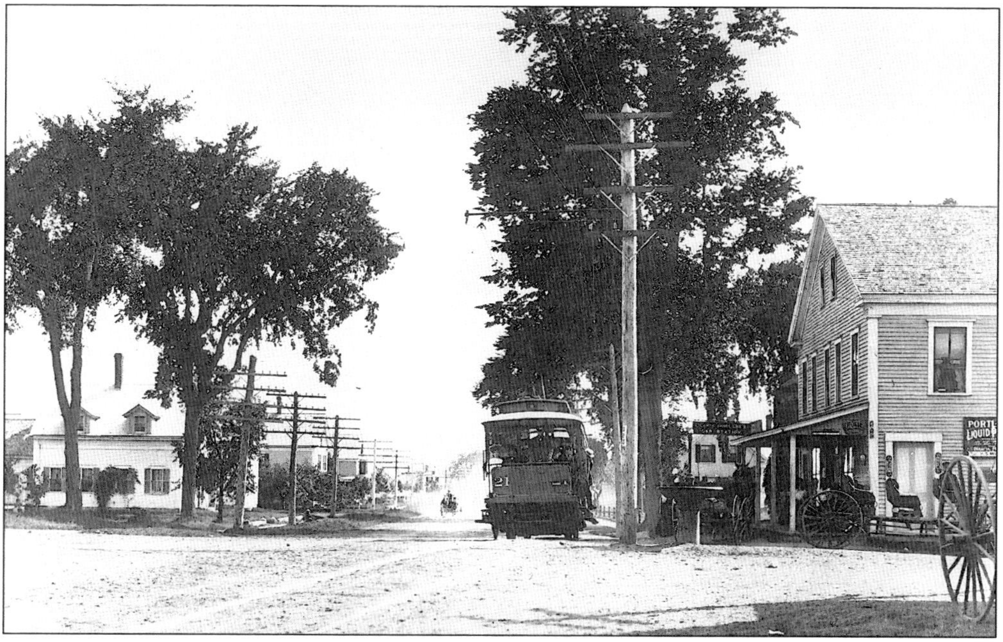

A northbound trolley on the York Beach-Kennebunk line pauses at the Wells Corner car station in 1907. This particular car, No. 21, was built for the Sanford & Cape Porpoise Railway and was taken over by the Atlantic Shore Line in 1904. Renumbered 51 prior to 1908, it was destroyed in a carhouse fire at Town House Junction in Kennebunkport on February 7, 1909.

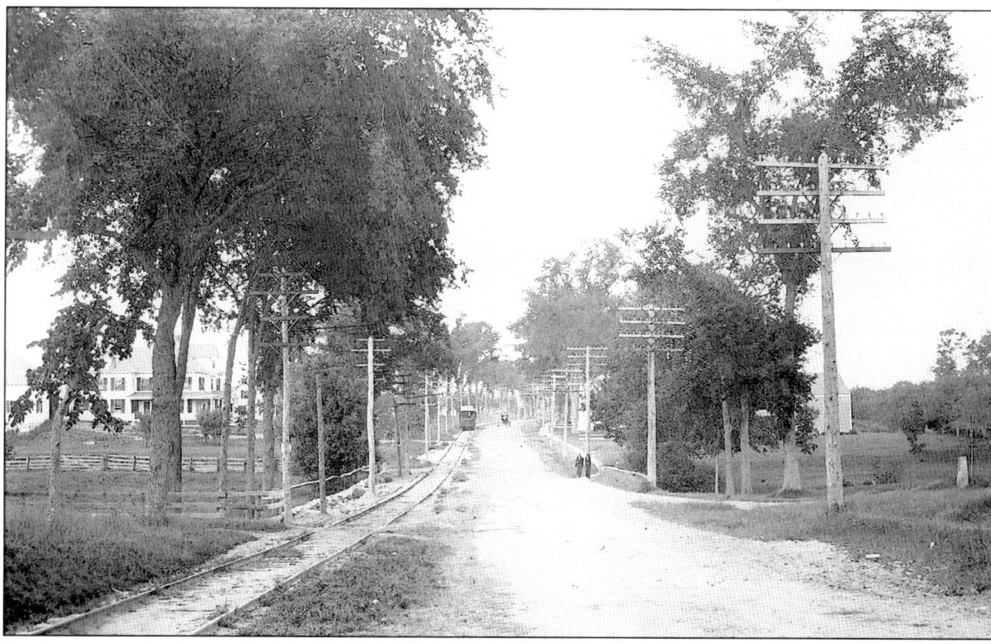

Looking north along the Post Road (U.S. Route 1) from Wells Corner. Atlantic Shore Line trolley tracks paralleled the west side of Route 1 from Ogunquit square northerly to Wells Corner and on to the Boston & Maine Railroad bridge spanning the highway and for many summers a portable substation was set up at The Elms to boost power on the Kennebunk-York Beach route.

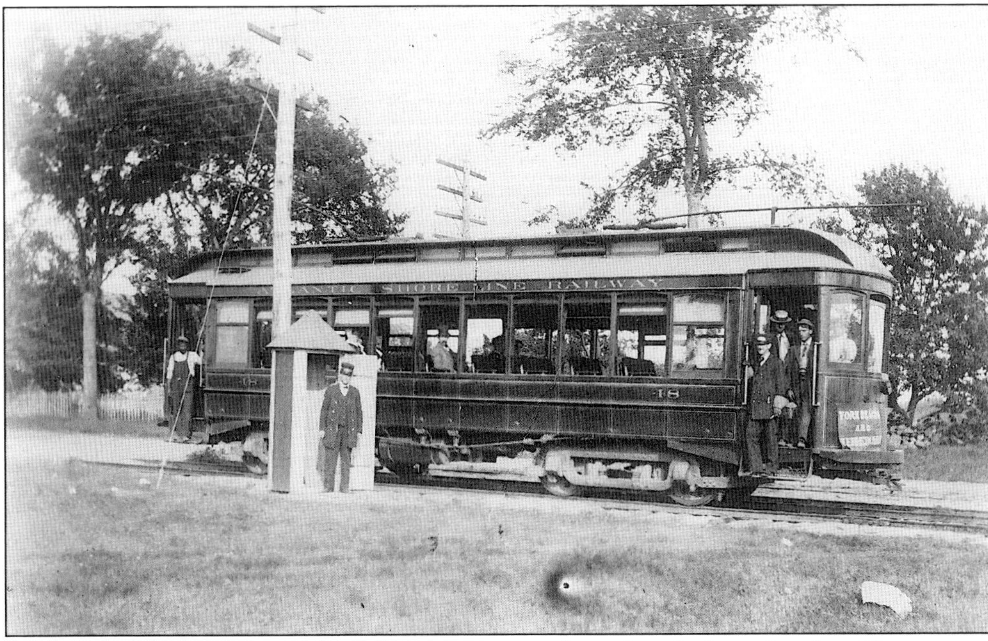

The conductor of York Beach-bound Car 48 emerges form the telephone booth at Elms turnout on the present Route 1, Wells. Nearby was the Boston & Maine Railroad's The Elms depot, built in 1888 and now part of Harding's Bookstore. This was a regular meeting point the year round for trolleys on the Kennebunk-York Beach route.

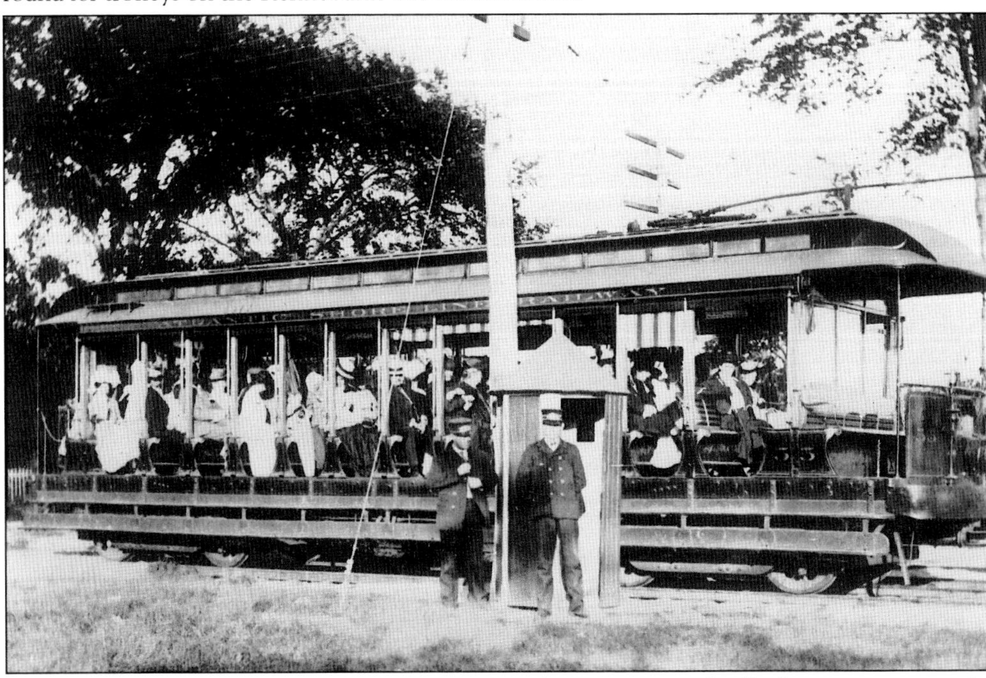

This 15-bench open car was one of two purchased in 1907 specifically for operation on the York Beach-Kennebunk line. Each had four 50-horsepower motors and could easily maintain the scheduled running time of one hour. Both were destroyed in the Town House Junction carhouse fire of February 1909.

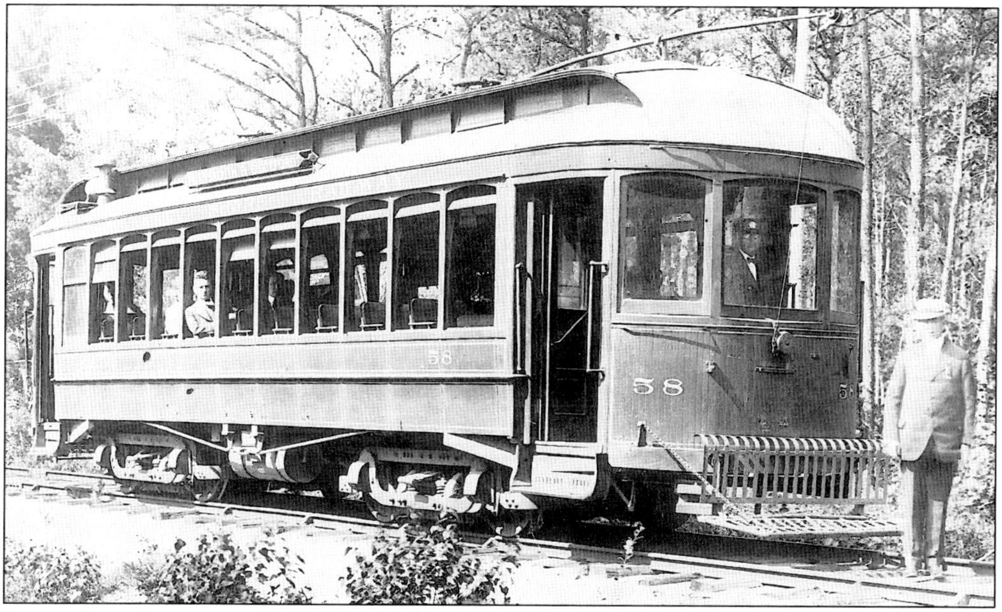

It must have been a warm day for nearly all the side windows of Car 58 are open as it headed north from Wells to Kennebunk about 1916. The man standing on the track is Eastern Division Superintendent George Hanscom and the device at the front of the car is a fender, designed to scoop up any person who stepped or fell in front of a moving trolley and prevent him or her from being run over by the wheels .

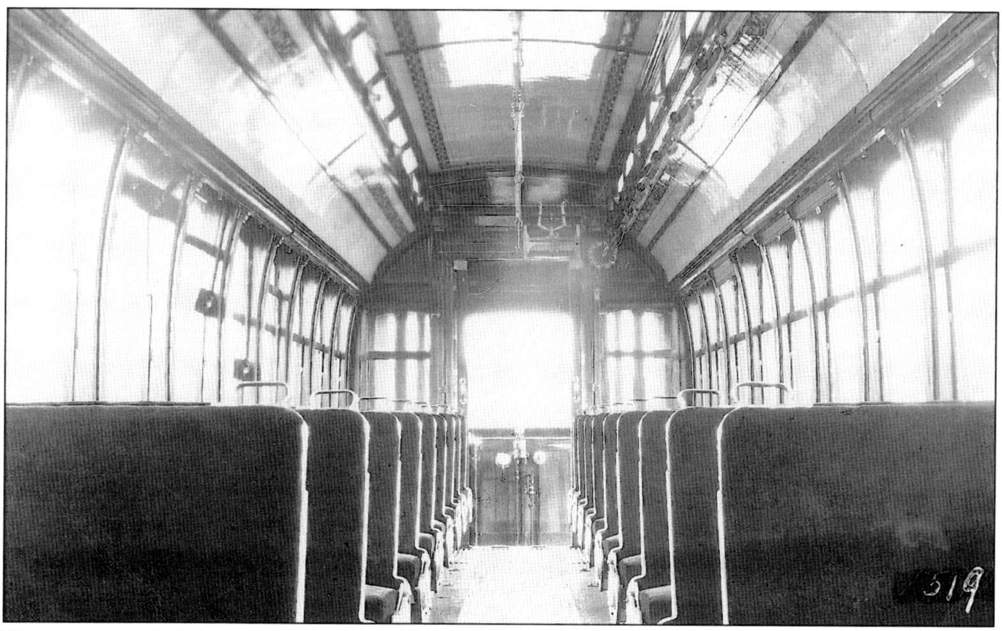

The interior of Atlantic Shore Line No. 60, which was identical to No. 58. Note the plush-upholstered seats and the curvature of the windows. The hot water heating system had not yet been installed but, when it was, would occupy the space of one corner seat.

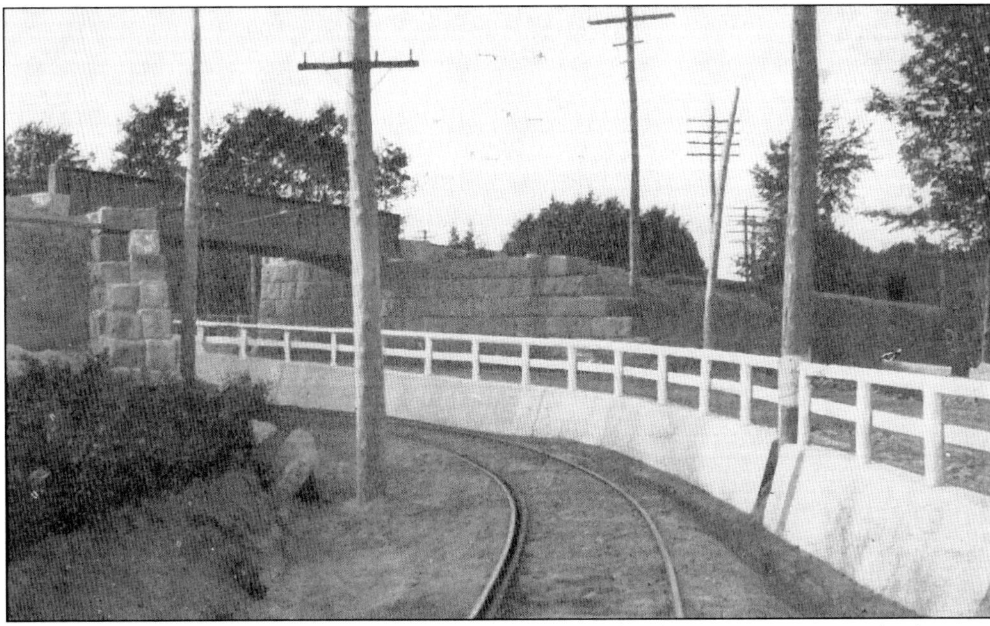

The tracks of the York Beach-Kennebunk line dipped under the Boston & Maine bridge near the northerly intersection of the present Routes 1 and 9 in Wells. There is known to have been at least on trolley-automobile collision under the span and the motor vehicle came off second best.

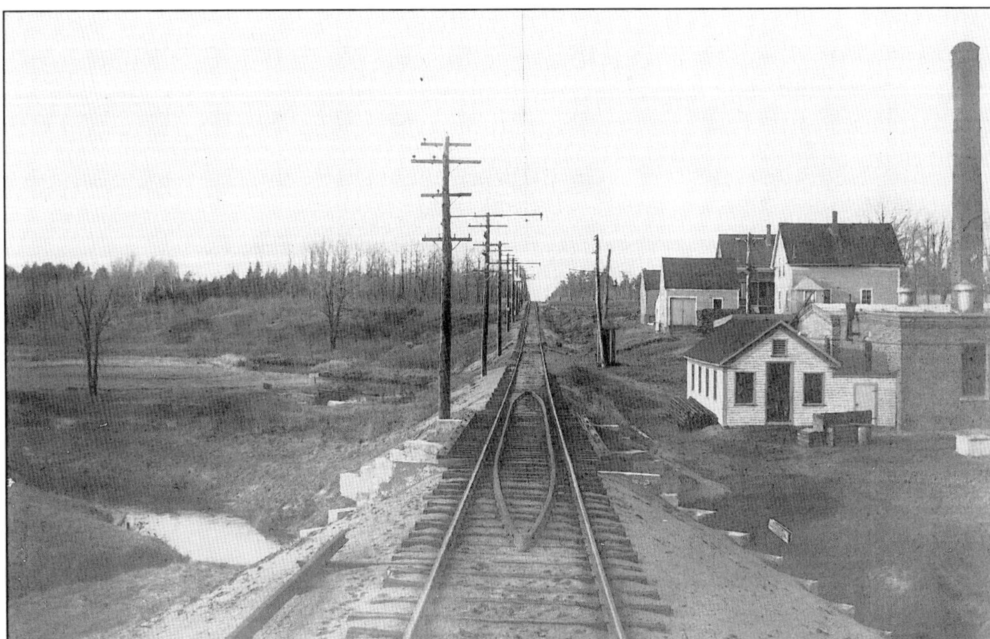

A short trestle carried the Atlantic Shore tracks across Branch Brook near the pumping station of the Mousam Water Company, now the Kennebunk, Kennebunkport & Wells Water District. An Atlantic Shore Railway freight tariff of 1917 quoted a rate of $6 for moving 15 gross tons of coal from the Kennebunk interchange with the Boston & Maine to this station and a nickel more for each additional ton.

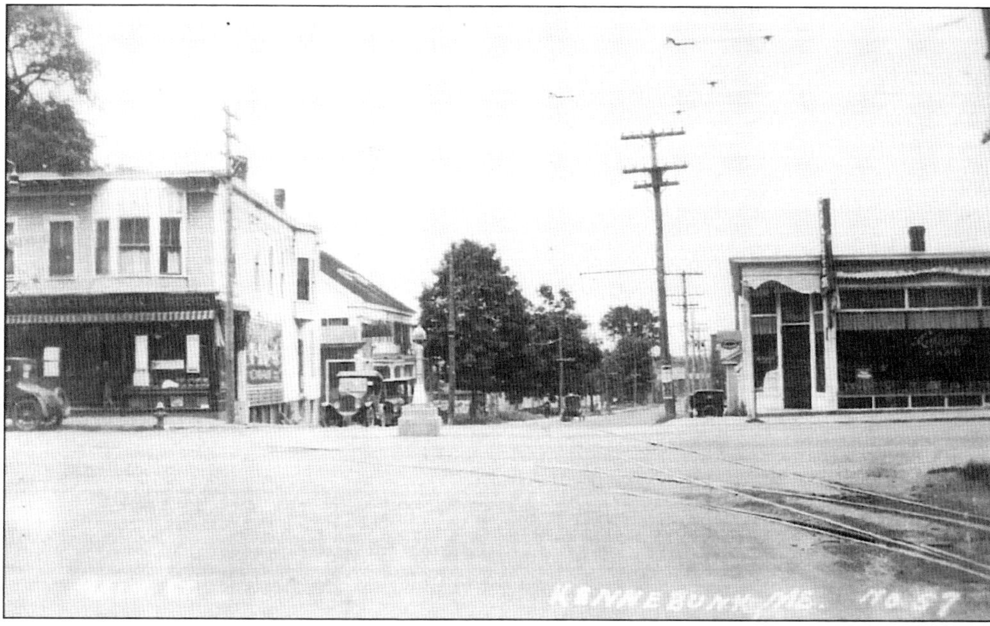

The only known view of the freight spur constructed on Water Street, Kennebuck, by the Sanford & Cape Porpoise Railway in 1901. We're looking from Storer Street. This spur initially served the plants of the Mousam Manufacturing Company, the National Fibre Board Company and the Leatheroid Manufacturing Company, one or more of which utilized trolley freight to receive raw materials and coal and ship finished goods.

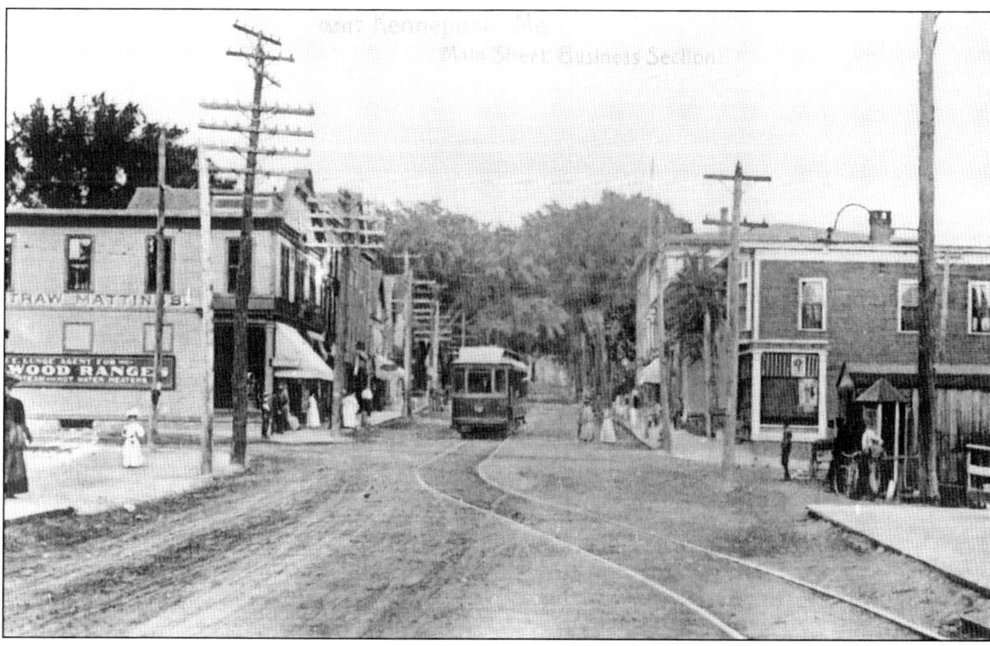

Looking north on Main Street, Kennebunk, from the Mousam River bridge about 1907. The J.W. Bowdoin drug store housed the Atlantic Shore Line ticket agency in 1909, on June 16 of which the basic cash fare was boosted from a nickel to six cents. This increase sparked a mighty uproar and in December the company began offering strips of five tickets for a quarter.

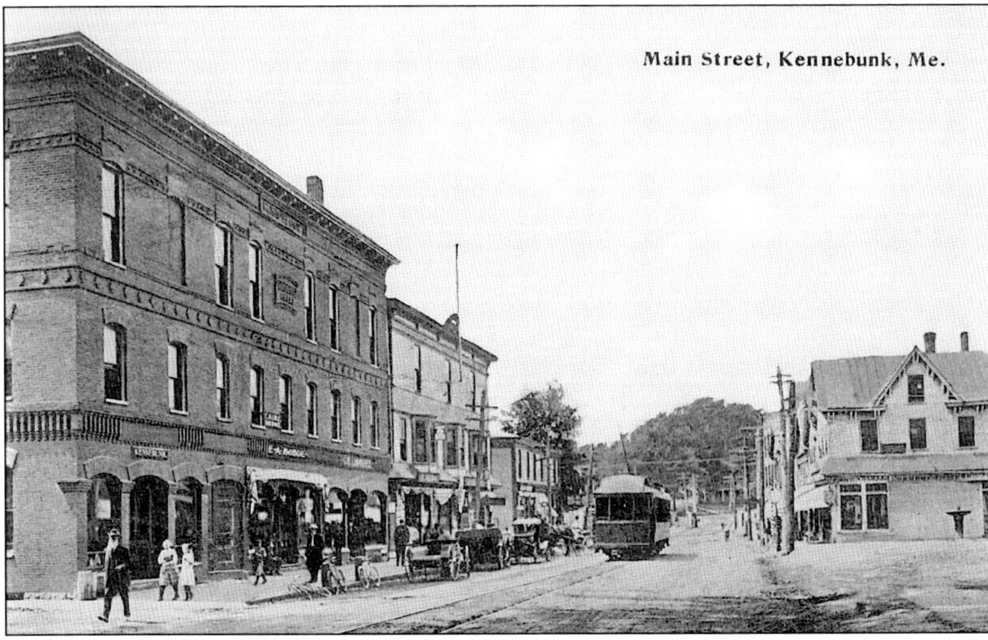

The Masonic Temple is at the left as an Atlantic Shore Line trolley runs southerly on Main Street, Kennebunk, on its way to either York Beach or Sanford. Cars ran in both directions on Main Street and their movements were controlled by a set of block signals installed in 1907 at Storer Street and at Summer Street.

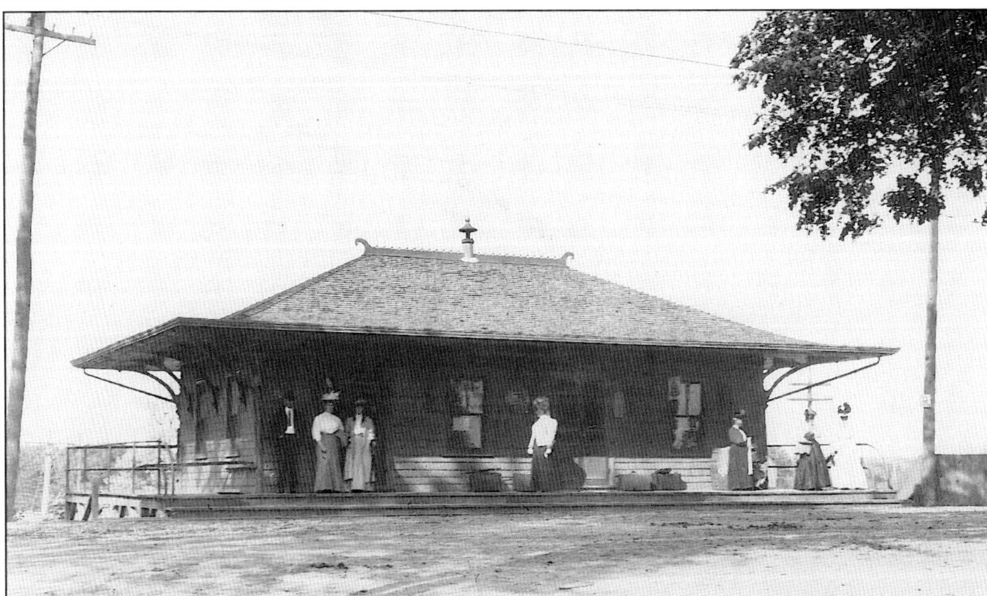

Erected by the Sanford & Cape Porpoise Railway in 1901, Kennebunk Station was on the north side of Summer Street at the west end of the bridge spanning the Boston & Maine Railroad. The overhanging roof eaves provided shelter on rainy days for passengers who did not wish to wait inside. Mrs. E.M. Chisholm was the ticket agent here and she also operated a refreshment stand. A proposed spur track from Summer Street to the Kennebunk passenger station of the B&M never materialized.

Four

The Kennebunks and Biddeford

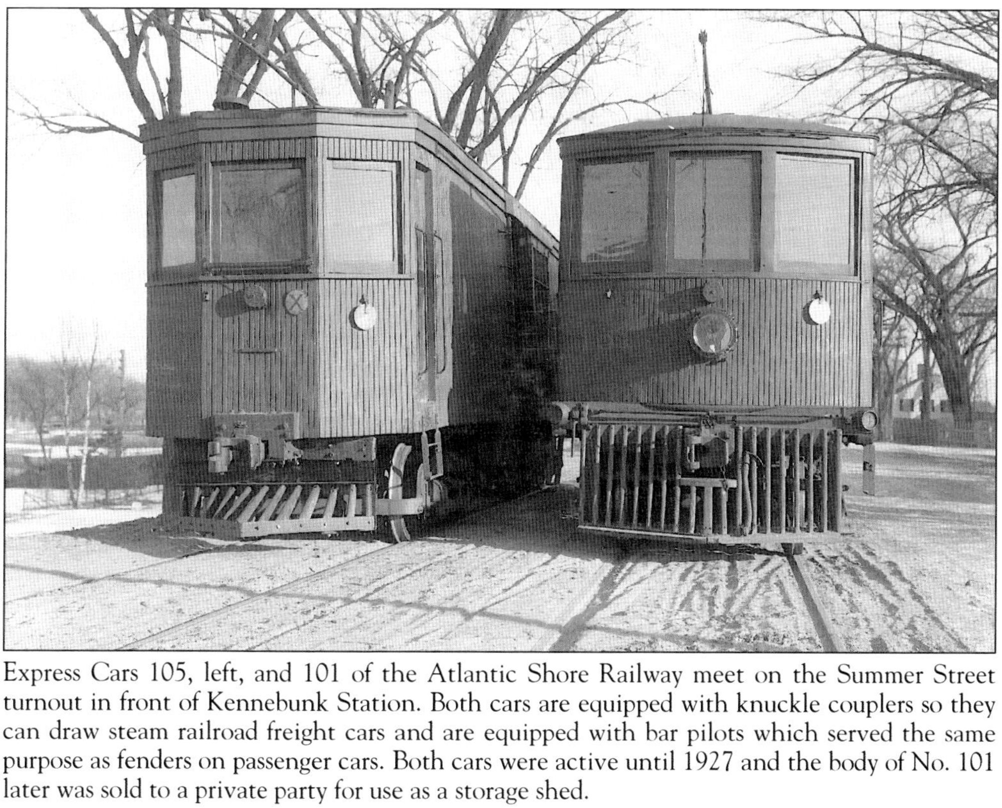

Express Cars 105, left, and 101 of the Atlantic Shore Railway meet on the Summer Street turnout in front of Kennebunk Station. Both cars are equipped with knuckle couplers so they can draw steam railroad freight cars and are equipped with bar pilots which served the same purpose as fenders on passenger cars. Both cars were active until 1927 and the body of No. 101 later was sold to a private party for use as a storage shed.

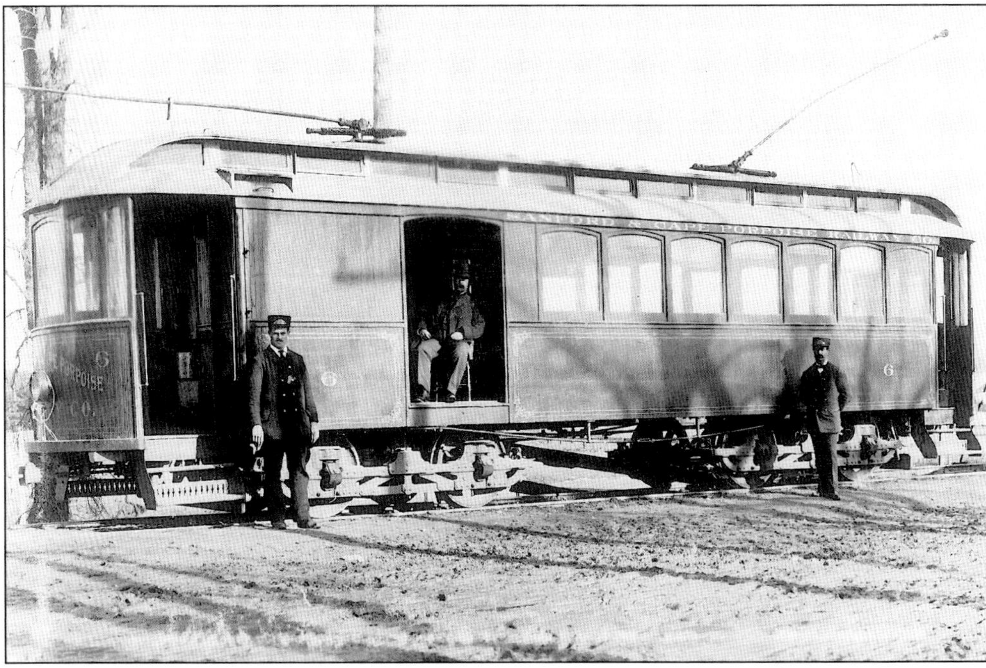

The Sanford & Cape Porpoise Railway (S&CP) was opened between Sanford and the Summer Street bridge, Kennebunk, on August 19, 1899, and was completed to Cape Porpoise in November. S&CP combination car No. 6 is at the Summer Street bridge. This car and two identical ones, Nos. 8 and 10, originally had hand brakes only, air brakes later being installed.

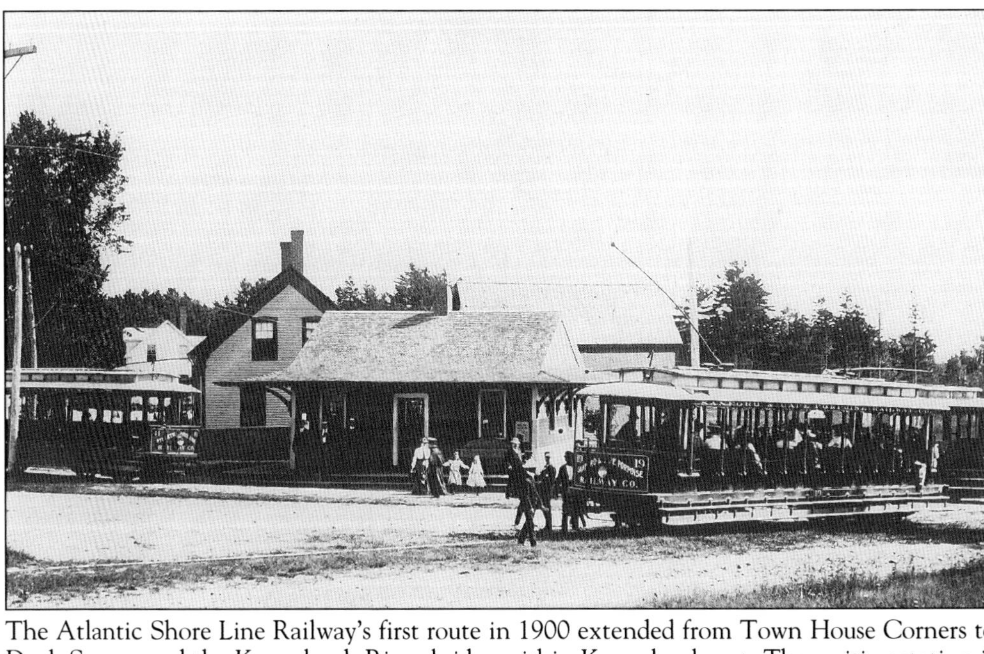

The Atlantic Shore Line Railway's first route in 1900 extended from Town House Corners to Dock Square and the Kennebunk River bridge within Kennebunkport. The waiting station is the former District 5 school, purchased from the town of Kennebunkport by the street railway. The trolleys are 15-bench opens Nos. 11 and 19 of the Sanford & Cape Porpoise Railway.

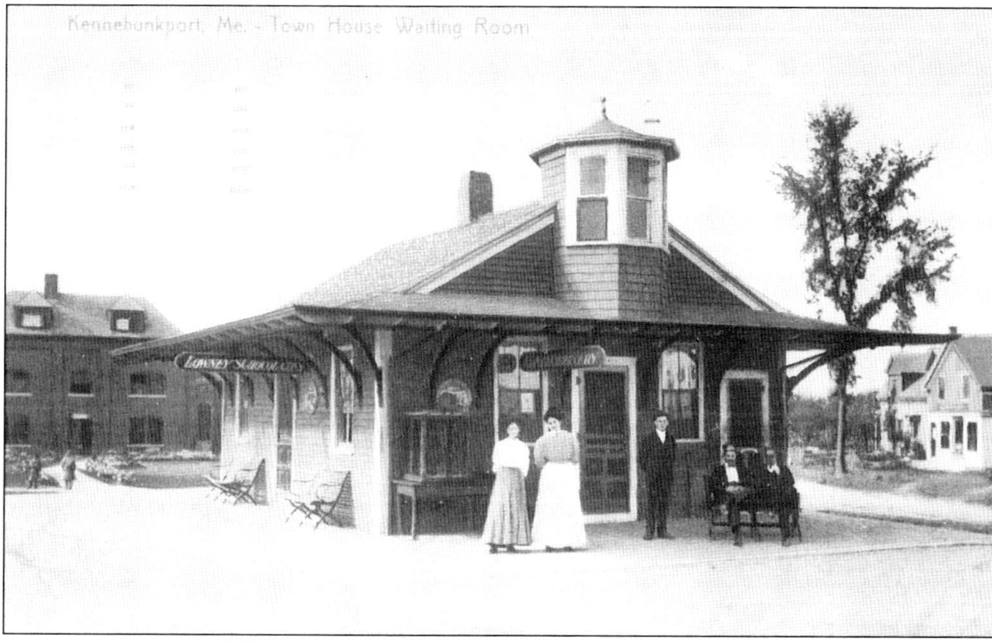

After the opening of the trolley line to Dock Square on July 4, 1900, Town House Corners was identified by the Atlantic Shore Line Railway as Town House Junction, from which an 8.5-mile line to Biddeford was opened on August 15, 1904. Coincident with the construction of a carhouse at Town House Junction, the waiting station was moved to a new location and extensively remodeled.

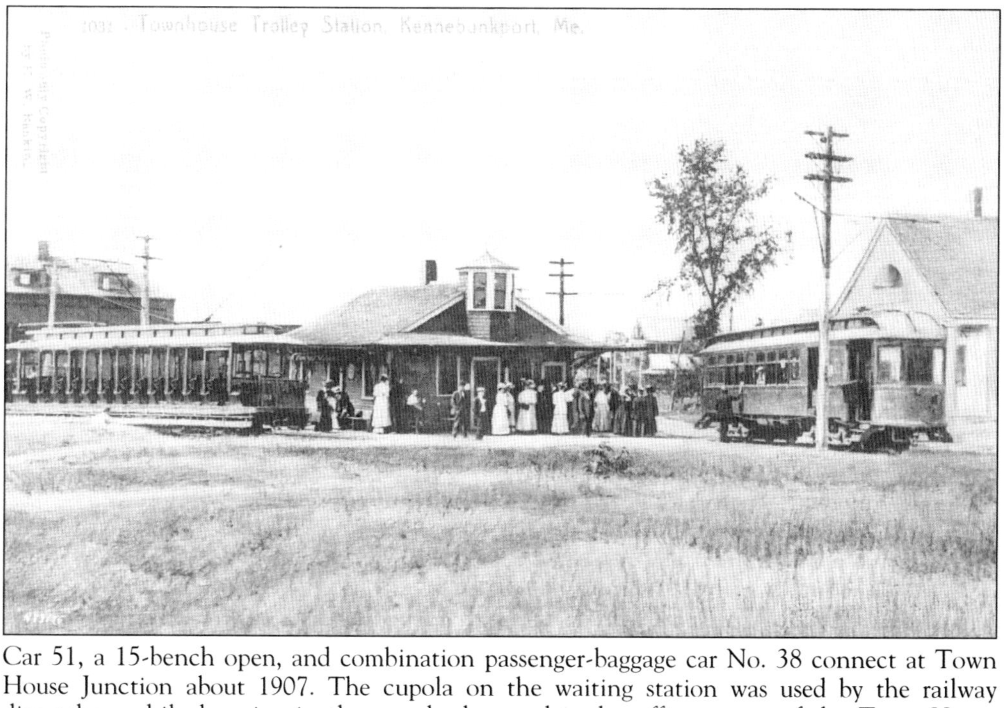

Car 51, a 15-bench open, and combination passenger-baggage car No. 38 connect at Town House Junction about 1907. The cupola on the waiting station was used by the railway dispatcher, while looming in the rear background is the office annex of the Town House carhouse.

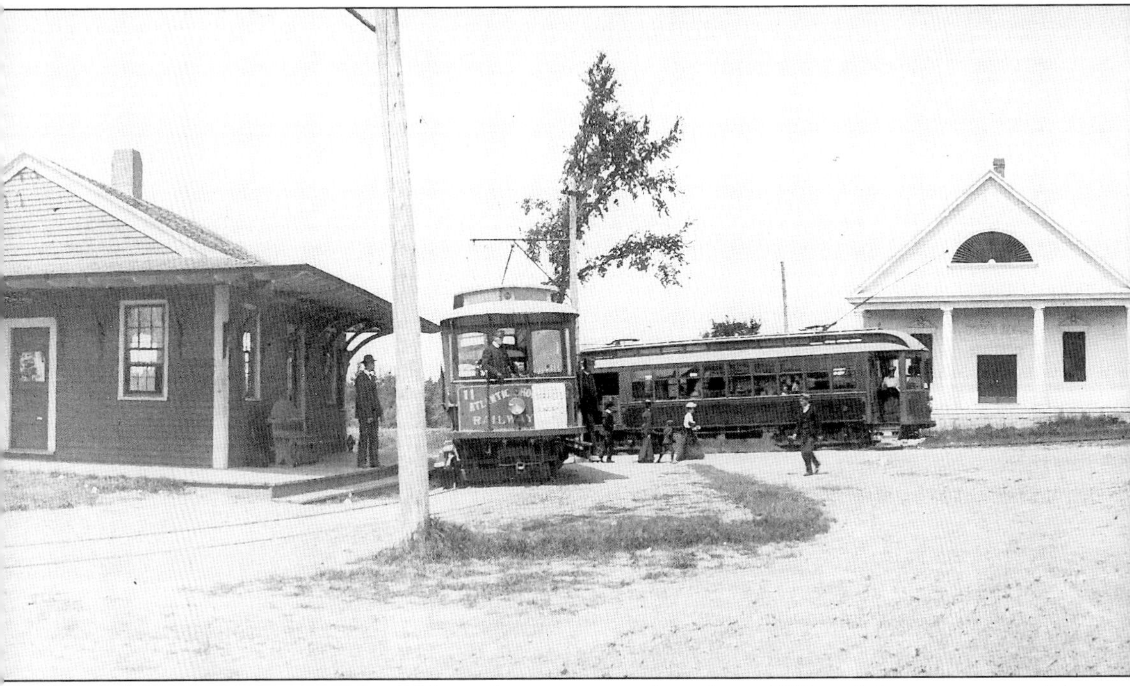

This panoramic view of Town House Junction was taken about 1902 and shows two cars of the Atlantic Shore Line Railway at the waiting station. The building behind the closed car is the Kennebunkport Town House while that at right center is the Poor Farm. The former was sold

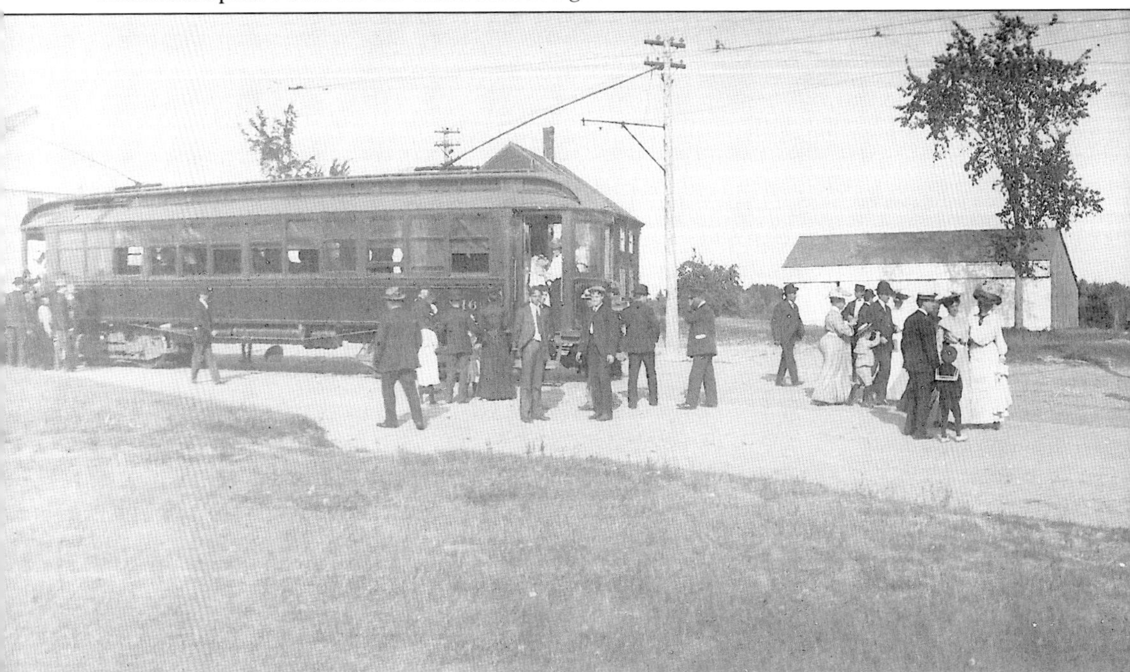

In this c. 1904 view of Town House Junction, Car 16 at left loads passengers for Biddeford while Cape Porpoise is the destination of the combination passenger-baggage car, No. 38, at right. Where the dog was bound is anybody's guess. This was a particular busy place in summer

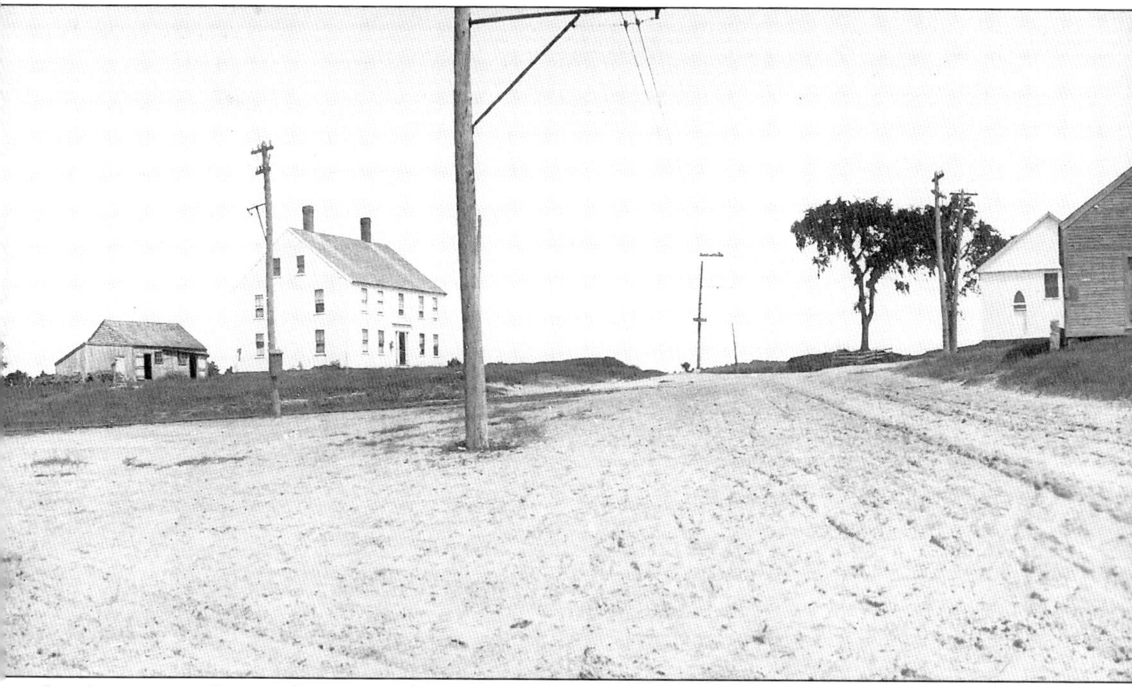

by the town and moved to a new location on North Street in 1954 and became the Arundel Opera Theater, which went out of business in 1963. A year later, it was resold to the Diocese of Maine and became St. Martha Roman Catholic Church.

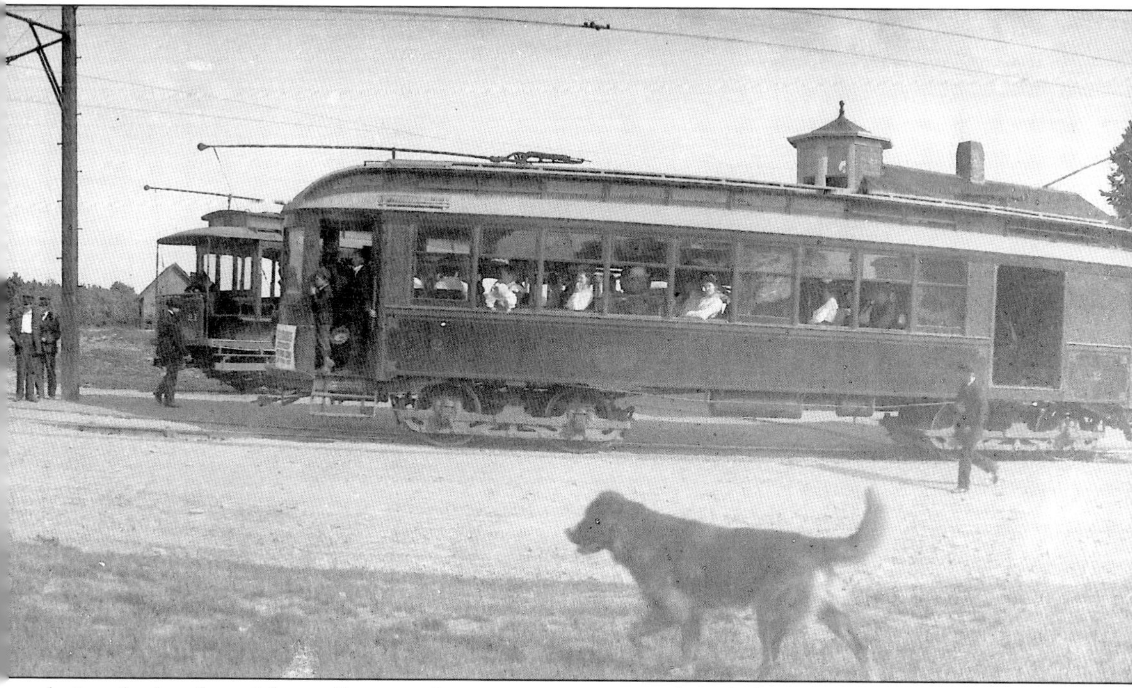

during the heyday of the trolley era when passenger cars ran hourly between Sanford and Cape Porpoise and every half hour between Kennebunkport and Biddeford.

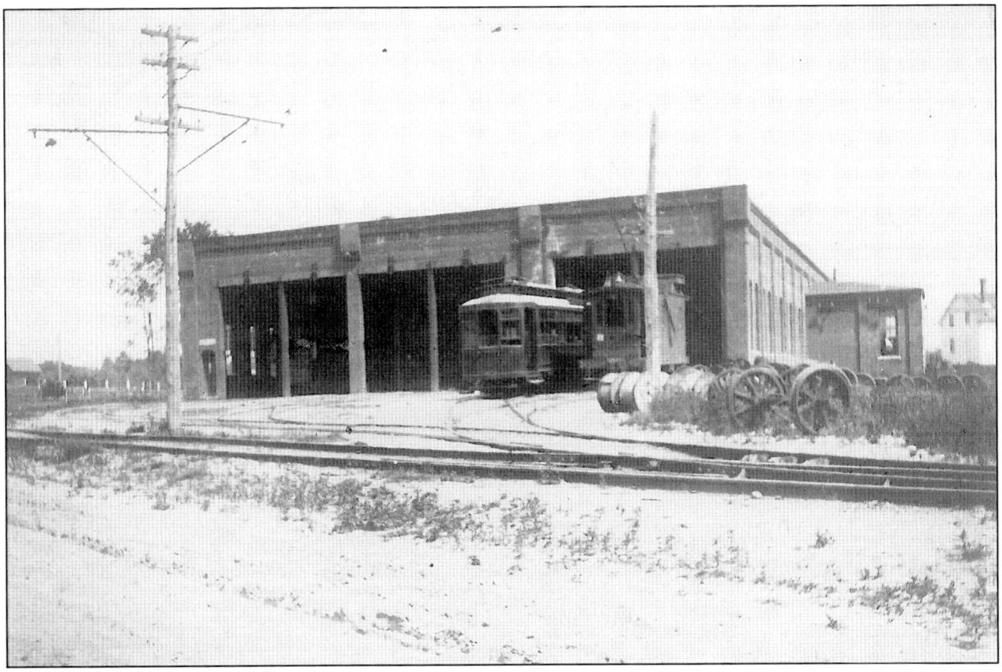

Opened at Town House Junction in 1904, this carhouse of the Atlantic Shore Line Railway was destroyed by fire on February 7, 1909, with a loss of seven passenger cars and a snow plow. This view shows the Arundel Road end of the barn. A number of cars were removed to safety after the fire was discovered shortly after midnight but then the power failed and nothing more could be done. When firefighters arrived, they could accomplish little except prevent the spread of the flames to nearby buildings because of a lack of water.

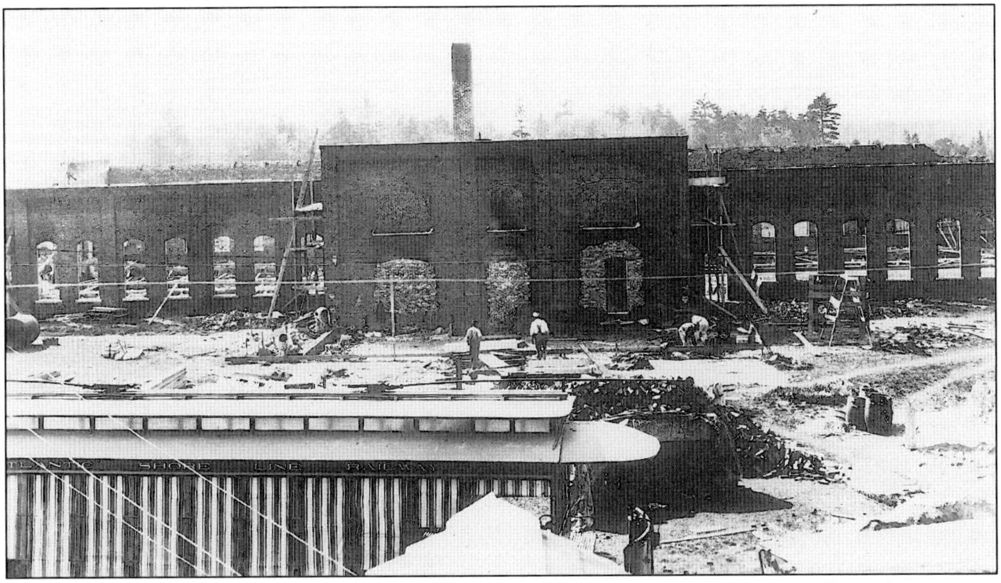

The Town House Junction carhouse is being reconstructed in this 1910 view from the waiting station. Atlantic Shore Line officials reportedly sought to erect a replacement facility in Kennebunk but no suitable site could be found. The rebuilt building was the same general design and size as the original and had the same track arrangement.

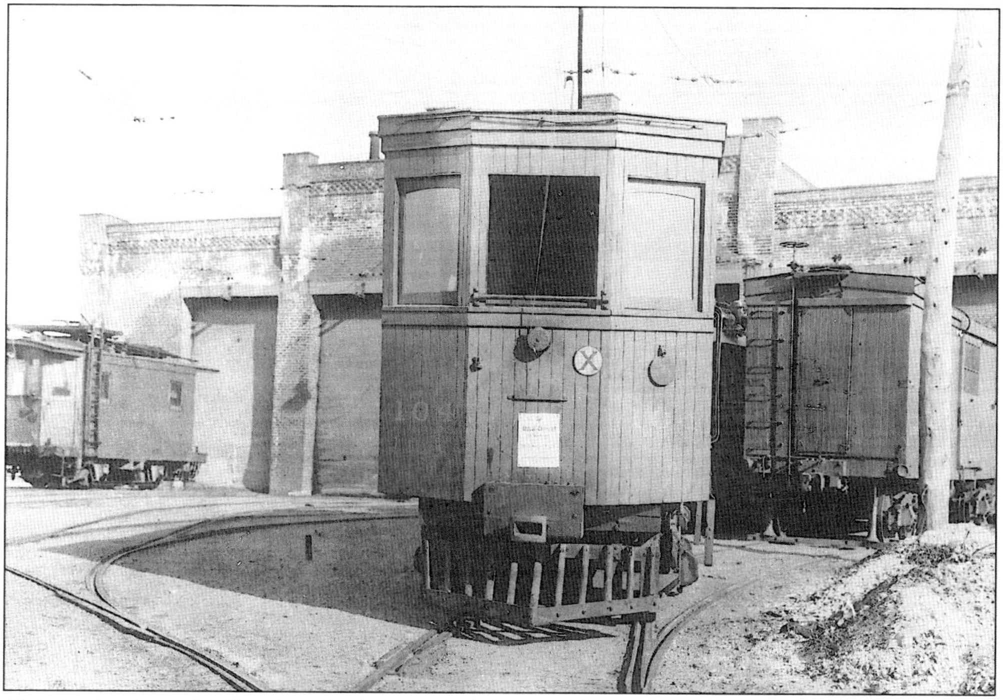

This is the Arundel Road end of the rebuilt Town House car barn about 1911. Shown are line car No. 97, express Car 104 and portable substation No. 103. The carhouse was closed in September 1927 after the end of trolley service between Sanford and Biddeford via Kennebunk and Kennebunkport and was sold to a private party, who allowed the building to deteriorate. An automotive garage occupies the site today.

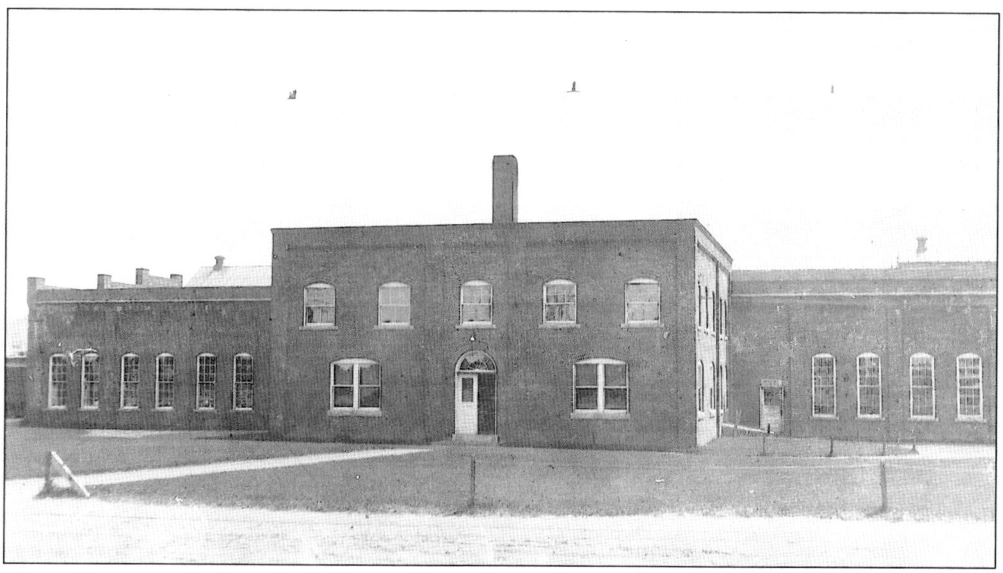

The office area of the rebuilt Town House barn about 1911. The Atlantic Shore Railway maintained its general offices here until August 1927 and then transferred them to Sanford. Abandoned during the move were large stocks of obsolete transfers, tickets, paper forms, and even cap badges and many of these are preserved today in the collections of trolley hobbyists.

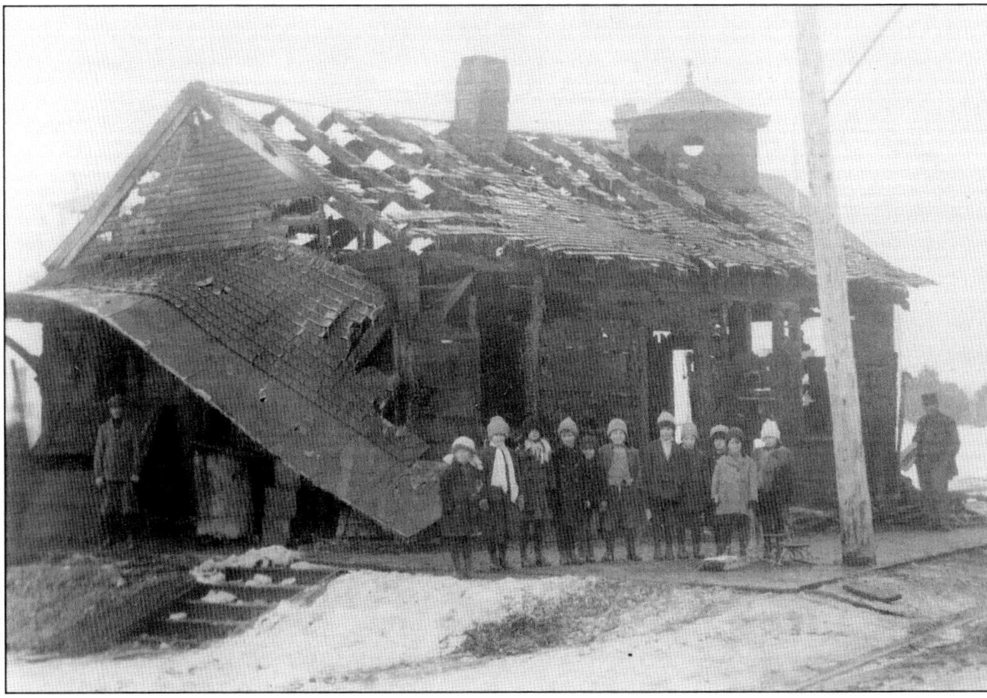

Little is left of the waiting station at Town House Junction after a 1914 fire. The fire loss and the cost of a replacement were not given in Atlantic Shore Railway financial reports.

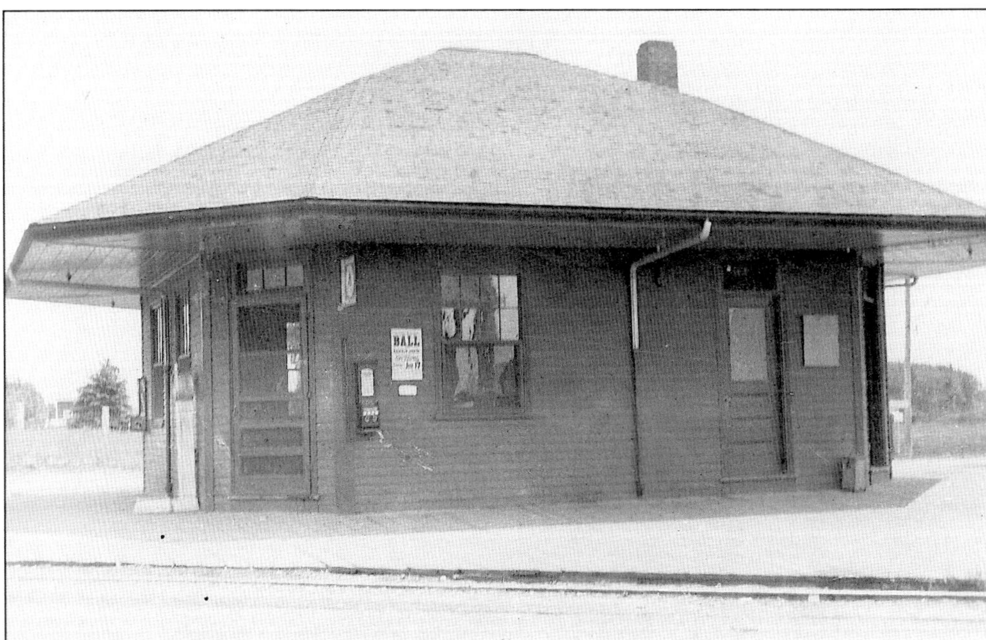

The new Town House Junction waiting station, completed in 1915, was in use until 1927 and then was either razed or sold. Like its predecessor, it had a refreshment stand but whether restrooms were provided is unknown.

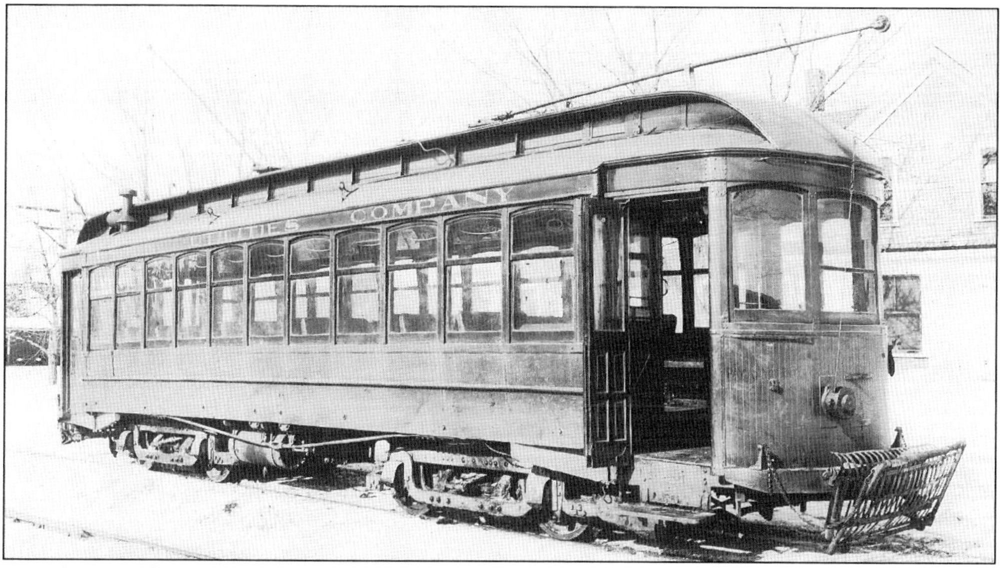

In order to reduce labor costs, the York Utilities Company revamped many of its double-truck closed passenger cars for one-man operation, dispensing with the services of conductors. No. 48, built in 1907 and resplendent in a new brilliant orange external livery, is on Arundel Road, near Town House Junction, about 1924.

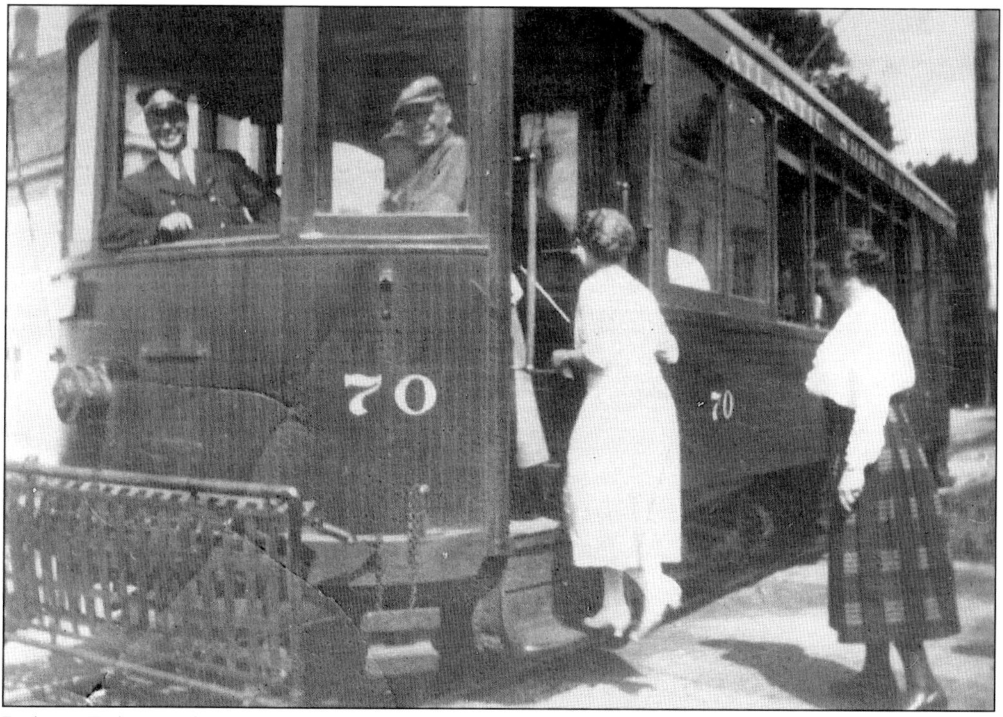

Robert Fiske is the motorman of Atlantic Shore Railway No. 70 on the North Street, Kennebunkport, about 1914. No. 70 and an identical car, No. 68, were the last new trolleys to be purchased by the company and were active until September 1927. Their bodies, sold to a private party, remained in the ruins of the Town House carhouse for many years and were destroyed by the elements.

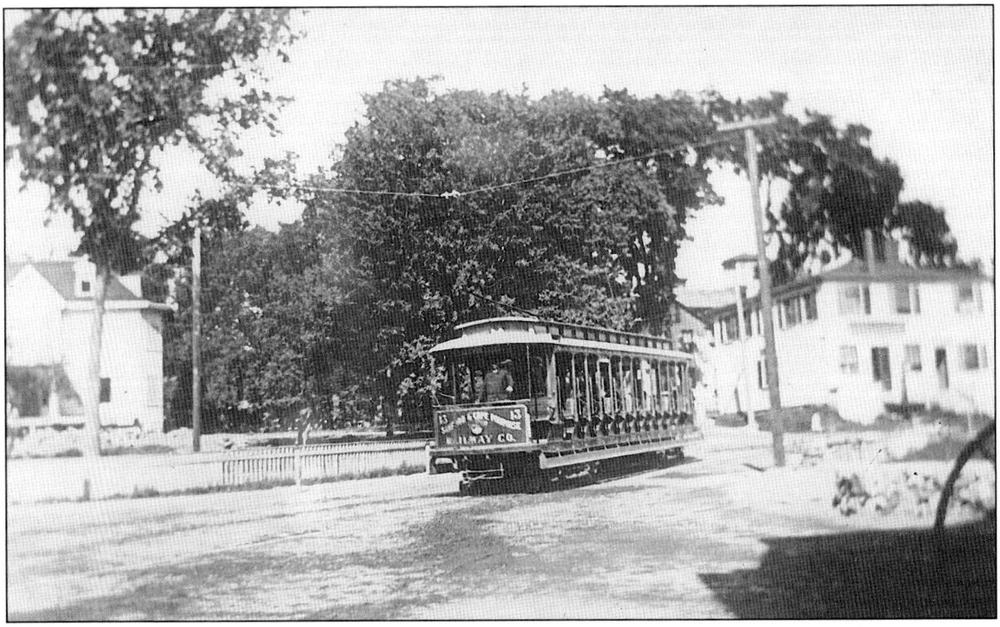

Entering Dock Square, Kennebunkport, about 1900 is Sanford & Cape Porpoise 15-bench open No. 13. These cars seated 75 passengers but were capable of carrying many standees if necessary. It was renumbered 43 by the Atlantic Shore Line Railway and was wrecked in a head-on collision with a freight car, No. 104, between Town House Junction and Cape Porpoise on June 4, 1908. One woman was killed and several other passengers on No. 43 were seriously injured.

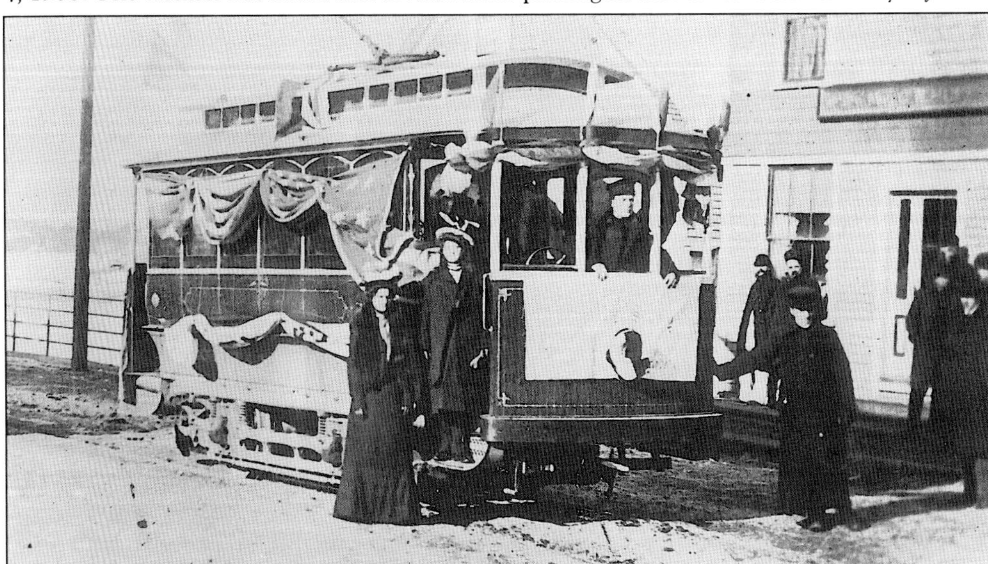

Adorned with bunting, Car 1 of the Atlantic Shore Line waits near the north end of the Kennebunk River bridge on February 28, 1901 to carry Miss Rose Seavey to the Kennebunk railroad station on the first leg of her journey to Washington, D.C. The Kennebunkport school teacher won all-expense paid trip to the National Capital in a contest sponsored by the *Boston Globe*. After a 1903 collision on North Street, Kennebunkport, No. 1 was withdrawn from service and its body became a waiting station on the Town House-Biddeford line in 1904.

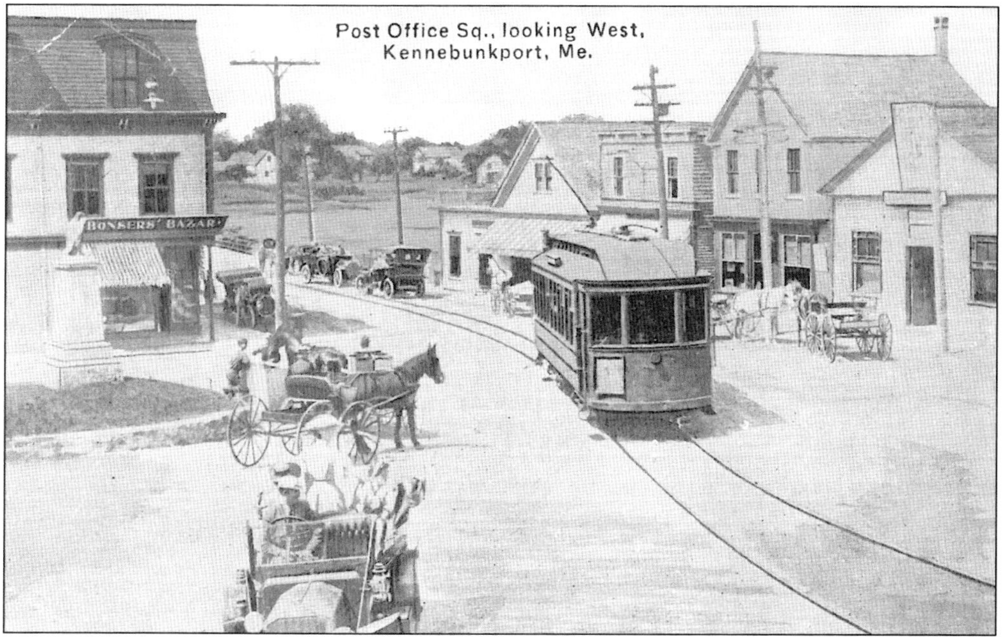

Biddeford is the probable destination of this Atlantic Shore Line closed car in Dock Square, Kennebunkport, about 1910. Through cars were run between this point and City Square, Biddeford, 10 miles, in summer for a number of years. Service was half hourly and the running time was 45 minutes. In other seasons, through cars were run between Dock Square, Kennebunkport, and Cape Porpoise.

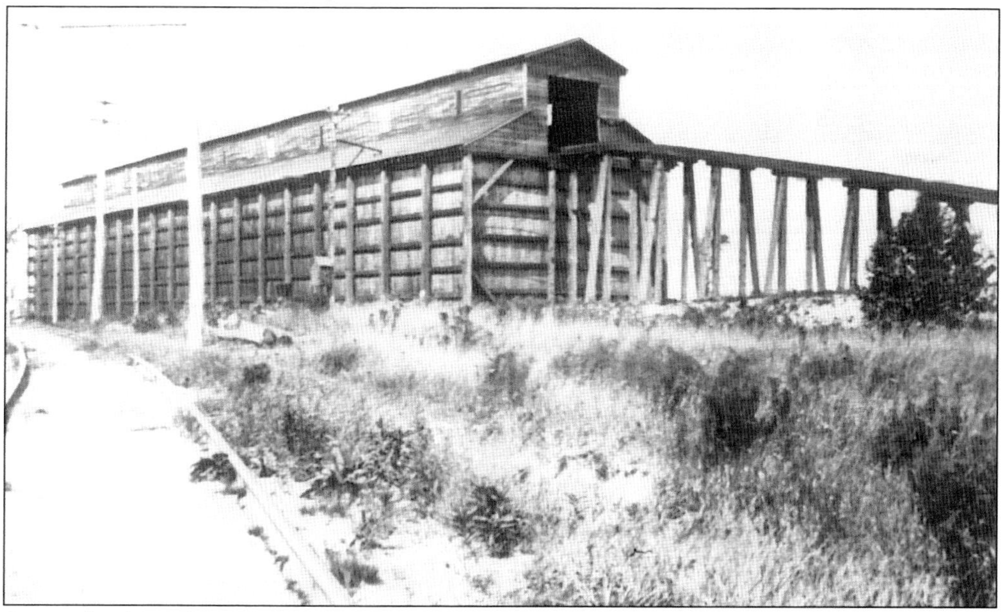

Situated a short distance east of Town House Junction was a 7,000-ton coal pocket erected in 1903 by the Sanford & Cape Porpoise Railway, which had begun moving the fuel from Cape Porpoise to Sanford two years earlier. Principal consignees were the Sanford Mills Company and the Goodall Worsted Company in Sanford village, who purchased the coal and paid the railway to transport it from tidewater to their textile complexes.

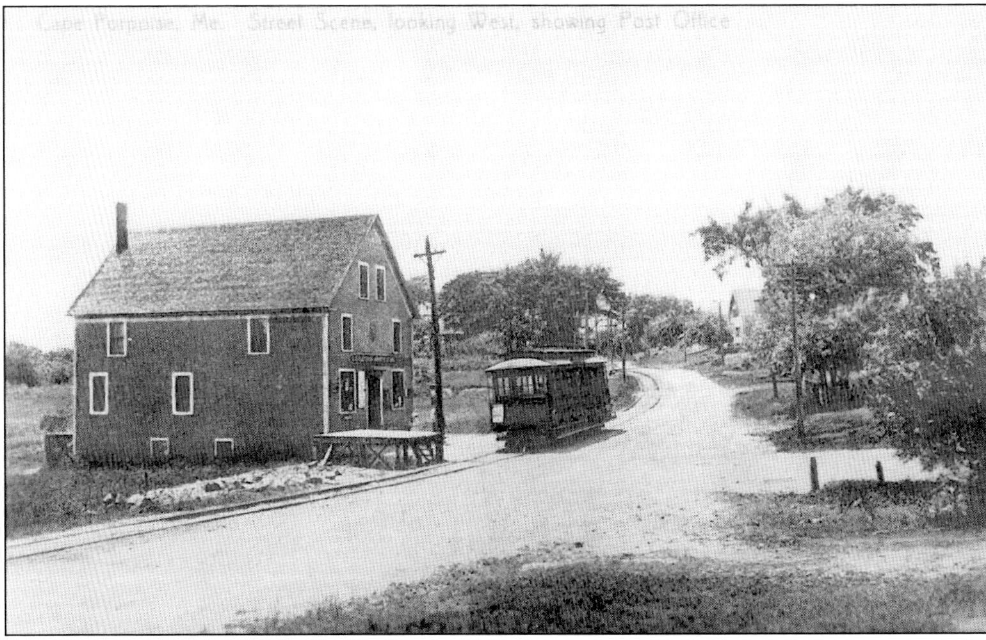

An open car passes the L.E. Fletcher store on its way to Bickford Island. Cape Porpoise's first telephone was installed here in July 1899, just a few months before the Sanford & Cape Porpoise Railway introduced trolleys to the village. Fletcher was the Atlantic Shore Line ticket agent at the Cape in 1908 and he still was listed as such four years later.

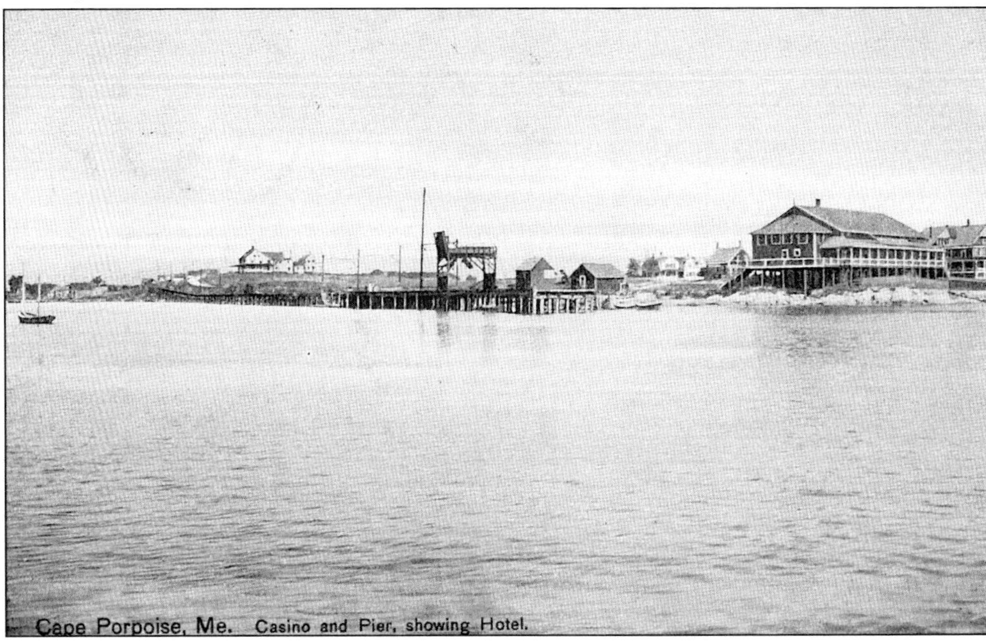

This 800-foot long trestle crossed Cape Porpoise inner harbor between the foot of Stone Haven Hill on Pier Road and Bickford Island. In the center can be seen the gantry used to unload coal barges and schooners arriving at the Cape. The fuel initially was carried to Sanford in four-wheel dump cars drawn by a double-truck locomotive, eight-wheel coal cars later being provided.

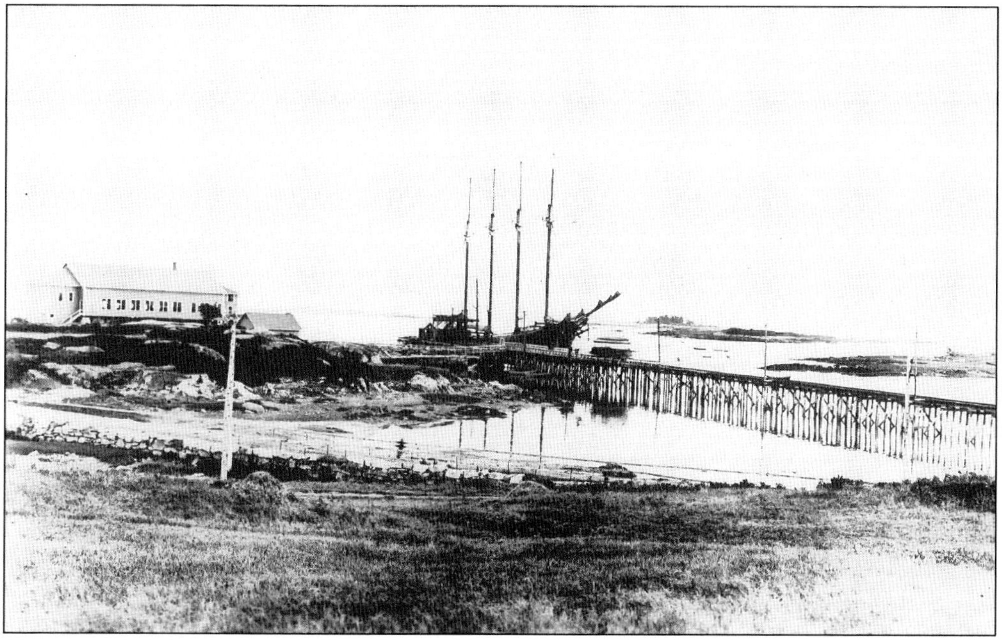

A four-masted schooner loaded with coal is docked at the Bickford Island end of the Cape Porpoise trestle. The outer harbor was dredged to a depth of 15 feet at mean low tide in June 1900, the U.S. Congress having appropriated $125,000 for the project after a lot of arm-twisting by the Maine delegation to Washington.

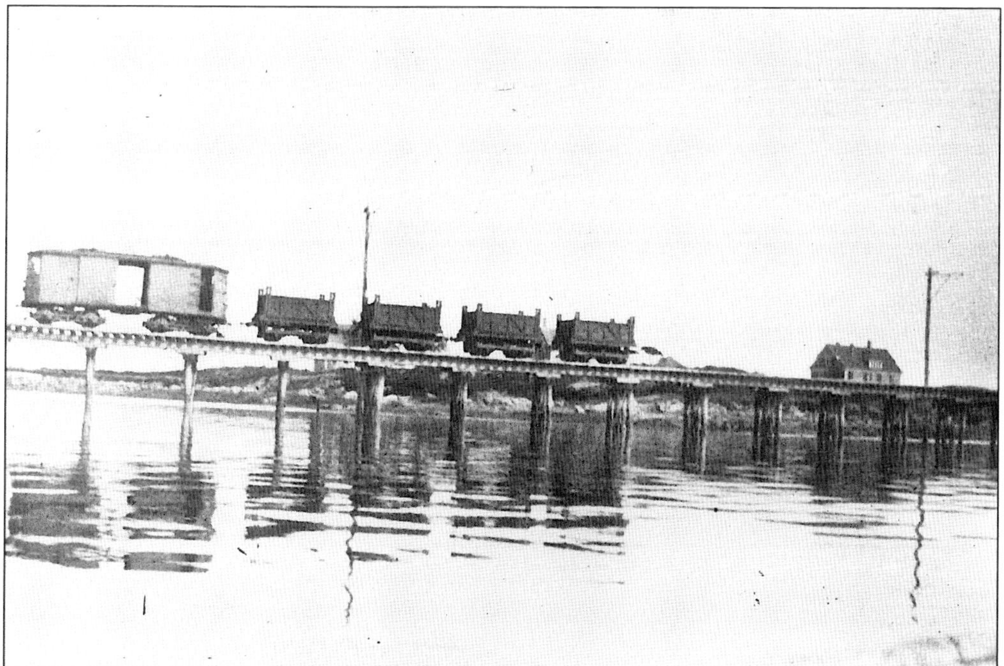

A Sanford-bound coal train about midway on the trestle crossing Cape Porpoise inner harbor about 1902. Coal shipments from the Cape to Sanford ended about 1910 due to the increased use of electricity by the Sanford village textile mills to power their looms and other machinery.

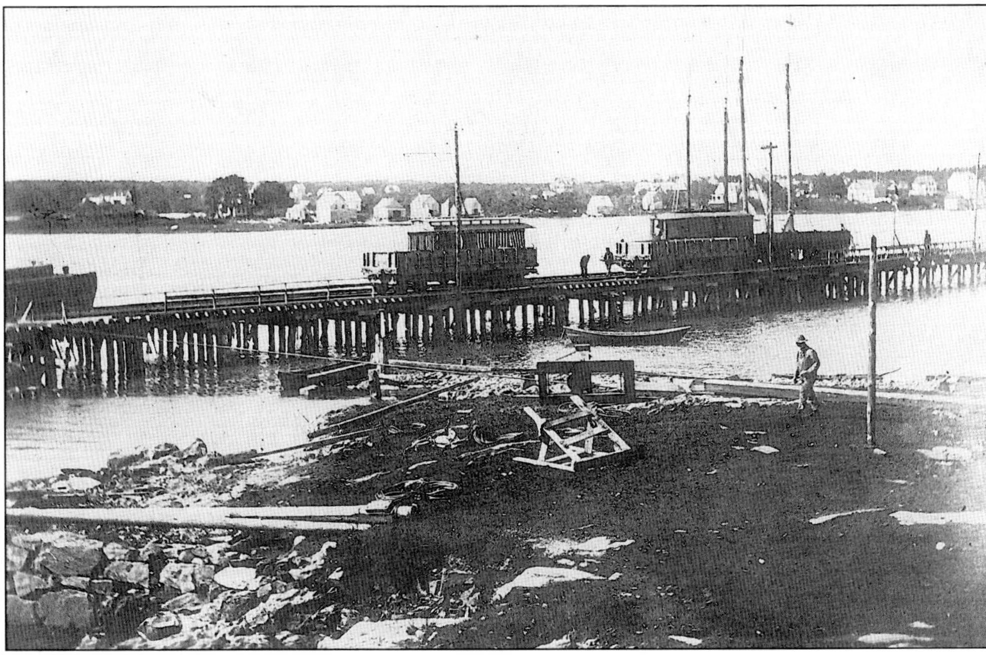

Another view of the Cape Porpoise trestle showing coal cars, a locomotive and a passenger car. Use of the trestle ended about 1914 after the track on Pier Road was extended to Bickford Island but its piles remained in evidence for many years thereafter. There's still a wharf on the island but it's now used by lobstermen and fishermen.

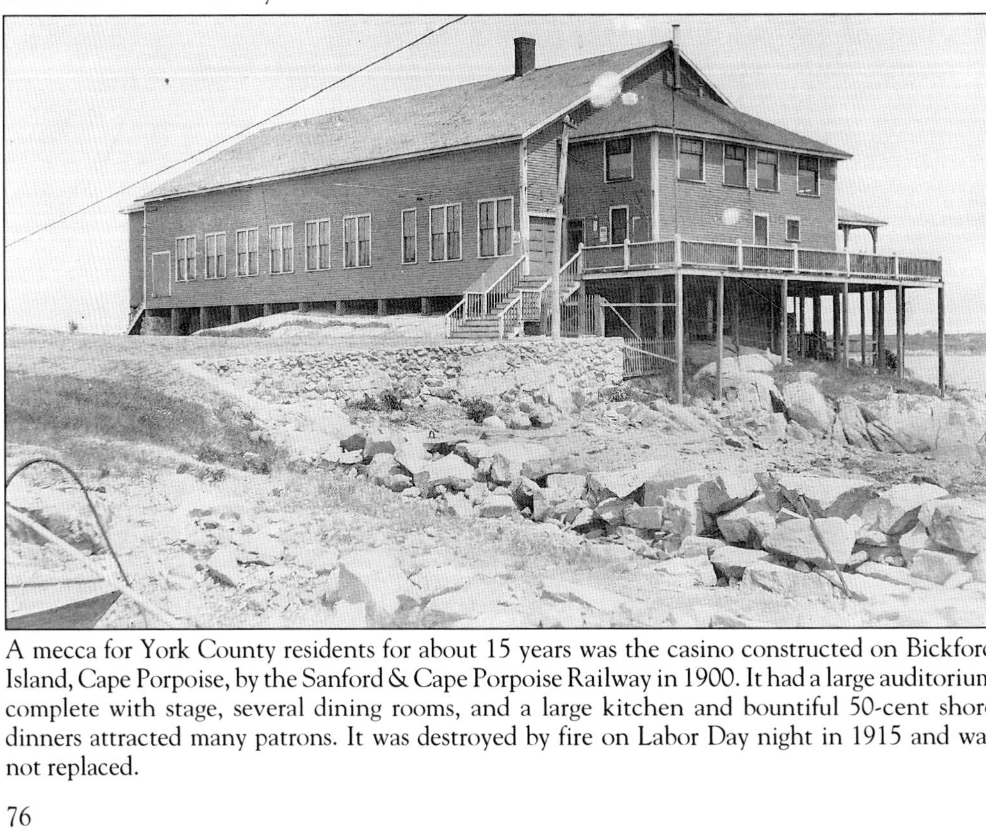

A mecca for York County residents for about 15 years was the casino constructed on Bickford Island, Cape Porpoise, by the Sanford & Cape Porpoise Railway in 1900. It had a large auditorium complete with stage, several dining rooms, and a large kitchen and bountiful 50-cent shore dinners attracted many patrons. It was destroyed by fire on Labor Day night in 1915 and was not replaced.

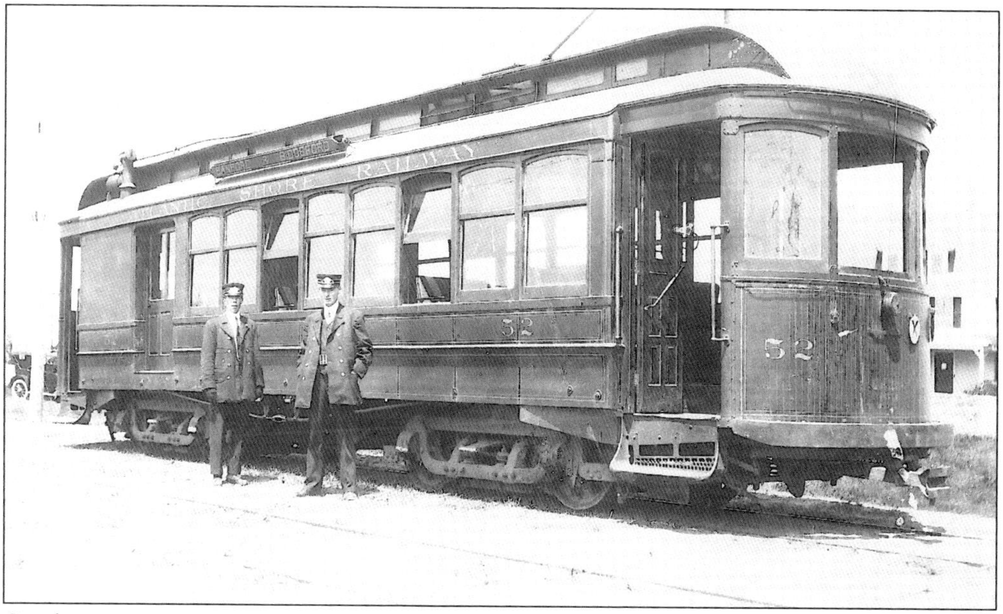

Combination passenger-express Car 52 of the Atlantic Shore Railway on Bickford Island about 1915. Everett Higgins, left, is the motorman while Eugene Merrill, right, is conductor. The round X sign on the dasher indicated that the car was being operated as an extra instead of on a regularly scheduled trip.

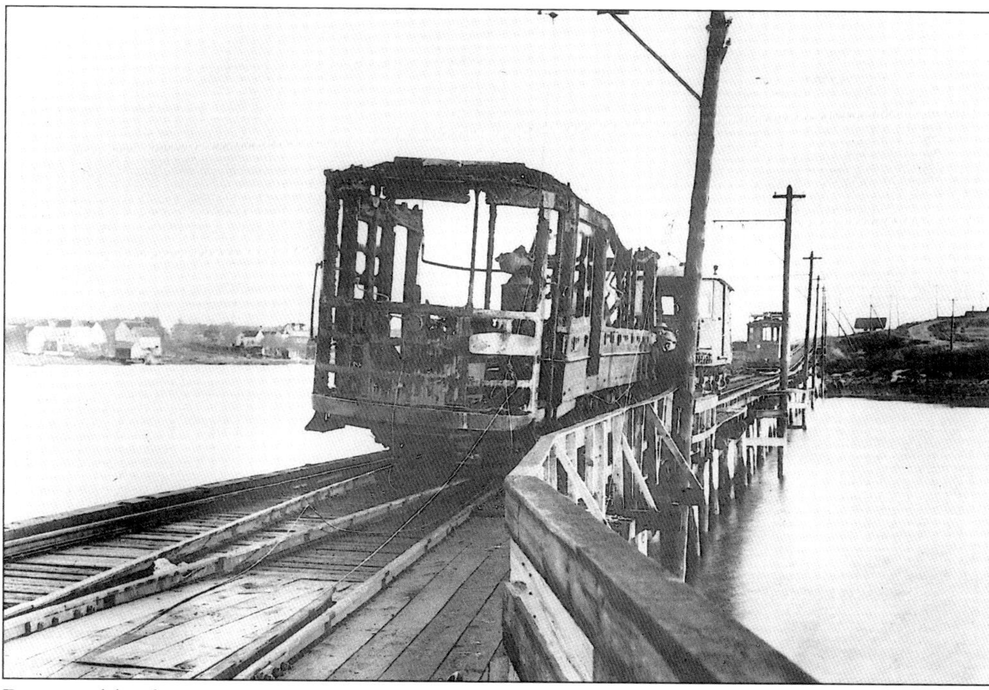

Destroyed by fire at Cape Porpoise on the evening of April 30, 1910, Car 54 is towed to the "boneyard" at the coal pocket for scrapping. A short circuit created when a trolley pole hit the stack of the hot water heater was believed to have been the cause of the blaze. Fortunately there were no passengers and the car crew escaped injury.

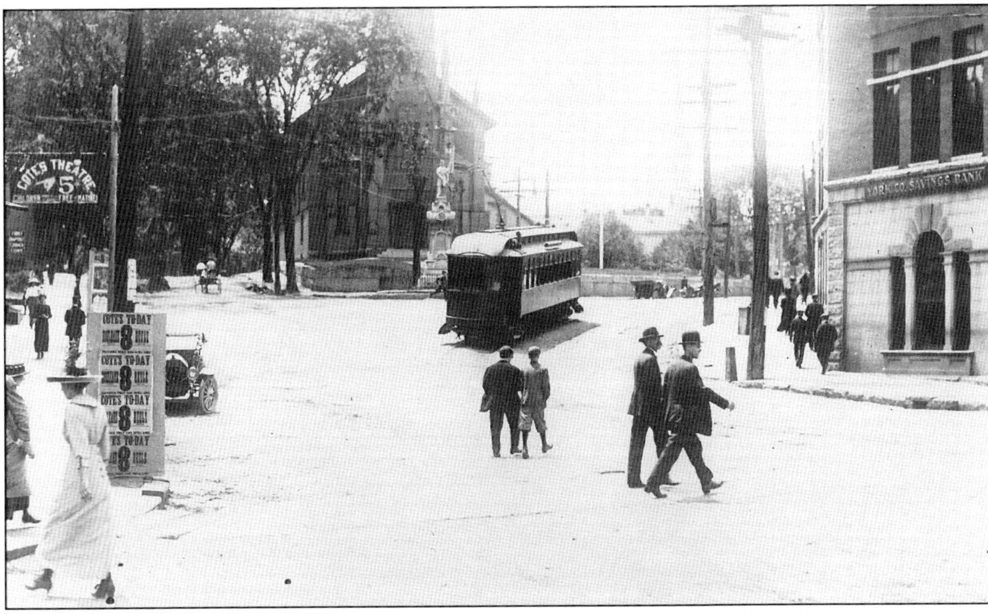

Ready to leave for Town House Junction is Atlantic Shore Line No. 40 in City Square, Biddeford. The building at right is the City Hall. A steep grade on South and Adams Streets approaching the square was the scene of several trolley runaways over the years and on one occasion, on October 29, 1909, a passenger car crashed into an express car standing at the end of track. Damage was minor and there were no injuries.

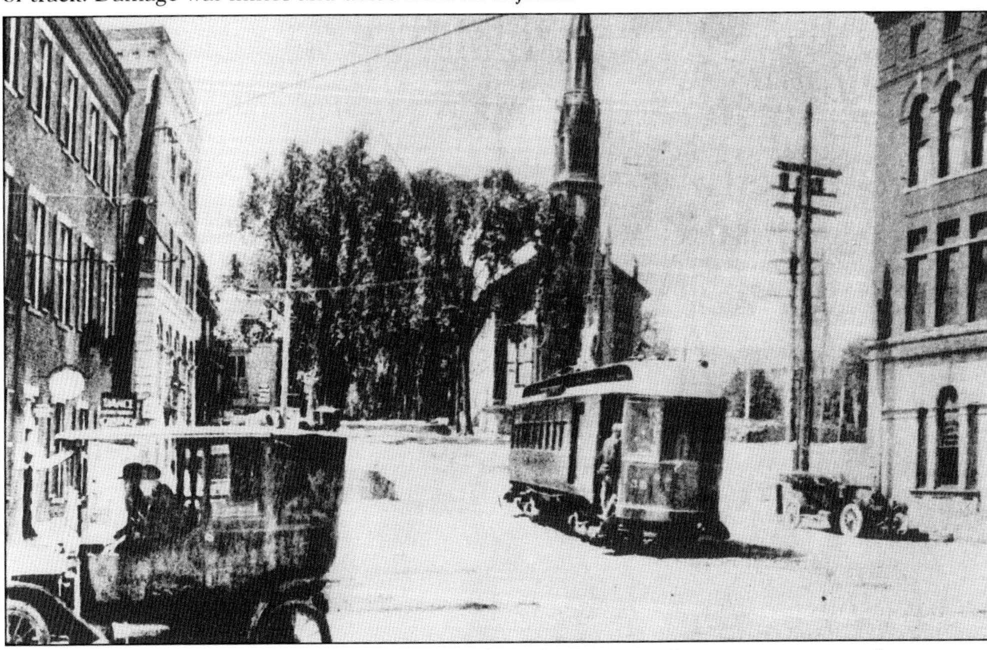

Standing beside the Biddeford City Hall on Adams Street is combination passenger-baggage car No. 38. Shipments of the Tarbox Express Company and its successors frequently were carried by this car. No physical connection between the Atlantic Shore and the Biddeford & Saco Railroad's track on Main Street ever was effected in City Square but one for express purposes only was provided at Birch and Alfred Streets in November 1915.

A new steam pumper is tested in City Square by the Biddeford Fire Department on May 24, 1909. At the extreme left is an Atlantic Shore Line express car. Yes, the streams of water did reach the cupola on the City Hall and the engine was accepted by the municipality.

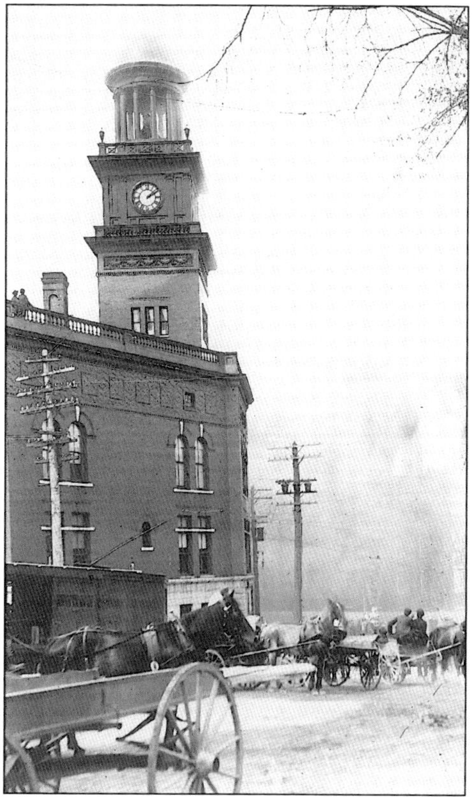

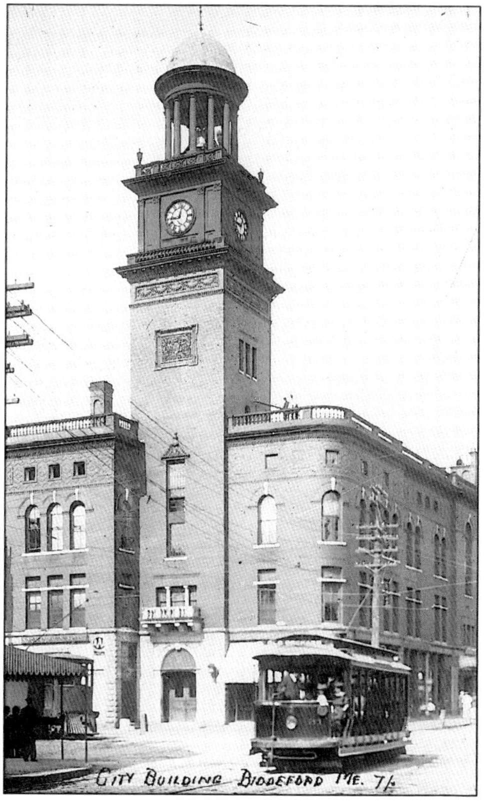

Nary an automobile is in sight in this view of the Biddeford City Hall. Atlantic Shore Express Car 101 is at the extreme left as Biddeford & Saco 12-bench open No. 31 heads for Old Orchard Beach. City Square was the point where Atlantic Shore passengers changed to Biddeford & Saco trolleys to continue on to Saco and Old Orchard Beach, the latter running every quarter hour in summer.

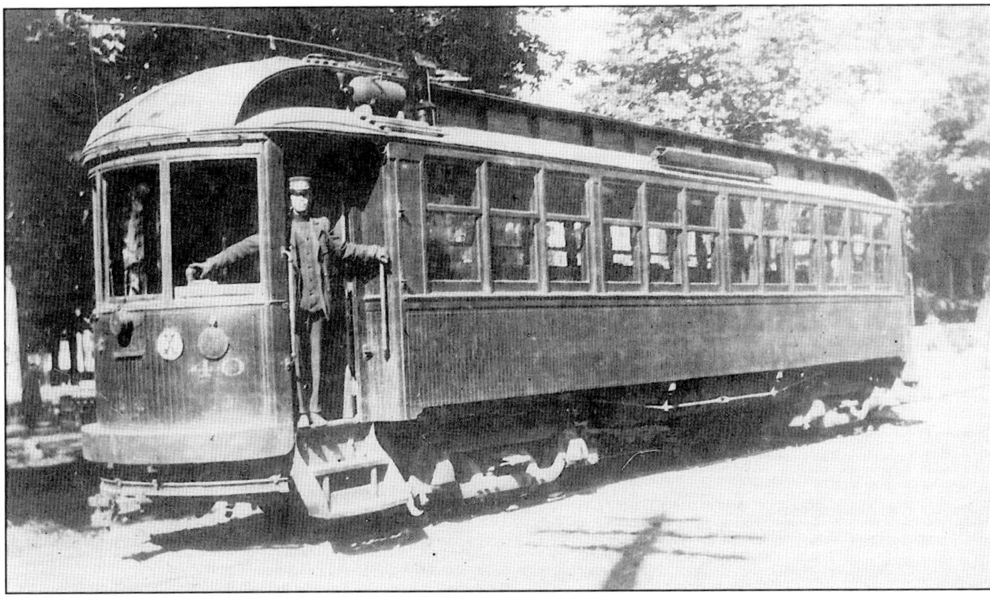

Everett Higgins was the motorman when this picture of Atlantic Shore Line No. 40 was taken on Granite Street, Biddeford. Cars from Town House Junction entered the city on a private right-of-way and Granite Street Extension and continued through Granite, Hill, Birch, Graham, Crescent, South, and Adams Streets to City Square.

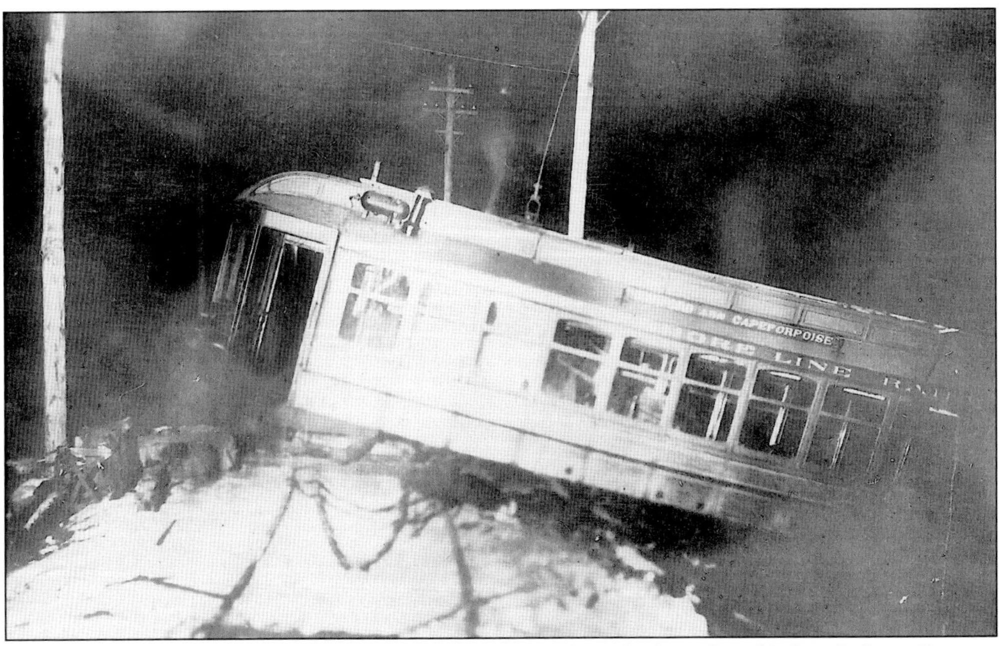

There were no serious injuries to the 27 passengers aboard when Car 56 derailed on Granite Street Extension, Biddeford, shortly before 2 p.m. on February 27, 1912. After being rerailed the next morning, the trolley was towed to the Town House carhouse for repairs. The accident was blamed on an accumulation of ice and snow on the rails and it was not until 10 a.m. on February 28th that the first regular passenger car arrived in City Square from Kennebunkport.

Five

Sanford and Springvale

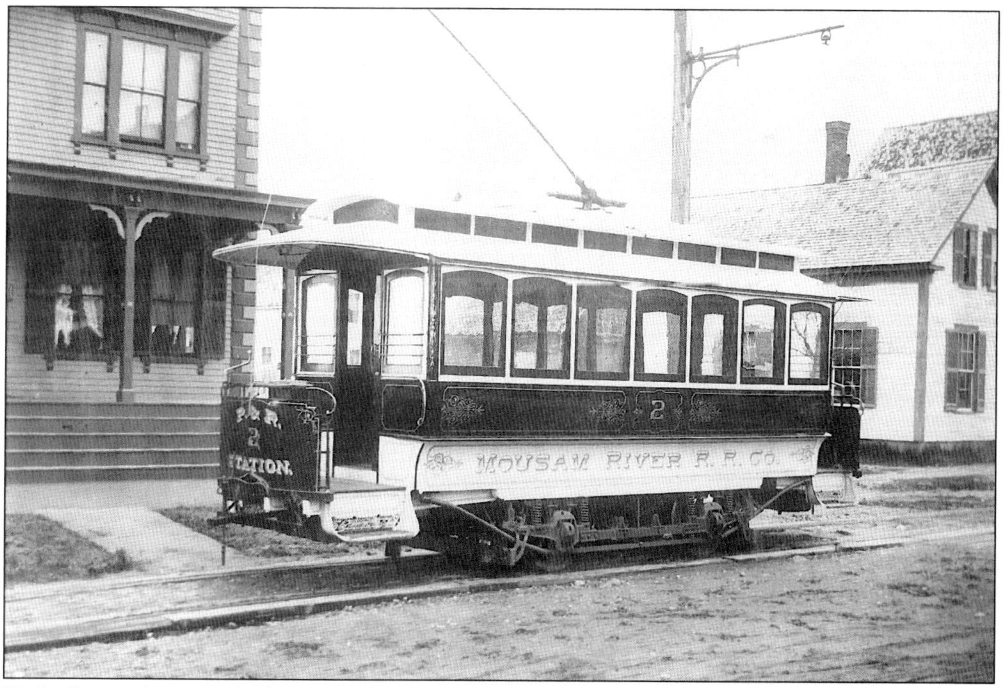

York County's second electric railway, the Mousam River Railroad, commenced operation between Sanford and Springvale villages in the industrial town of Sanford on April 1, 1893 with two four-wheel closed cars, Nos. 2 and 4, built by the Briggs Carriage Company of Amesbury, Massachusetts No. 2 is at the Hotel Sanford on Main Street, Sanford Village. While the interiors of the cars were heated and lighted by electricity, portable headlights of the oil-burning type were used, being shifted from one end of the car to the other at each terminal.

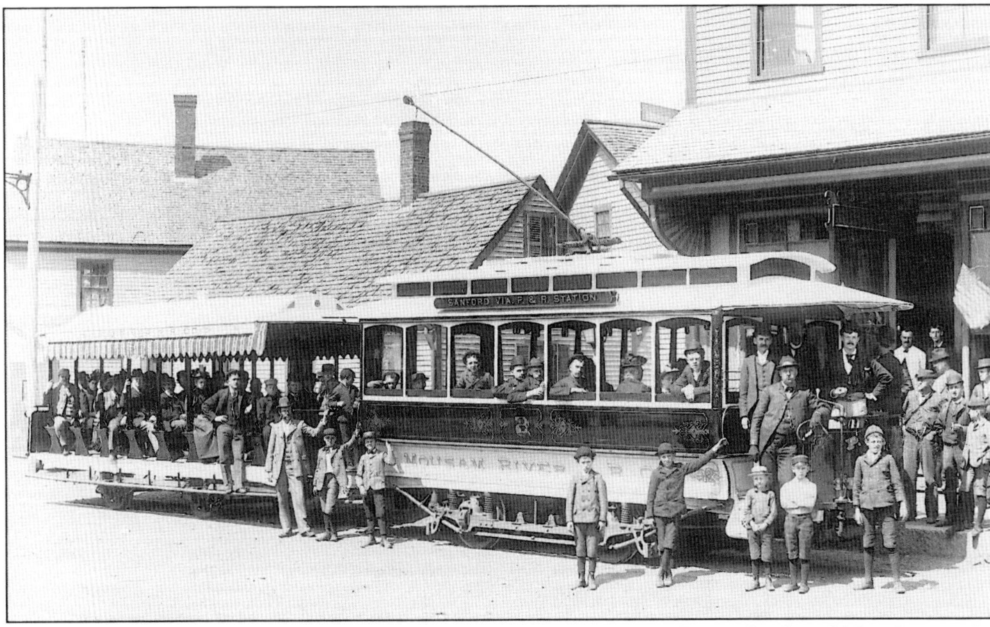

Towing an 8-bench open trailer purchased in Boston, Mousam River Railroad No. 2 is at the end of the line in Springvale village. Altogether four open trailers, all acquired in the Hub, were owned by the company in 1898 but were discarded after the MRRR was leased to the Sanford & Cape Porpoise Railway in August 1899.

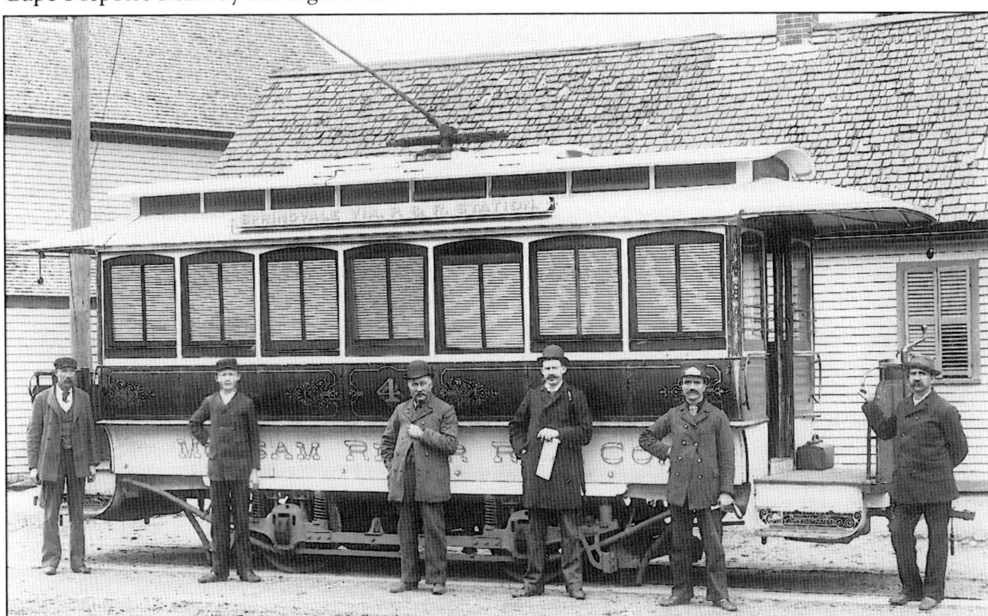

The men standing beside the car are unidentified but Mousam River Railroad No. 4 is at Springvale. Note the blinds at the windows in lieu of curtains. Nos. 2 and 4 each had longitudinal seats for 24 passengers and until their open end platforms were partially enclosed about 1898, motormen had a rough time in winter. Many of them wore fur boots, coats, and caps in an effort to keep warm and grew thick beards to protect their faces against rain, sleet, snow, and freezing rain.

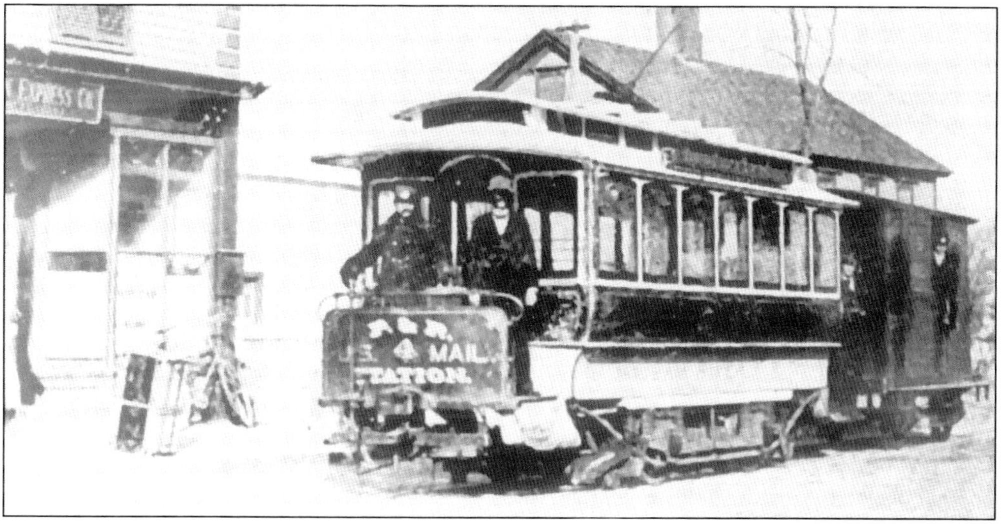

Two four-wheeled baggage and mail trailers, Nos. 6 and 8, were owned by the Mousam River Railroad and one of them is towed by No. 4 somewhere between Sanford and Springvale villages. No. 8 is now preserved at the Seashore Trolley Museum. The MRRR was awarded a contract on August 3, 1893 to carry the mail between the Portland & Rochester station at Springvale and the Springvale and Sanford post offices and was paid a flat $250 annually for doing so.

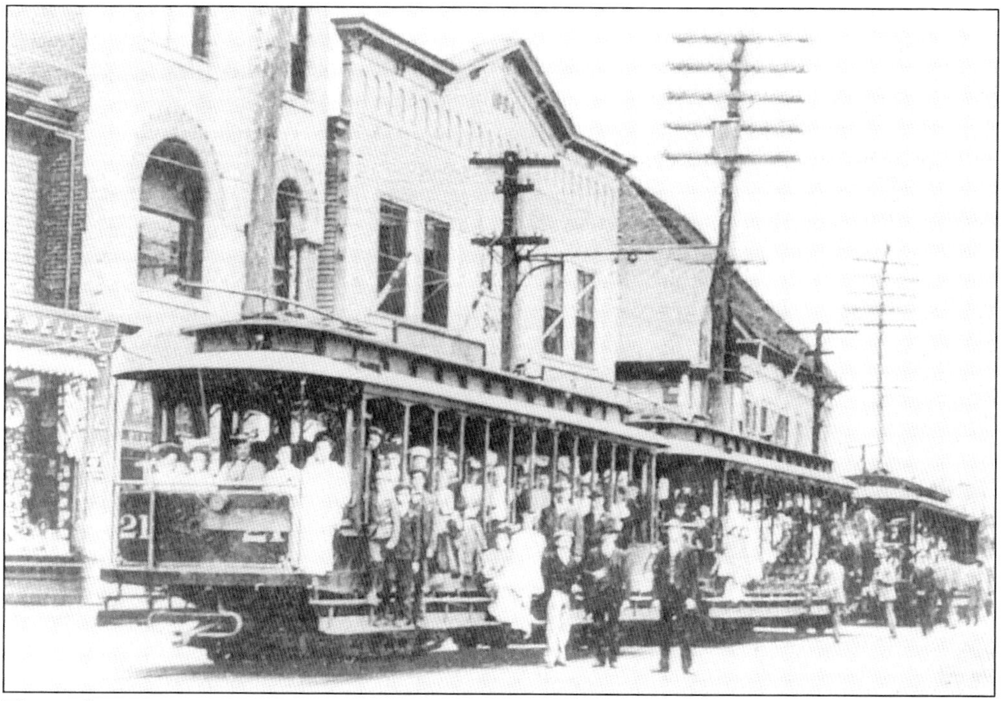

The trolley waiting room in Sanford village was situated on the first floor of the Smith Block at 12 Washington Street, the second accommodating the general offices of the Sanford & Cape Porpoise (S&CP) and Atlantic Shore Line Railways for a number of years. Three fully loaded open cars of the S&CP are ready to leave on the 21-mile, 90-minute trip to Bickford Island at Cape Porpoise.

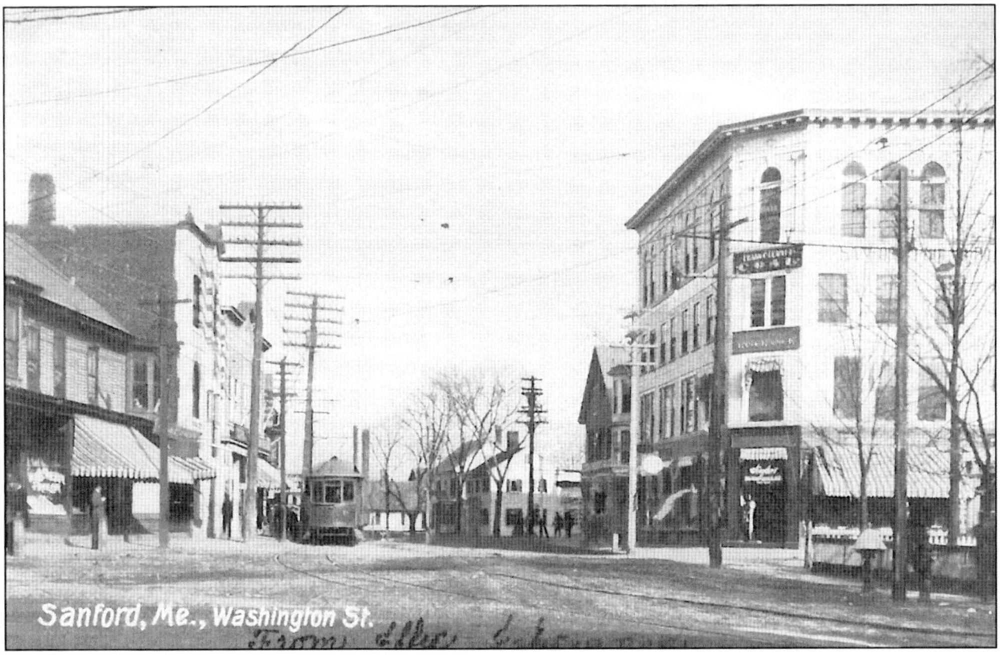

Biddeford may have been the destination of this Atlantic Shore Line closed car at the waiting room in Sanford village. Until the destruction of the Cape Porpoise Casino in 1915, through service was provided between Sanford and the Cape in summer and between Sanford and Biddeford in other seasons. Thereafter Sanford-Biddeford trips were run the year around.

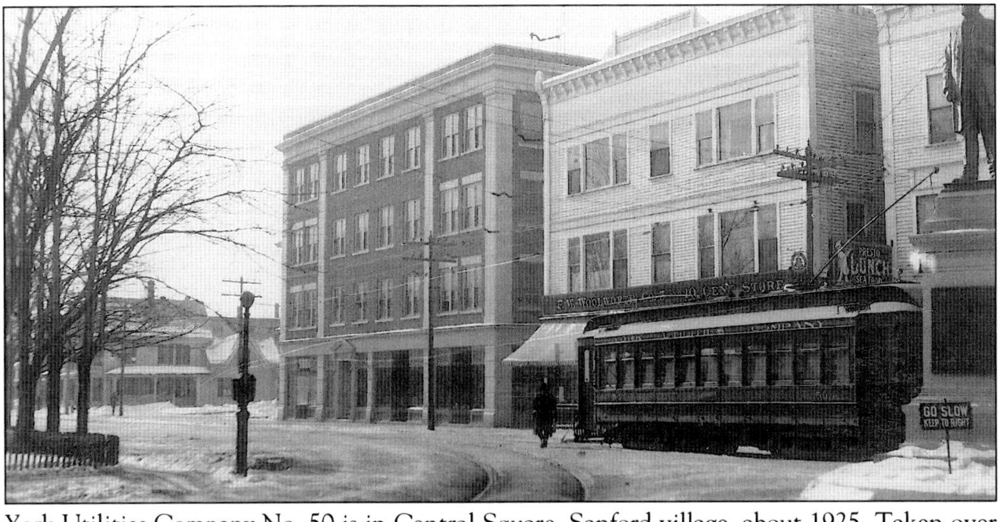

York Utilities Company No. 50 is in Central Square, Sanford village, about 1925. Taken over from the Atlantic Shore Railway in 1923, the car has been equipped for one-man operation but appears to carry its original green exterior livery.

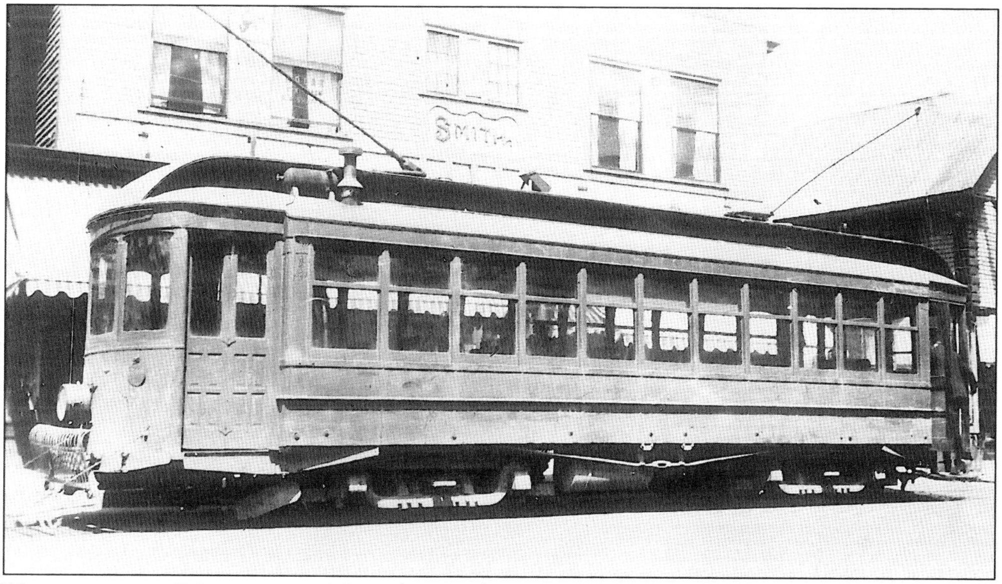

The operator is "changing ends" at the Washington Street waiting room as a York Utilities Company trolley prepares to leave for Springvale village via River Street about 1927. The running time for the 2.44-mile trip was 15 minutes but there usually was time for a quick cold drink or cup of coffee at each end of the line.

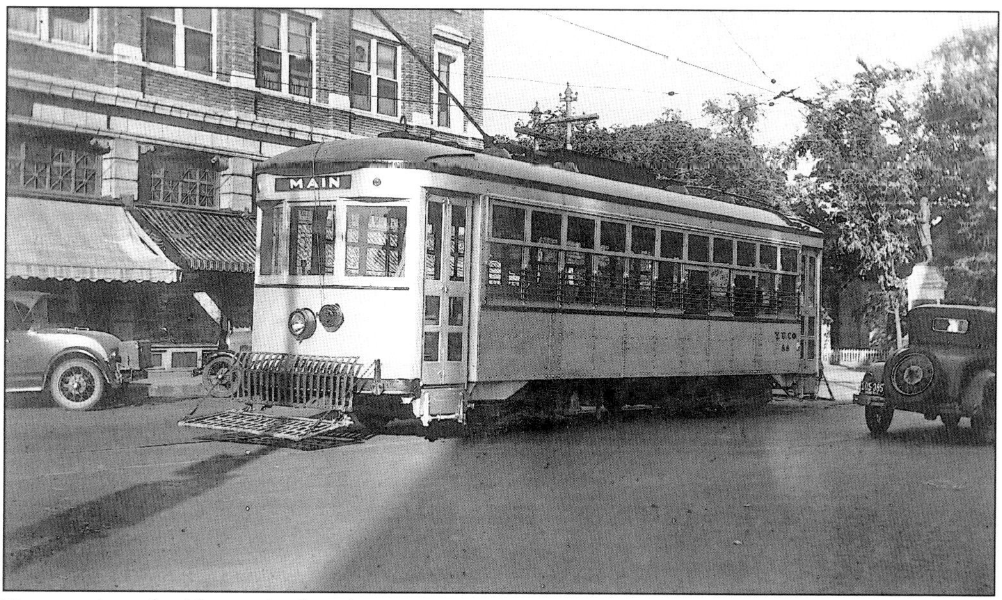

Two modern double-truck closed cars equipped for one-man operation were acquired second-hand from the East Taunton (Massachusetts) Street Railway by the York Utilities Company in 1934 and were numbered 88 and 90. No. 88, now preserved at the Seashore Trolley Museum, is running on the Main Street line between Sanford and Springvale villages. At this time the exterior of the car was painted aluminum with blue striping.

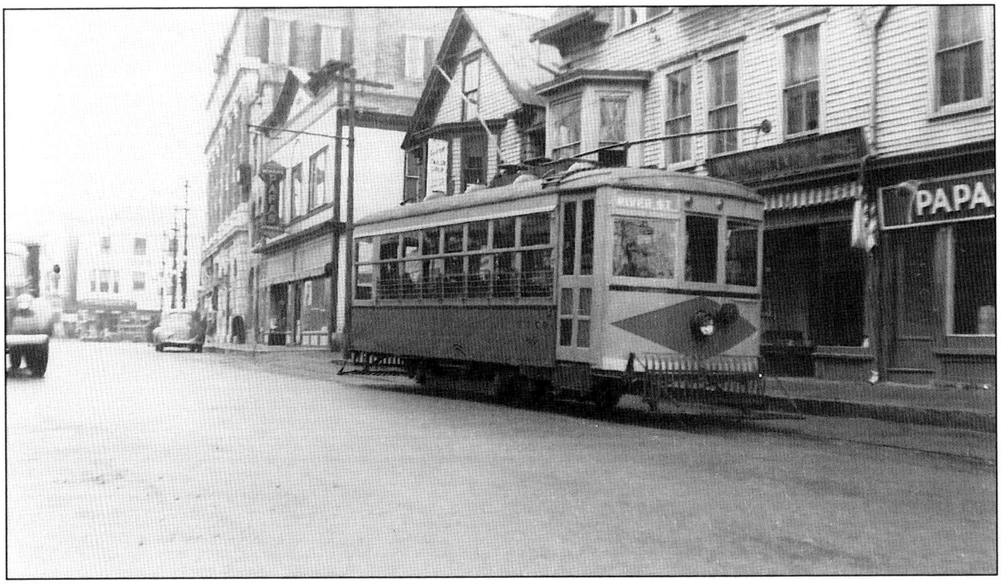

Purchased second-hand from the Denver & South Platte Railway of Littleton, Colorado, in 1927, Birney one-man safety car No. 80 is on Washington Street, Sanford Village, en route to Springvale. The car and a mate, No. 82, are now at the Seashore Trolley Museum. When this picture was taken, the body color was red and beige.

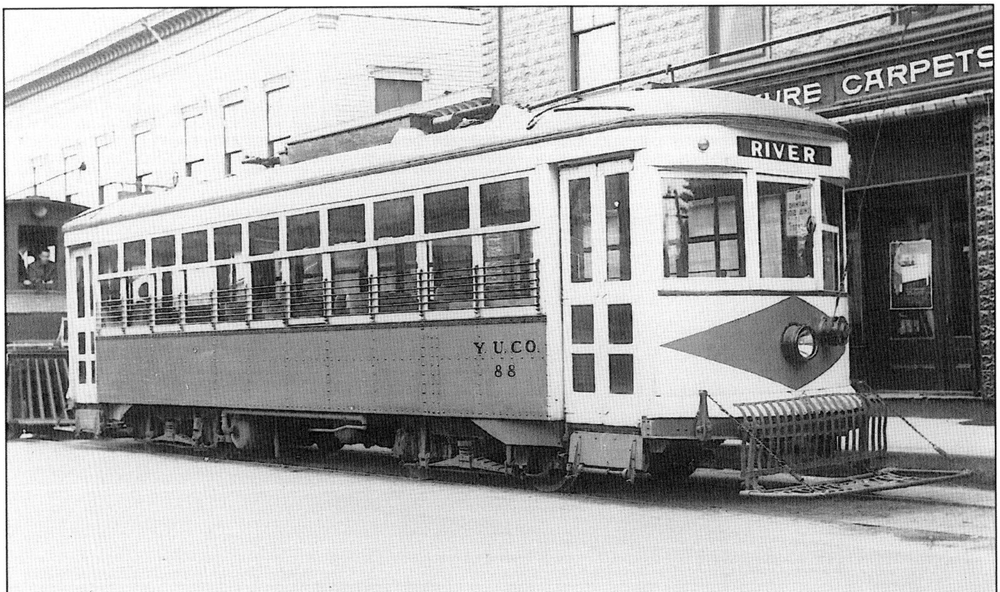

Trolley passenger service between Sanford and Springvale villages ended April 1, 1947 but on April 27th a special farewell excursion was run for the Railroad Enthusiasts. No. 88 is followed by freight locomotive 102 at Springvale.

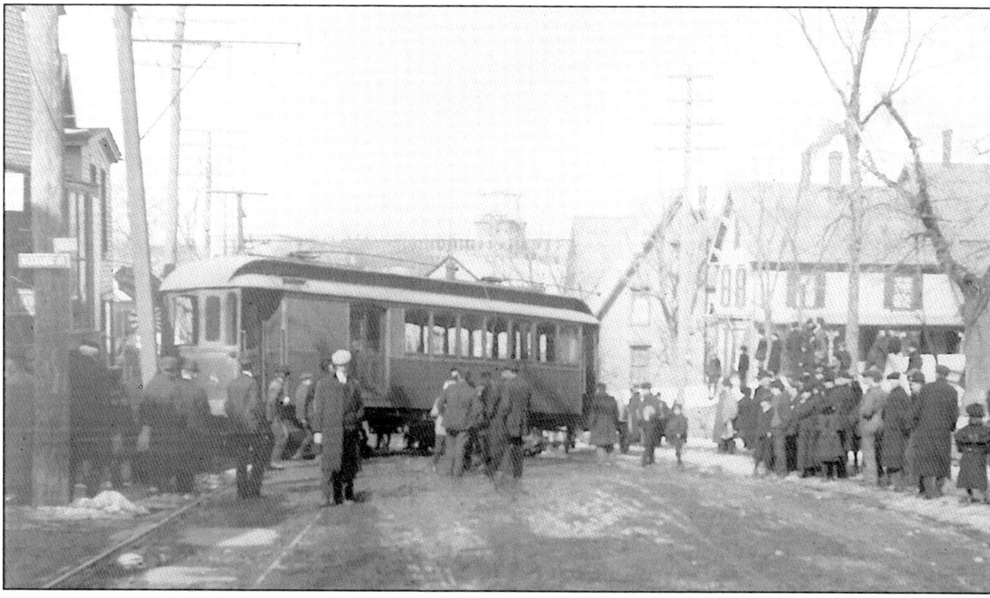

Plenty of sidewalk superintendents are on hand to view the rerailing of Sanford & Cape Porpoise No.8 on Washington Street, Sanford village, about 1900. The car became No. 34 of the Atlantic Shore Line Railway about 1907 and was in active service, mostly on the Eastern Division, through 1916. By then it had seen much better days.

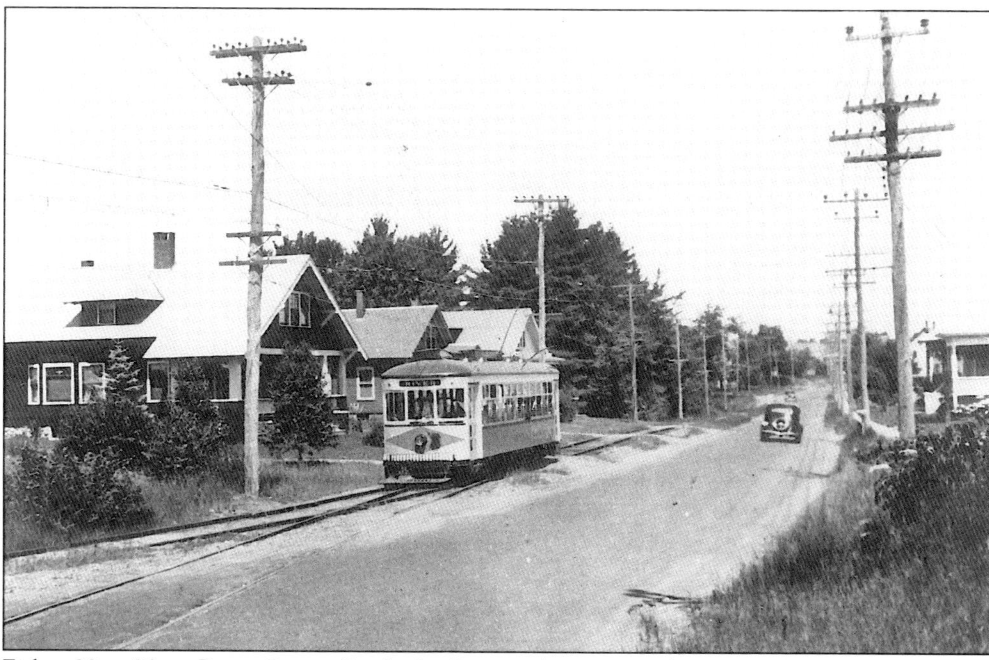

Either 88 or 90 on River Street, Sanford village, is shown near the new carhouse erected by the York Utilities Company in 1923. Some of the heavier timbers used in constructing the building came from the former coal pocket, which had been razed the previous year, near Town House Junction. There were originally three tracks, a fourth track being added later.

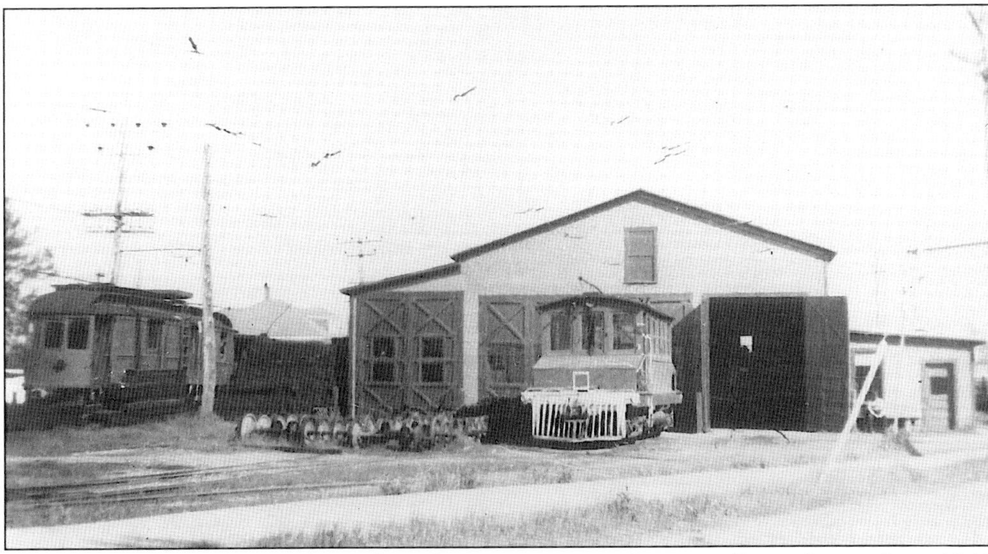

Locomotive 102 in front of the York Utilities Company carhouse on River Street about 1946. After the end of trolley freight service between the Springvale depot and Sanford Village in 1949, the building served as a bus garage for many years.

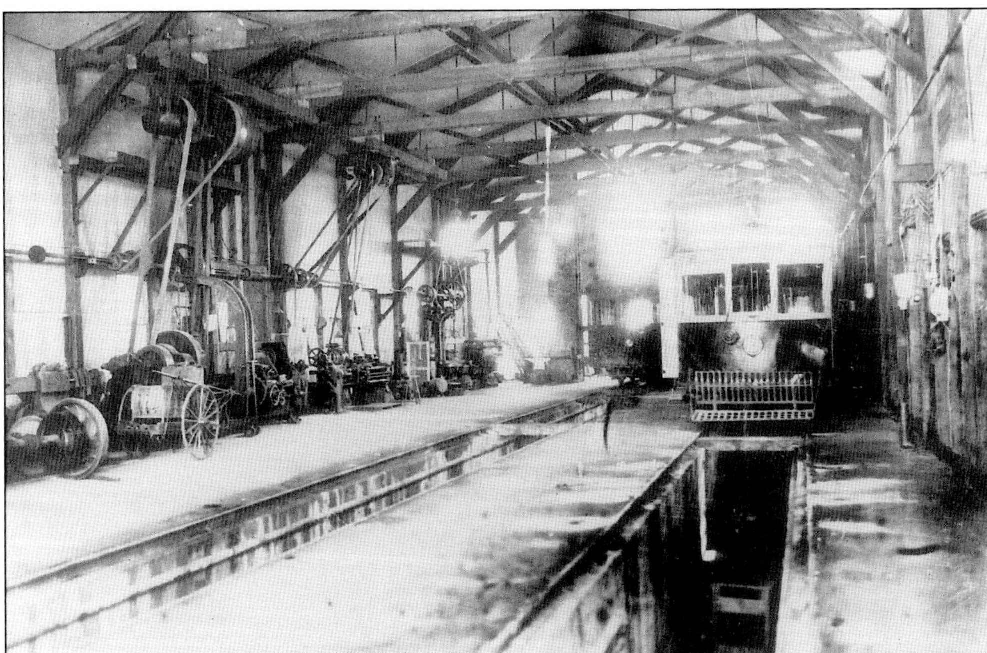

The interior of the York Utilities carhouse on River Street, Sanford. Two Birney cars are on repair and maintenance pits. Some of the repair shop machinery came from the Town House barn after its closure in 1927.

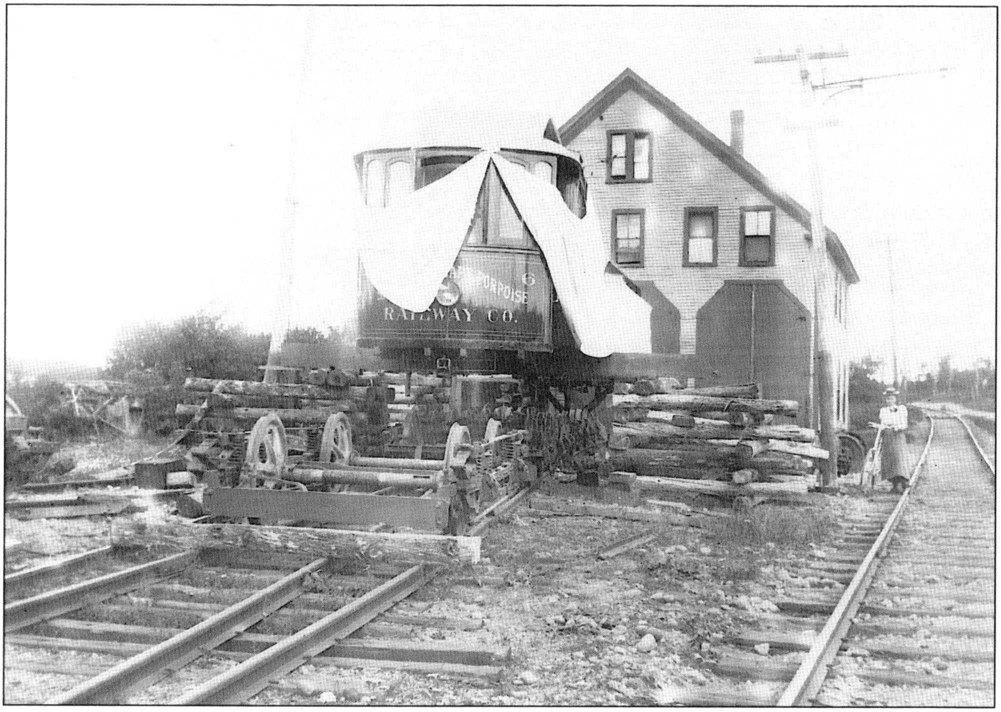

The 1893 carhouse of the Mousam River Railroad on upper River Street, Sanford. Combination car No. 6 of the Sanford & Cape Porpoise Railway is being placed on its trucks in this 1899 view. Reportedly the carhouse originally was part of a discontinued railroad station in Portland and was moved in sections over the Portland & Rochester to Sanford. The upper floor housed tenements are believed to have been occupied by the carhouse foreman and the chief engineer of the nearby power station.

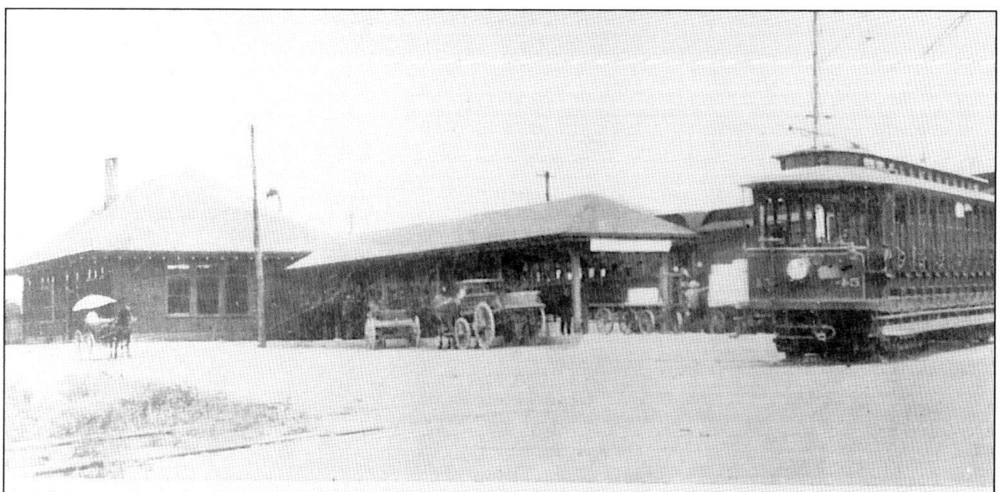

Fifteen-bench open car No. 45 is at the Sanford-Springvale depot of the Boston & Maine Railroad's Worcester, Nashua & Portland Division. Trolley schedules on the Sanford-Springvale via River Street line were arranged to provide positive connections with all passenger trains at the station.

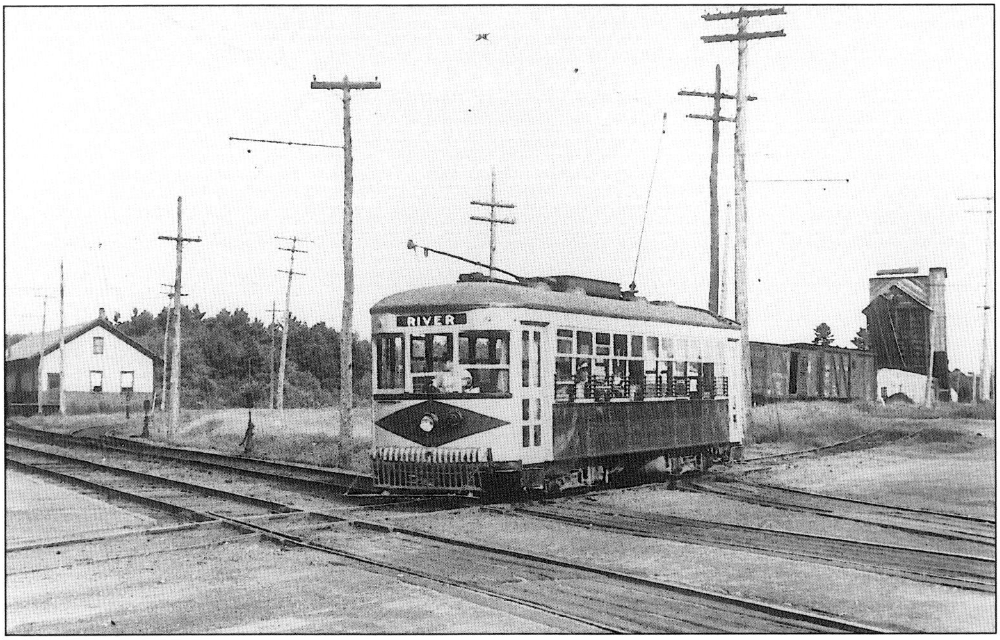

Crossing the Boston & Maine near the Sanford-Springvale depot on September 4, 1939 is Car 90. The crossing was protected by automatic wig-wag signals but operators still had to stop their cars within a prescribed distance from the railroad tracks, look to the left and right to satisfy themselves that the way was clear, and then proceed.

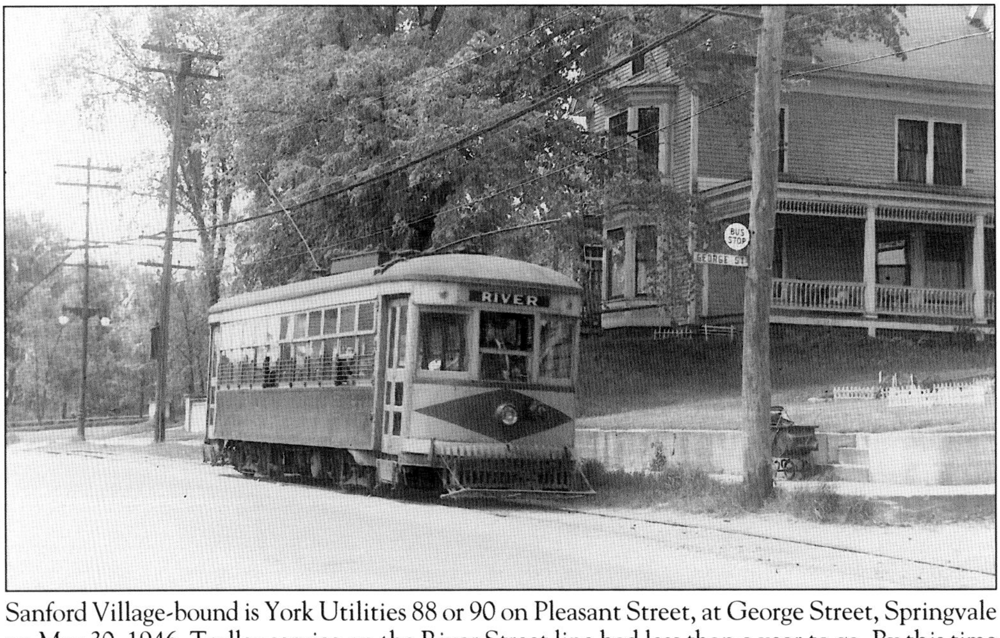

Sanford Village-bound is York Utilities 88 or 90 on Pleasant Street, at George Street, Springvale on May 30, 1946. Trolley service on the River Street line had less than a year to go. By this time destination signs had been removed and "River" had been painted in white letters on a black background on the front of the sign box.

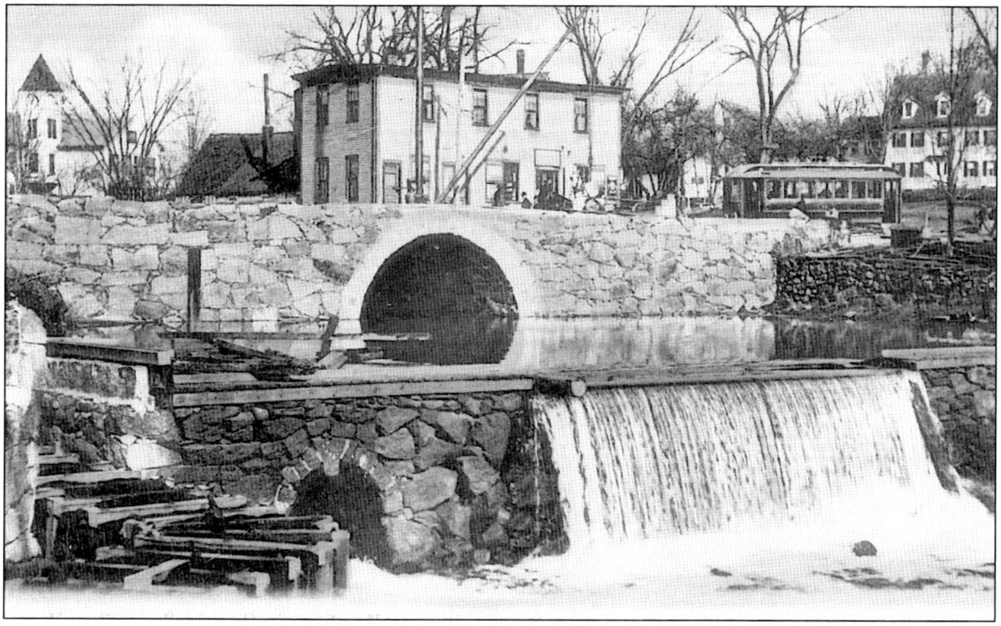

Approaching the stone arch bridge spanning the Mousam River in Springvale is Car 14 of the Sanford & Cape Porpoise Railway about 1899. The building at right still stood when Sanford-Springvale trolley service ended 48 years later but was in a rather dilapidated condition.

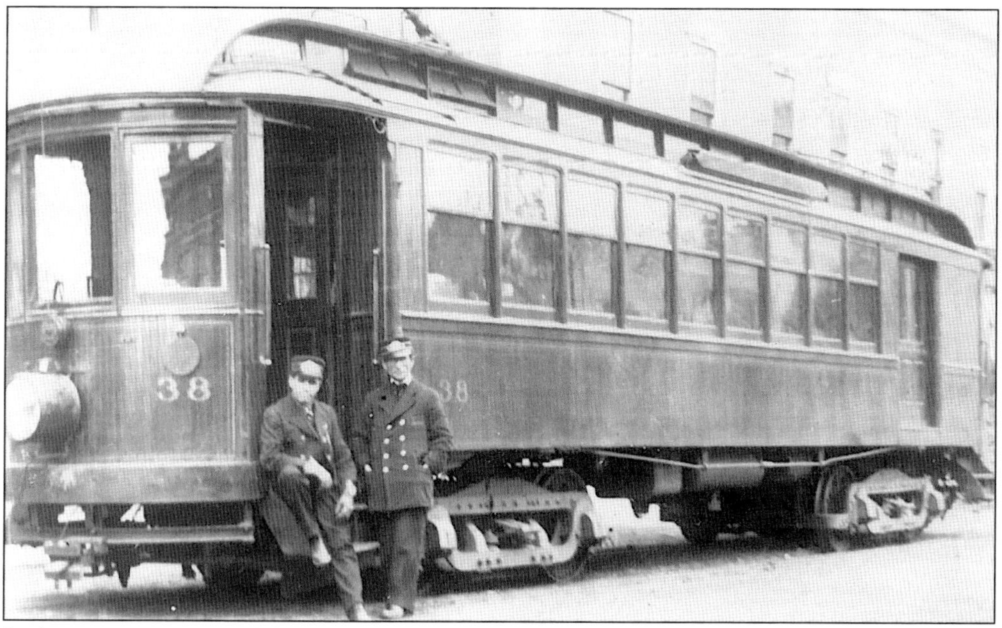

Built in 1902 as No. 2 of the Atlantic Shore Line Railway, this combination passenger-baggage car, shown at Springvale, was renumbered 20 in 1904 and became No. 38 three years later. It became the property of York Utilities Company in 1923 but appears to have been retired a few years later.

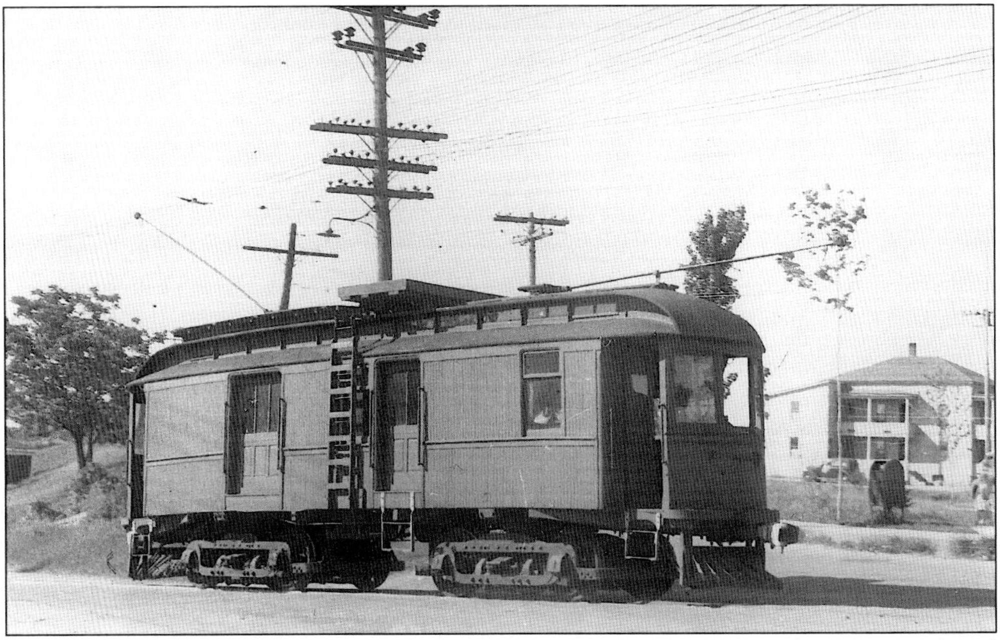

Former Mail and Express Car 108 of Portsmouth, Dover & York Street Railway was purchased by the York Utilities Company in 1925 and served as a line car and auxiliary locomotive until 1949. Acquired by the Seashore Trolley Museum that same year, it has since been restored to its original configuration and livery.

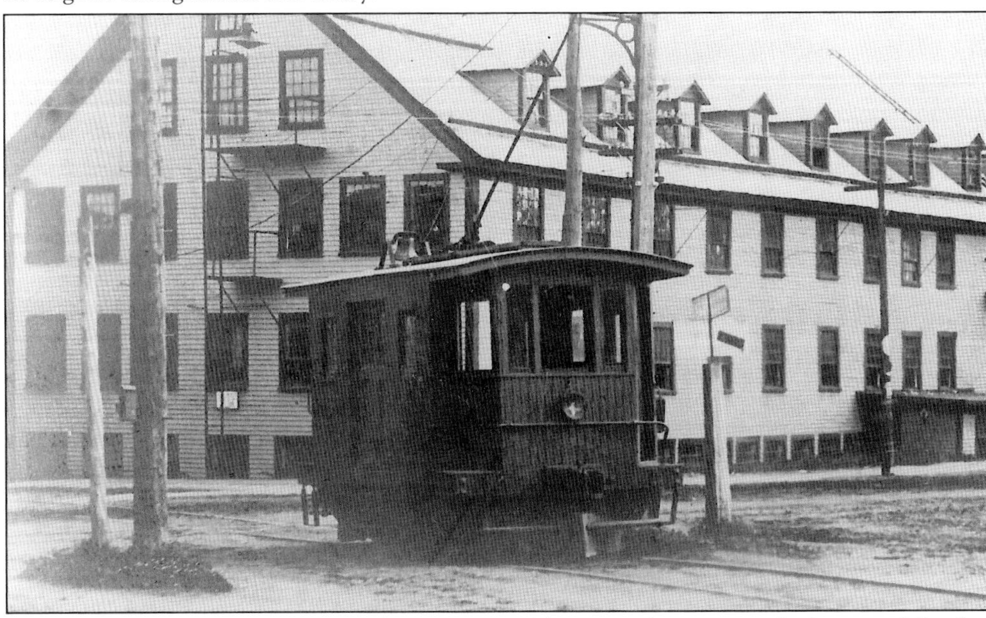

Substantial amounts of carload freight were moved between the Springvale depot and Sanford village from 1893 through 1949. The freight locomotive, No. 1, of the Mousam River Railroad approaches the No. 1 mill of the Sanford Mills Company near Mill Square about 1899. It later became line car No. 97 of the Atlantic Shore Line Railway and still later the body was dismantled and the underframe and truck became a trailer equipped with a frame for holding reels of trolley wire.

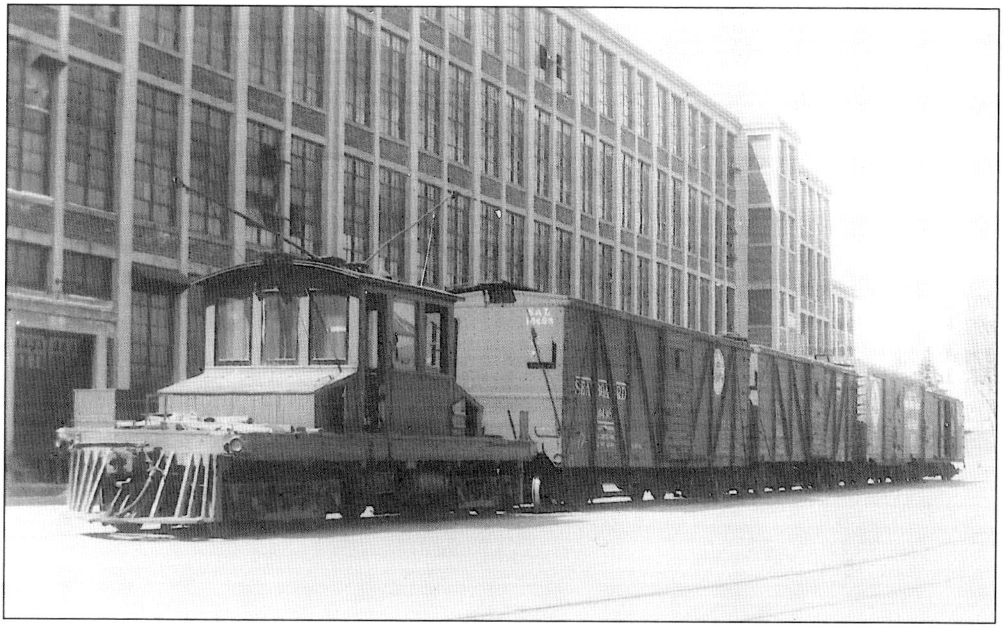

Three identical freight locomotives, Nos. 100-102, were purchased by the Atlantic Shore Line Railway in 1906. No. 100, shown drawing four freight cars to the Springvale interchange with the Boston & Maine. It was the last electric locomotive in active service in Sanford and was conveyed in 1949 to the Seashore Trolley Museum, where it awaits restoration.

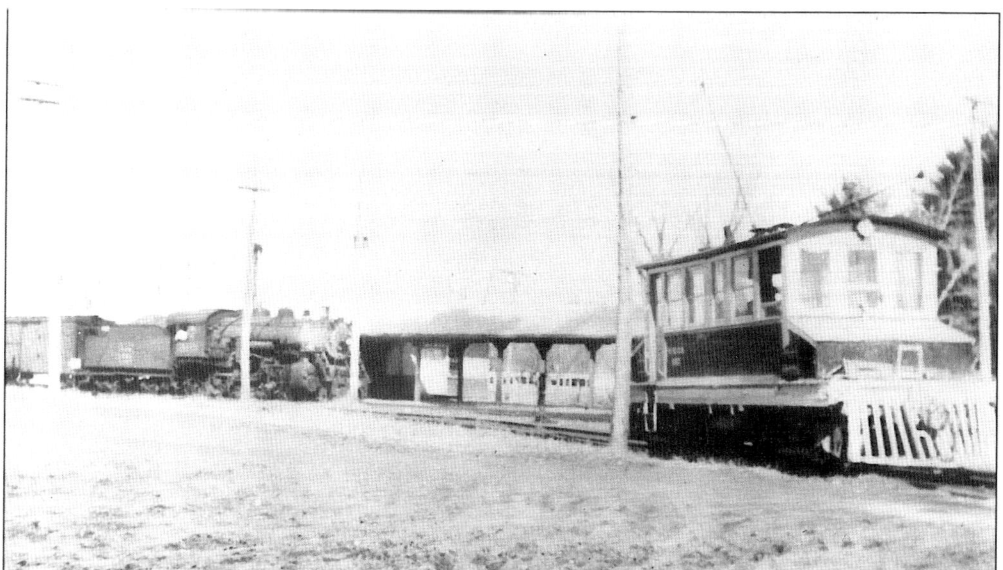

Locomotive 102 is at the Springvale depot to pick up cars from the freight train drawn by Boston & Maine engine 2459. The original cab of this locomotive was nearly doubled in size by adding that of No. 101 when the latter was converted to a box express car by the Atlantic Shore Line Railway in 1908.

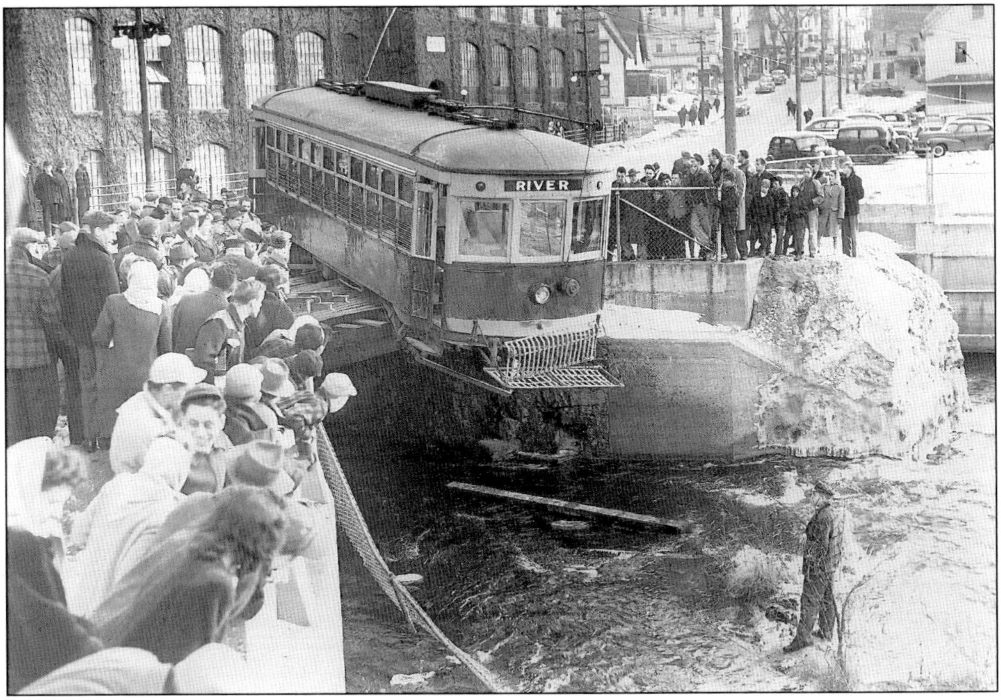

The destination sign was appropriate when Car 90 derailed on Mill Square bridge in Sanford village on February 6, 1947 and almost plunged into the Mousam River. Operator Stanley Cram jumped to safety and 17 passengers escaped through a rear door. This accident left the York Utilities Company with only one passenger car, resulting in the start of bus service on the River Street line on April 2nd.

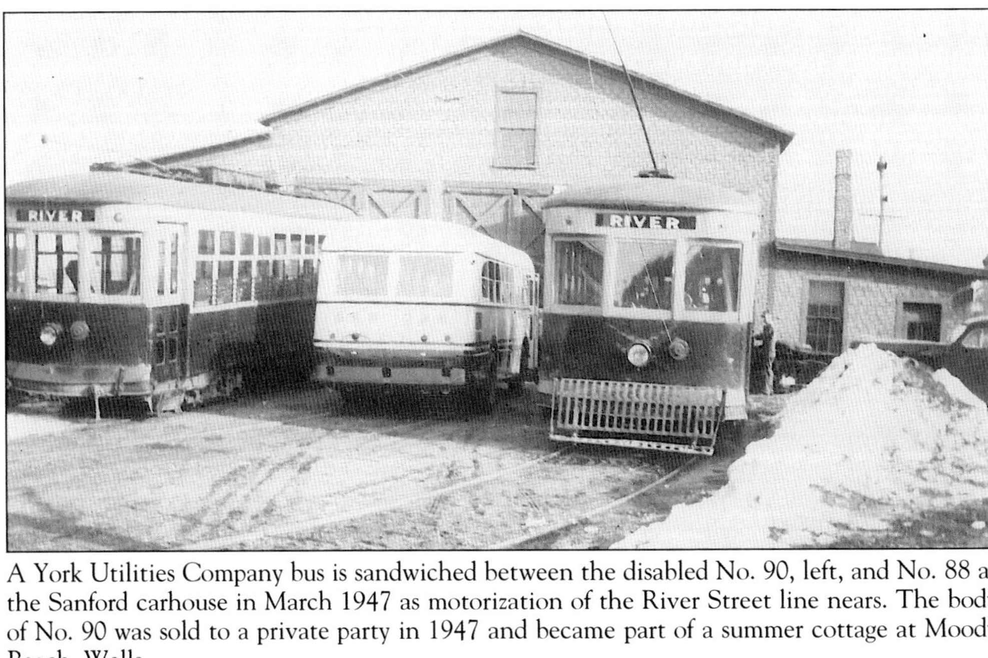

A York Utilities Company bus is sandwiched between the disabled No. 90, left, and No. 88 at the Sanford carhouse in March 1947 as motorization of the River Street line nears. The body of No. 90 was sold to a private party in 1947 and became part of a summer cottage at Moody Beach, Wells.

Six

BIDDEFORD & SACO RAILROAD: BIDDEFORD-OLD ORCHARD BEACH

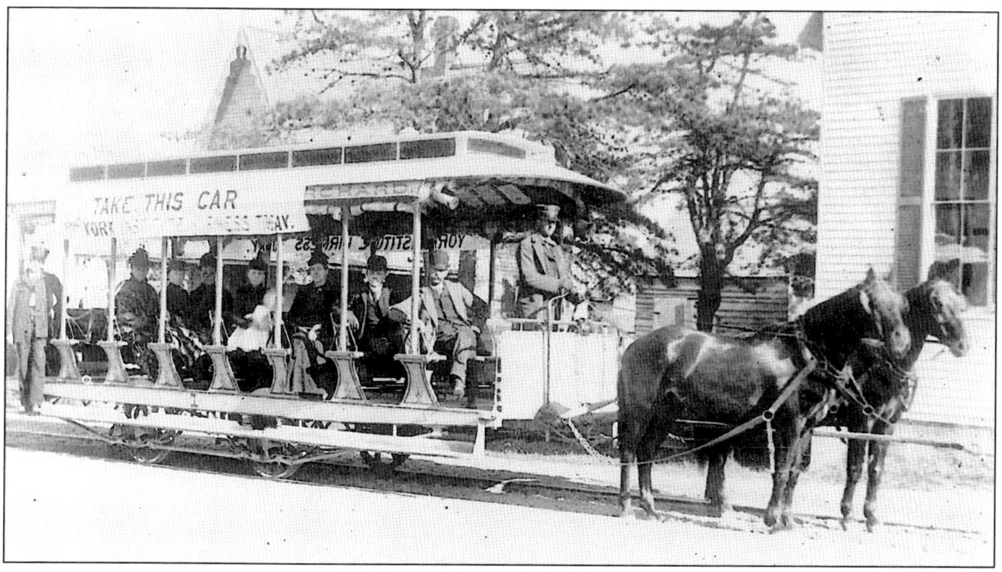

York County's first street railway, the Biddeford & Saco Railroad, commenced operating horsecars between Biddeford and Old Orchard Beach via Saco on July 15, 1888. No. 1 is at the Advent Church in Old Orchard The car may have been electrified in 1892 but it definitely was retired after the B&SRR began acquiring 12-bench, double-truck opens in 1900.

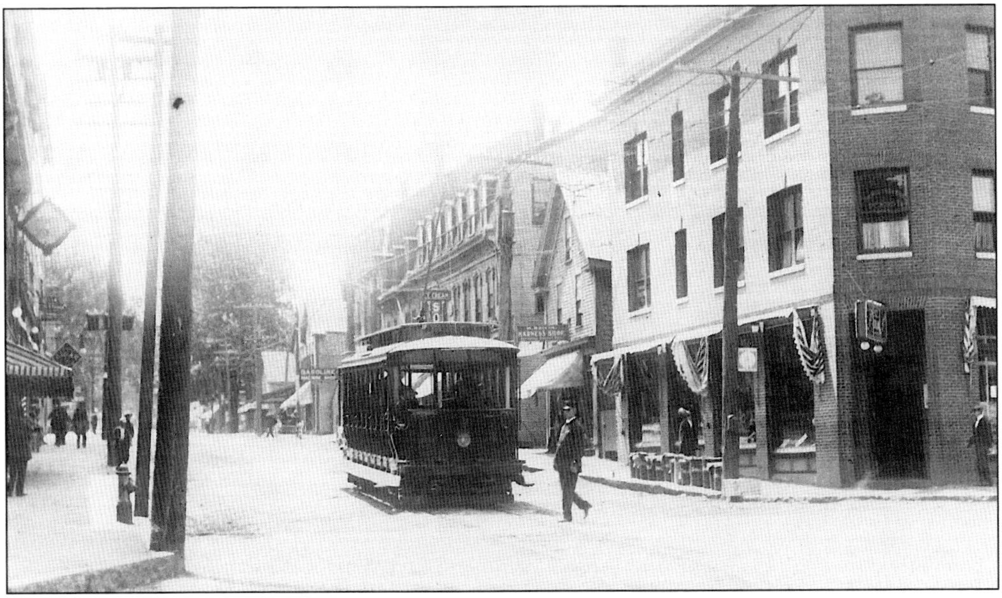

The corner of Main and Alfred Streets in Biddeford was the starting point for Old Orchard Beach cars after September 1900. Twelve-bench open car No. 43 prepares to depart for the resort in the summer of 1901. The route in Biddeford was along Alfred Street to Five Points; on Elm Street to Main Street at Harmon's Corner and on Main Street, through City Square, to the Saco River bridge.

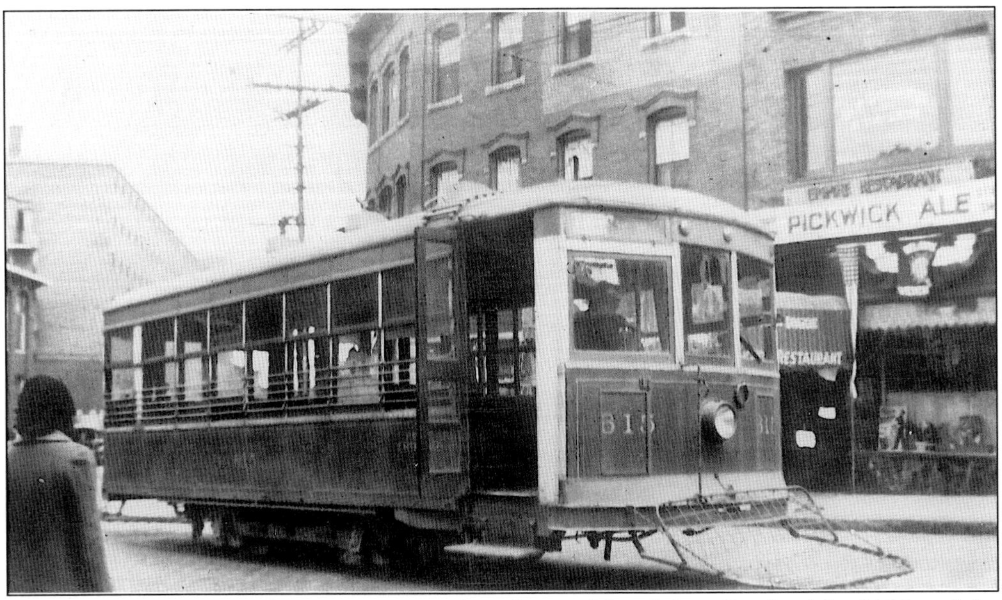

Eight Birney one-man safety cars were purchased second-hand from Portland for $100 each by the Biddeford & Saco in September 1936. These were numbered Nos. 615-622 and, with low mileage, were a great bargain! No. 615 is at the corner of Main and Alfred Streets, Biddeford, shortly after its arrival from the Forest City. The body of this car is at the Seashore Trolley Museum.

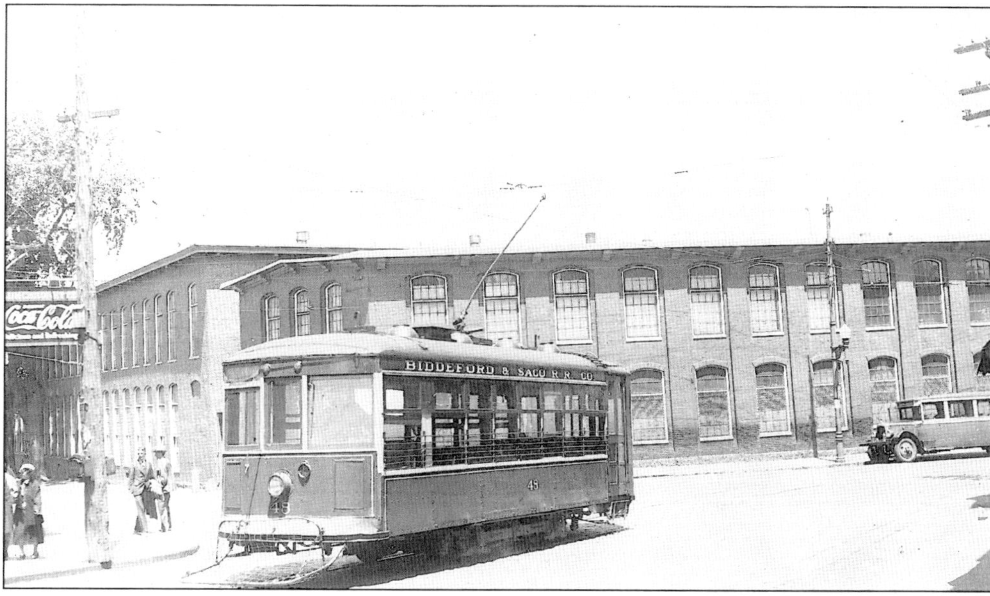

A motor bus of the York Utilities Company is at the extreme right as Biddeford & Saco No. 46 waits at the Biddeford terminus to load passengers. The car was one of six purchased secondhand for $400 each in 1931 from the receiver of the Massachusetts Northeastern Street Railway, which had discontinued trolley service a year earlier. Spare parts were included in the transaction.

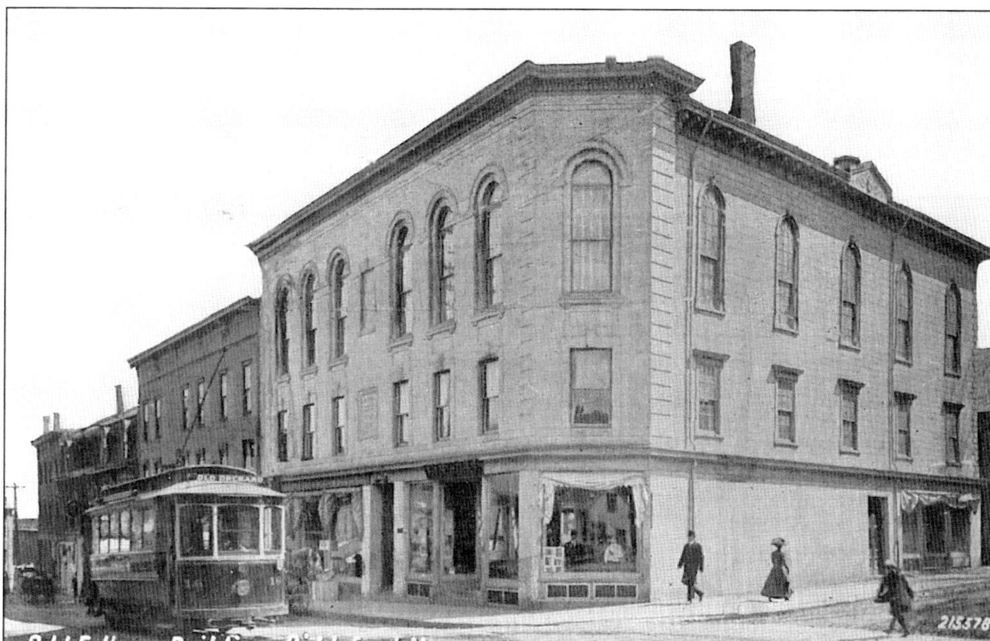

Northbound on Alfred Street, Car 16 passes the Odd Fellows Building in Biddeford. Built for the Biddeford & Saco in 1899, this trolley became a line car in 1931 and was still active when buses took over in July 1939.

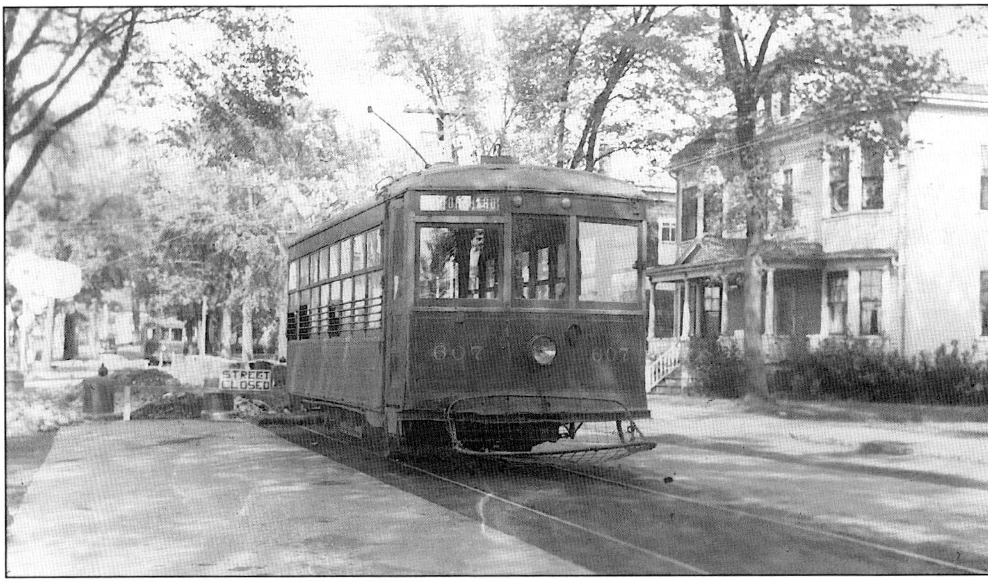

A sewer project on Alfred Street. Biddeford, disrupted service on the Biddeford & Saco in June 1939. No. 607 waits near Ray Street for a shuttle car from the downtown terminus. Passengers had to transfer around the excavation for several days until the work was completed by a Works Progress Administration (WPA) crew.

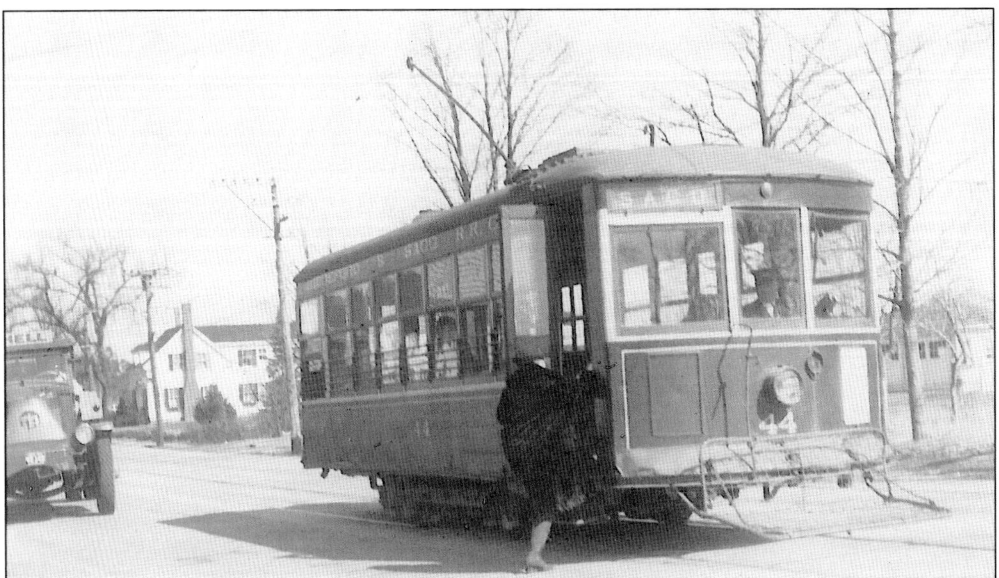

Birney Car 44, bound for Laurel Hill Cemetery in Saco, is at Five Points turnout on Alfred Street on March 26, 1936. Note the approaching "Bulldog" Mack of Shell Oil Company at the extreme left. Traces of this turnout, paved with concrete, were in evidence until the early 1970s when Alfred Street was rebuilt by the city.

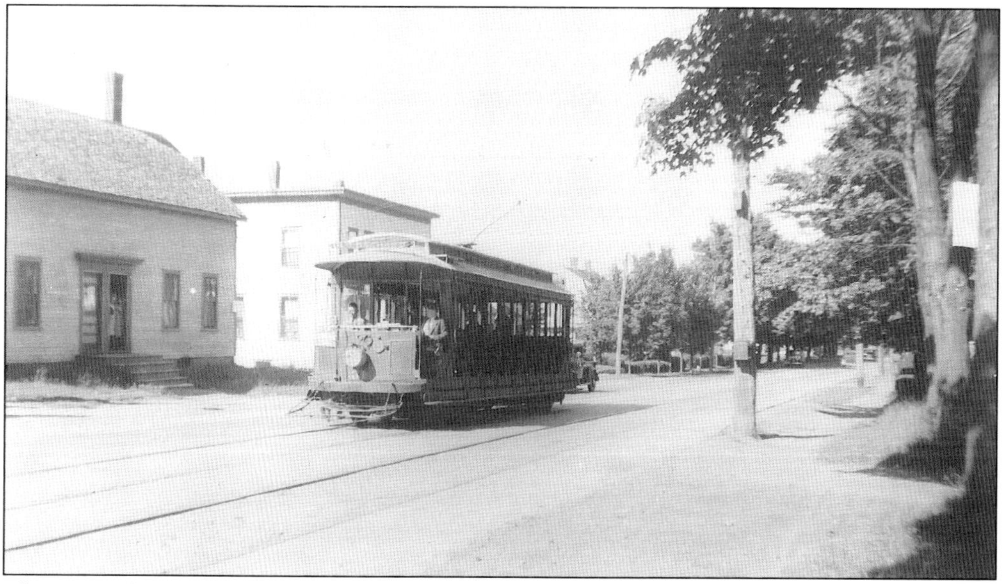

The start of bus service on the Biddeford & Saco was less than a month away on June 18, 1939 when 12-bench open No. 31 was photographed at Five Points turnout in Biddeford. The car has been restored to its original appearance at the Seashore Trolley Museum and will be a century old in 2000.

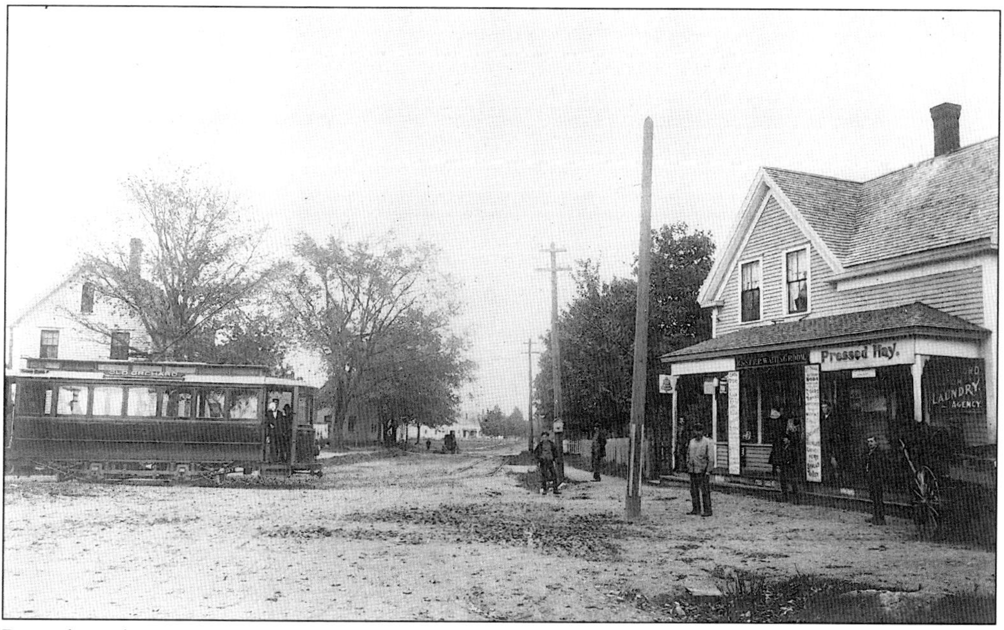

Rounding the curve at Five Points, Biddeford, Car 20 moves into Alfred Street in this c. 1903 photograph. The store at right doubled in brass as a Biddeford & Saco waiting station. No. 20 was active until the Biddeford & Saco acquired the six Birney cars from the Massachusetts Northeastern and then was scrapped.

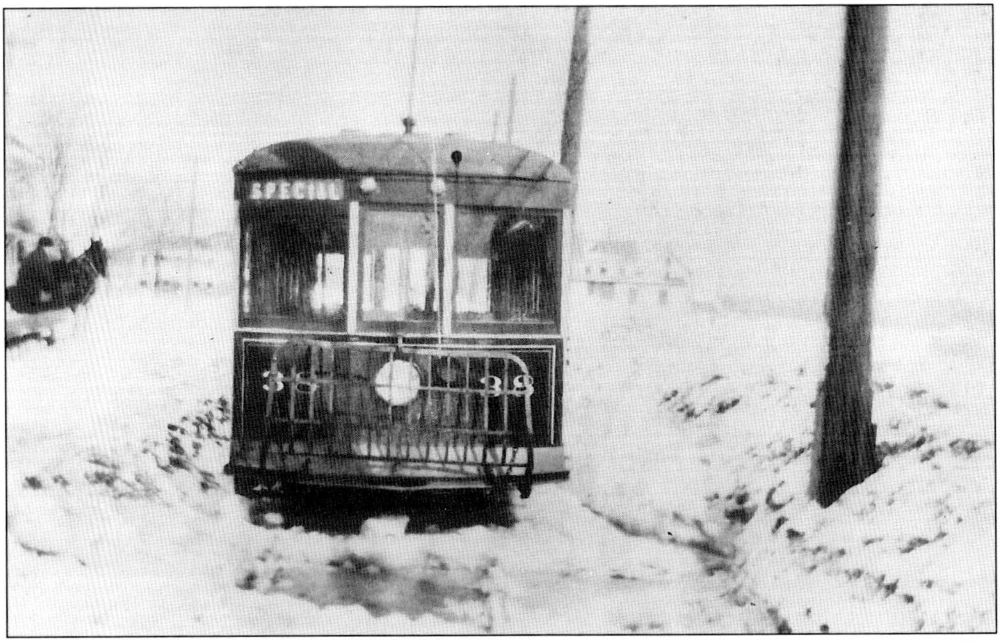

Snowed in on Elm Street, near Five Points, Biddeford, in March 1920 is one-man car No. 38, acquired by the Biddeford & Saco in 1919. A large group of men and boys, all volunteers, cleared the tracks so the trolley could be returned to the car barn. A snowstorm beginning March 4 was particularly severe and Car 38 was stranded from March 6th until the 12th.

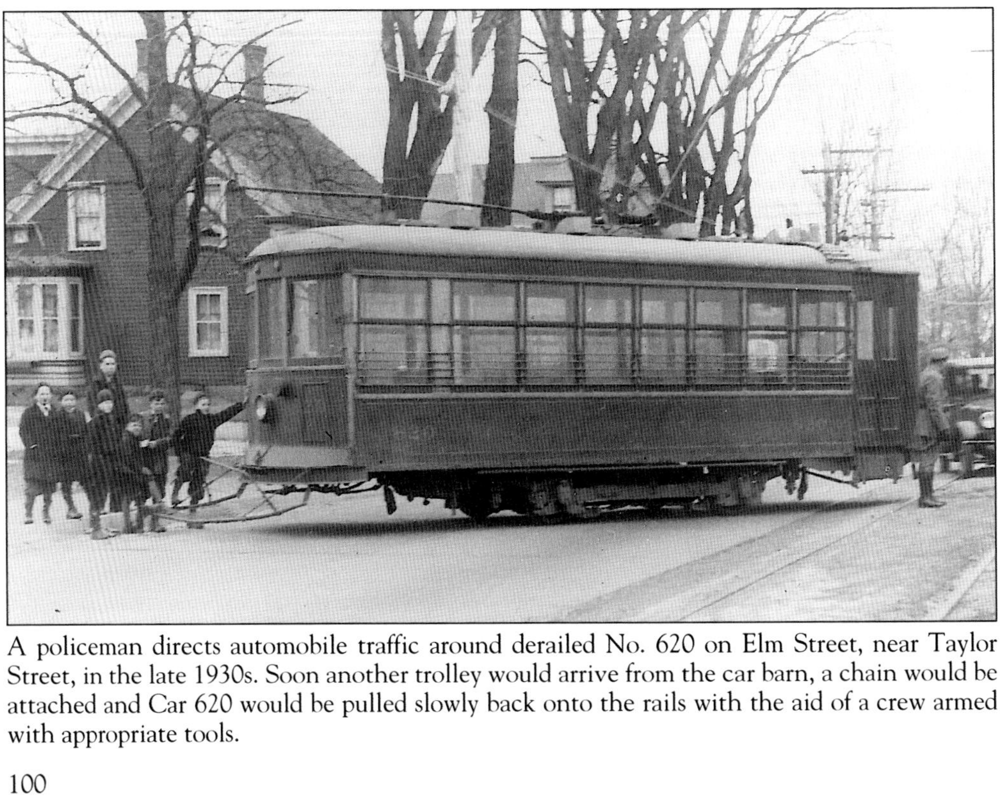

A policeman directs automobile traffic around derailed No. 620 on Elm Street, near Taylor Street, in the late 1930s. Soon another trolley would arrive from the car barn, a chain would be attached and Car 620 would be pulled slowly back onto the rails with the aid of a crew armed with appropriate tools.

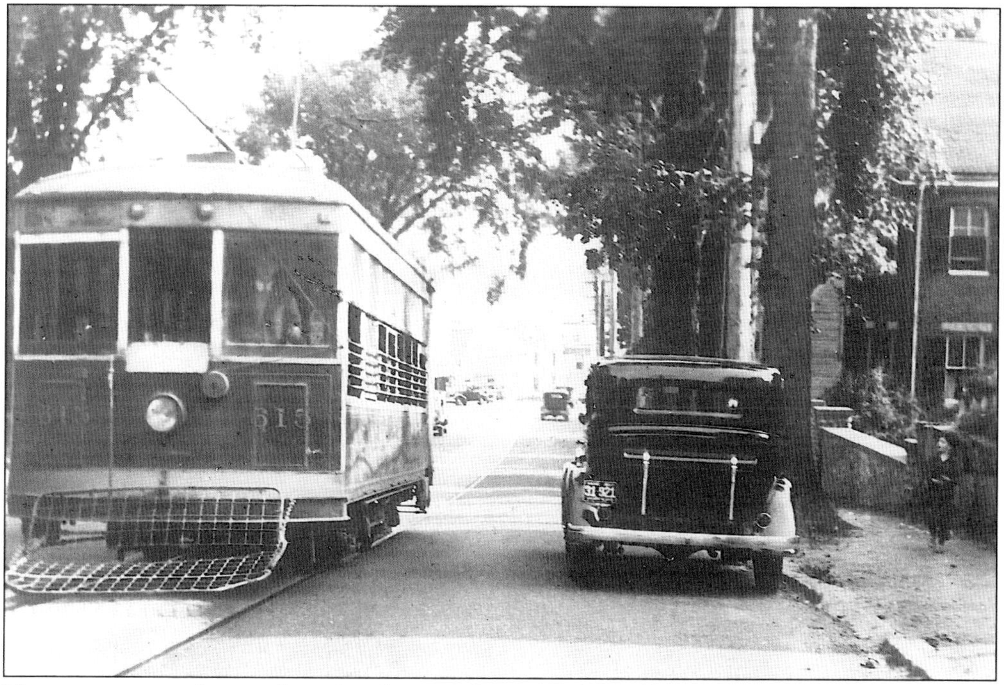

This picture was taken to show the clearance between the trolley track and a parked automobile on Elm Street, Saco, after a streetcar-automobile accident in the late 1930s. The sedan was the property of Biddeford & Saco superintendent Eugene O. Hill, who had been named to the post in 1919.

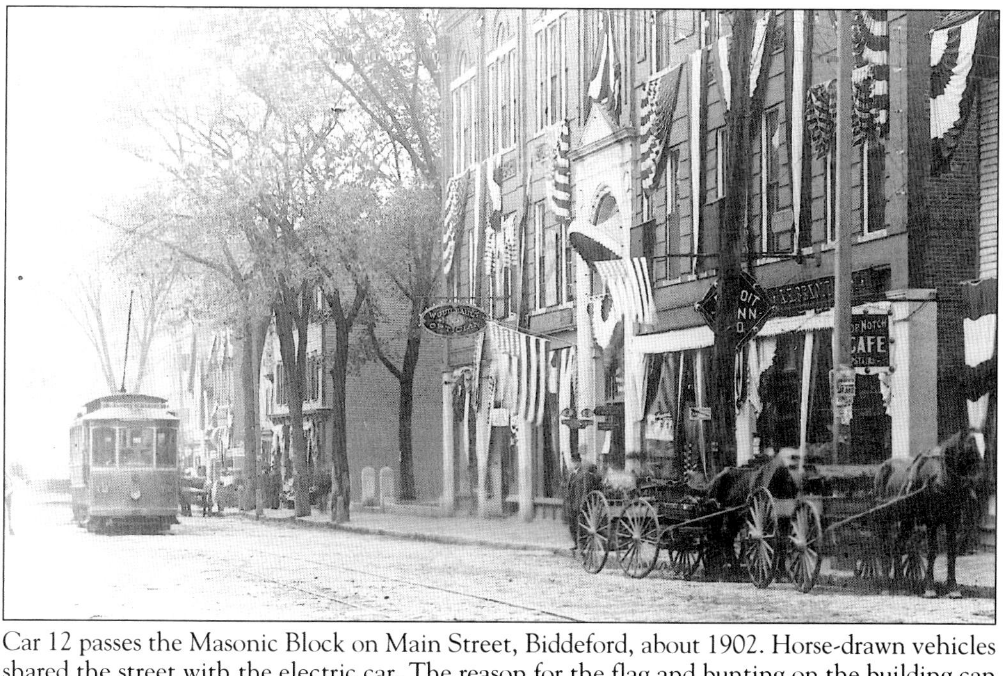

Car 12 passes the Masonic Block on Main Street, Biddeford, about 1902. Horse-drawn vehicles shared the street with the electric car. The reason for the flag and bunting on the building can only be speculated but possibly a national holiday was approaching or being observed when the photograph was taken.

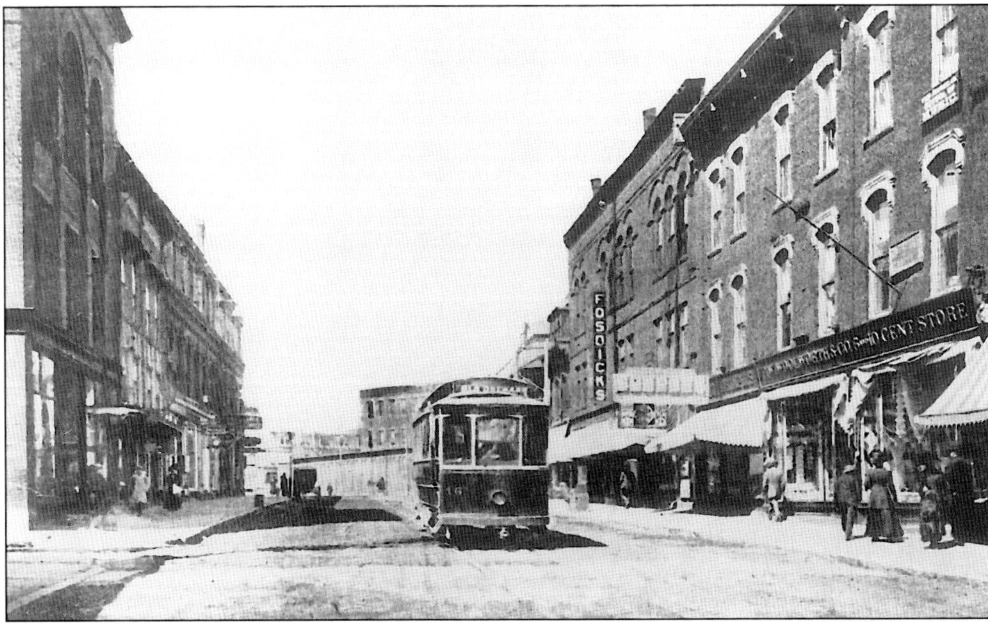

Starting to descend Dean's Hill on Main Street, Biddeford is a Car 16, carrying an Old Orchard destination sign. A F.W. Woolworth store is at the right. The trolleys are long gone and the Woolworth "five and dime" stores also are no more.

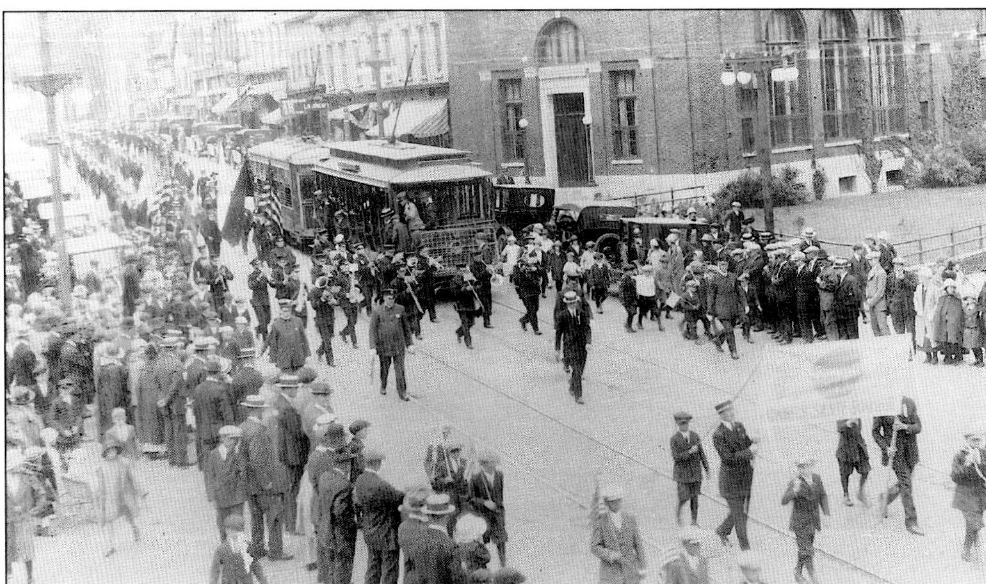

Two Biddeford & Saco trolleys wait on Main Street, Biddeford, as the annual LaKermesse Parade passes in 1923 or 1924. The parade, held annually in late June, honors the city's Fanco-American heritage. Double track laid on Main Street in 1913-14 extended from Laconia Street through City Square to Lincoln Street.

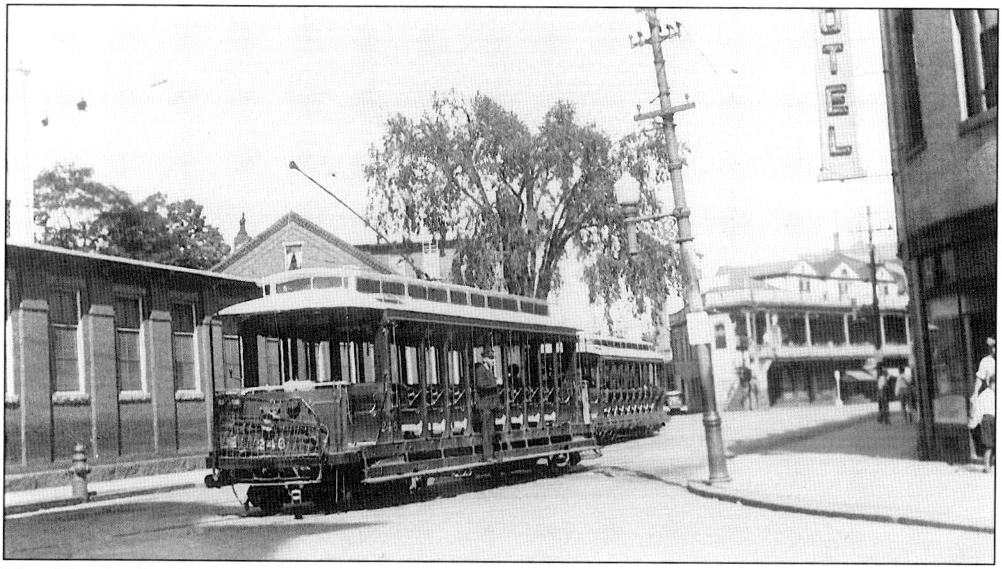

The Hotel Thacher is at the right as two Biddeford & Saco open cars meet on Main Street, Biddeford, near Adams Street on July 14, 1935. Trolley enthusiasts "discovered" the B&SRR in the mid-1930s and enjoyed many charter trips over its rails until the end in 1939. Frequently the "fans" changed from one type of car to another when they passed the car barn.

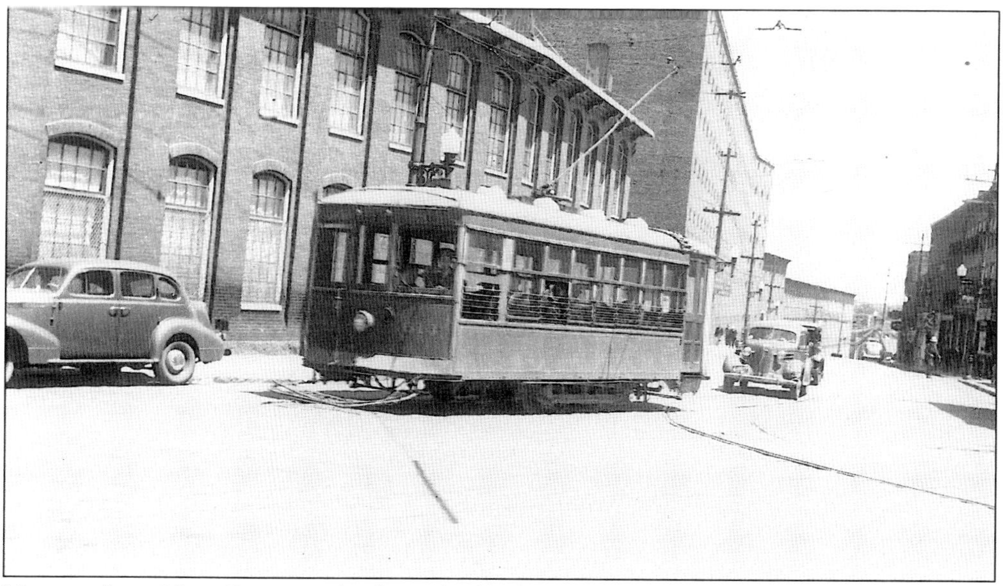

Moving along Main Street at the foot of Alfred Street is ex-Portland Birney Car 613 about 1937. After the purchase of Nos. 615-622 in 1936, another 13, Nos. 602-614, were acquired from the Forest City in 1937 and all 21 were moved on flat trailers over the highway from Thornton Heights, South Portland, to Saco.

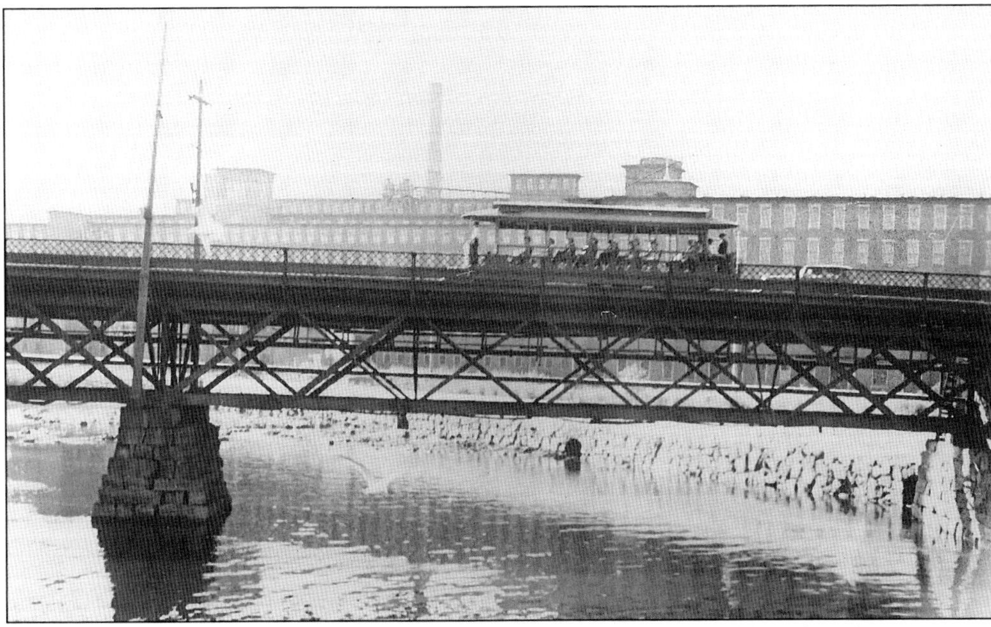

Crossing the bridge spanning the Saco River between Main Street, Biddeford, and Main Street, Saco is a Biddeford & Saco 12-bench open car, No. 29. Because of extremely high water in Saco River, this bridge was closed to all trolley traffic for a few days in March 1936, Birney cars being run to each end of the span and passengers walking across.

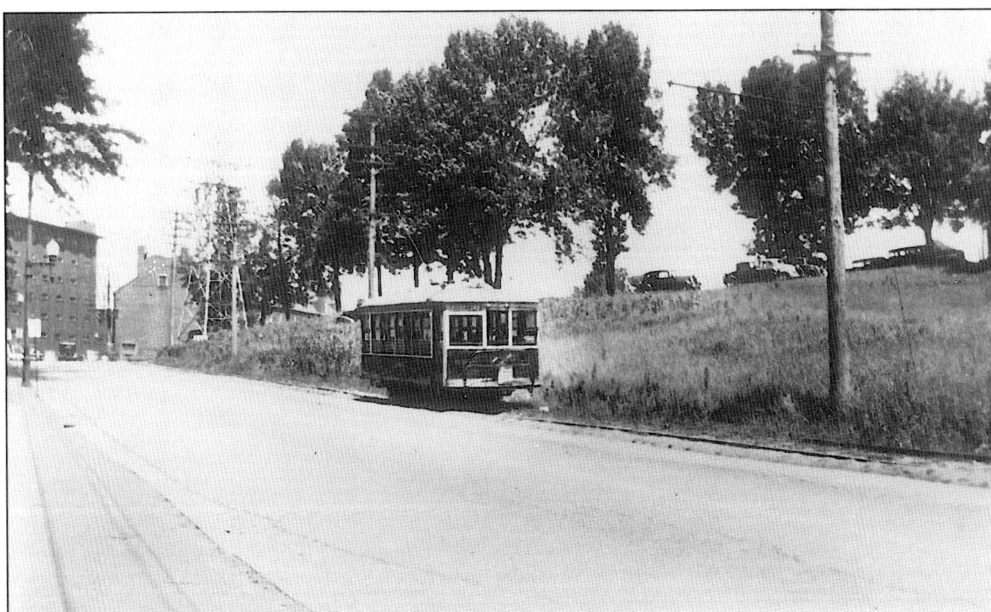

Descending York Hill on Factory Island, Saco, Car 610 is bound for Biddeford on July 21, 1937. When the Biddeford & Saco operated horsecars, an additional horse was attached to cars ascending this grade so the regular two-horse team would not be overburdened.

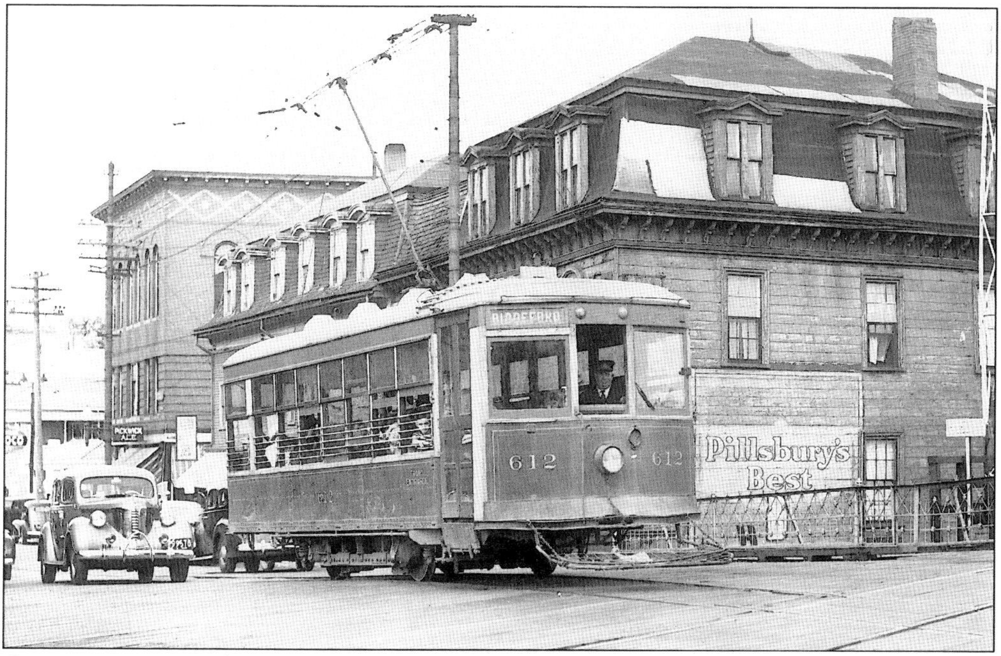

Operator George Perkins is at the controls as Car 612 crosses the Boston & Maine's Portland Division tracks on Main Street, Saco, about 1938. Conductors of open cars were required to "walk the crossing" before the trolleys could pass over the railroad tracks.

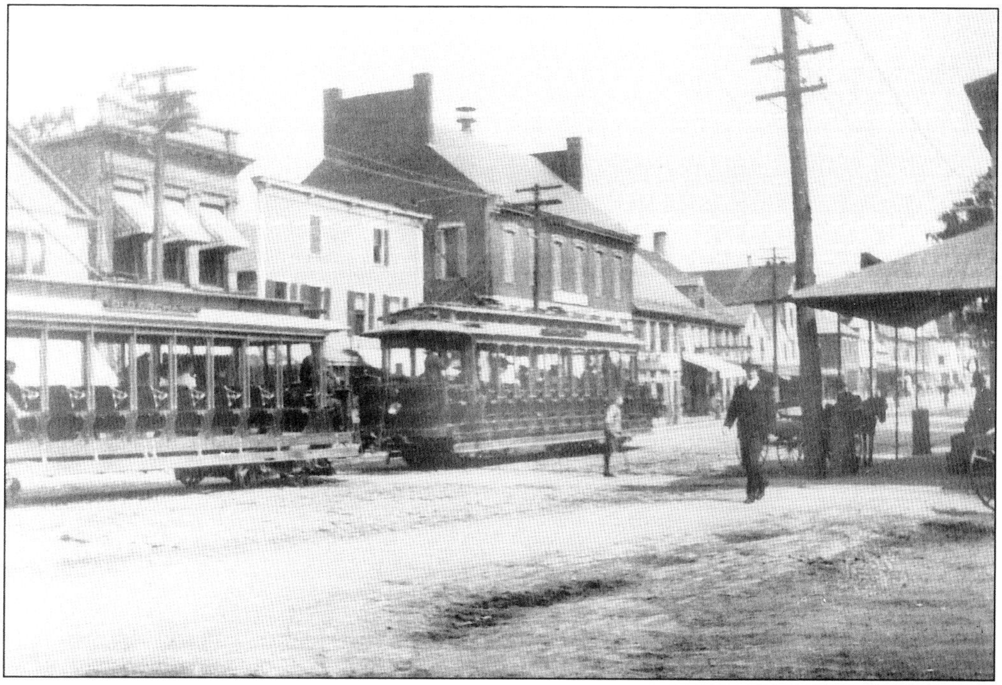

Biddeford & Saco and Portland Railroad open cars are shown here at Peperell Square on Main Street, Saco, *c.* 1905. The PRR held trackage rights over the Biddeford & Saco on Main Street between Beach Street and the square for three decades and maintained a storefront waiting room near the latter point for a number of years.

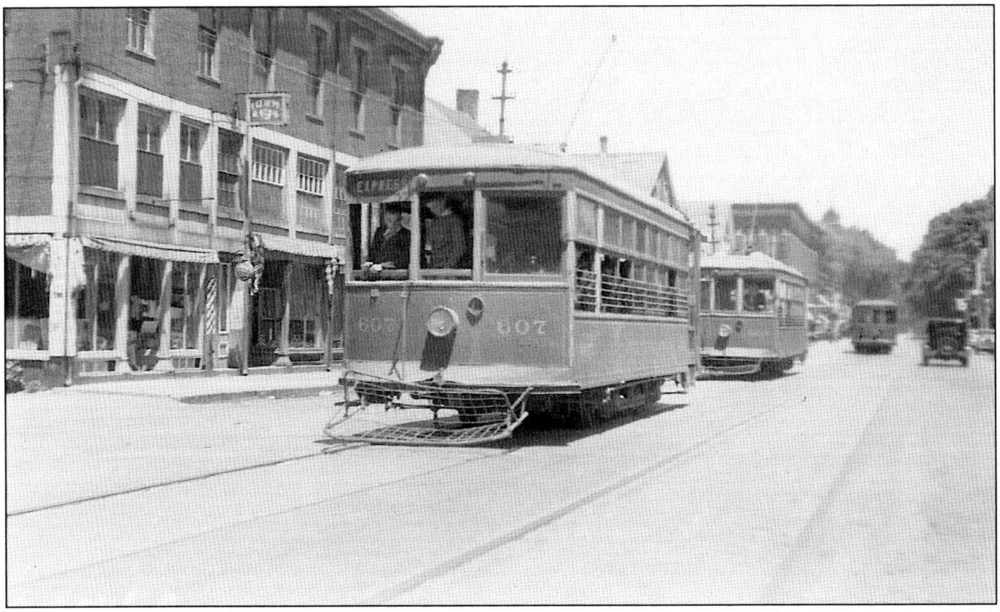

A long-needed turnout was constructed on Main Street, Saco, by the Biddeford & Saco Railroad in 1923. The two cars on the left-hand track are bound for Biddeford while a car headed for Old Orchard Beach can be seen in the background. No block signals ever were installed by the B&SRR but it did provide telephones at each turnout so crews could contact the dispatcher.

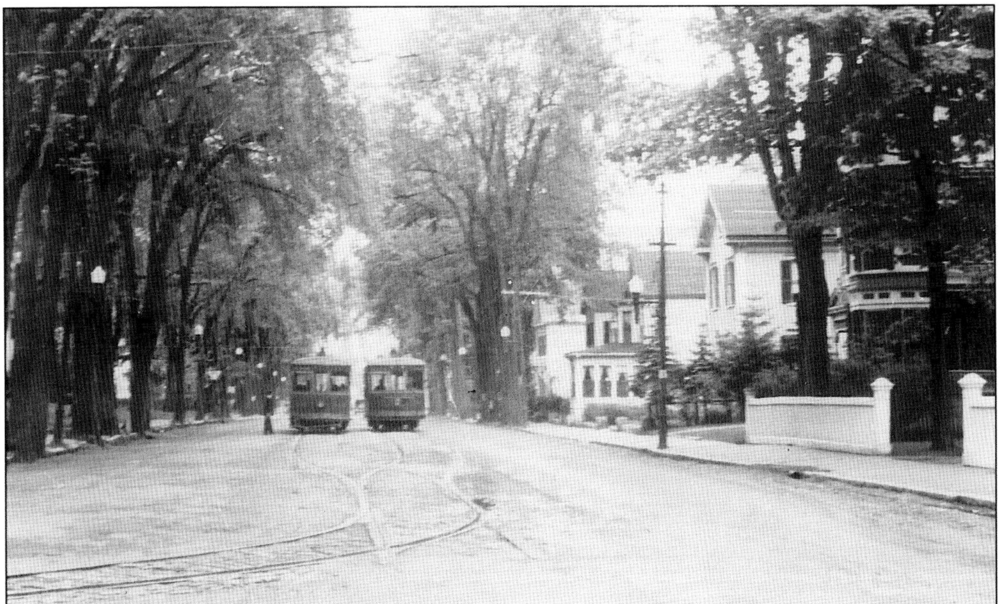

This is a *c. 1936* view of Nourse's turnout on Main Street, Saco, near its intersection with Beach Street. Still in place is the switch connecting the Biddeford & Saco rails with those of the Portland Railroad Company. The track on Main Street north of Beach Street remained in place for quite a few years after Portland-Saco trolley service ended in 1932 but was finally torn up when the street was repaved.

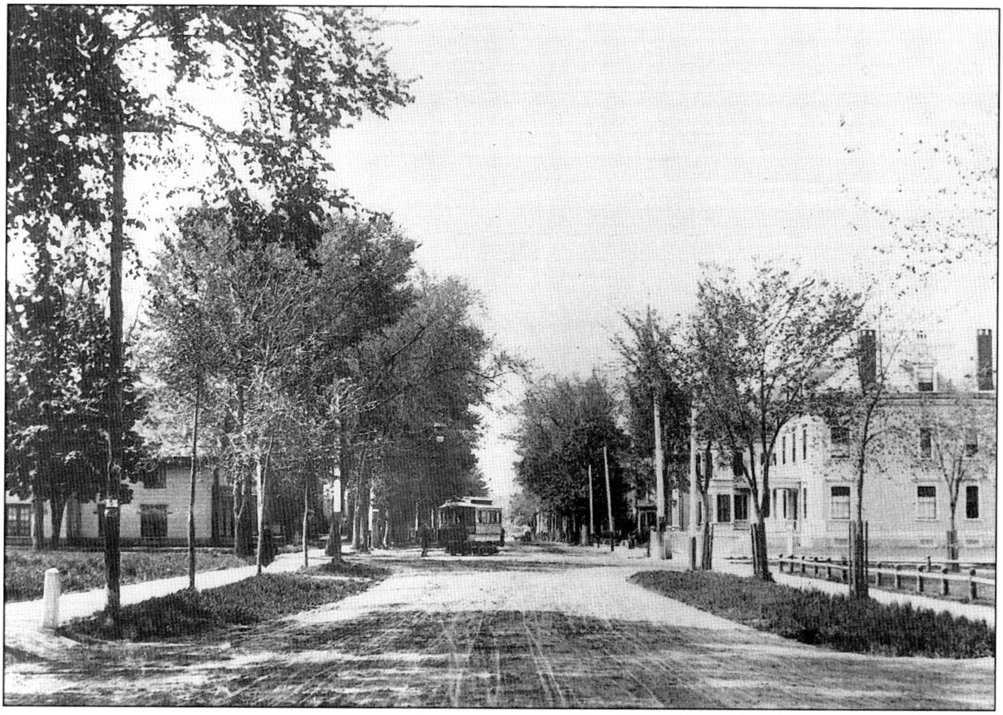

Four closed horsecars were motorized when the Biddeford & Saco Railroad adopted electricity as its motive power in 1892. One of them is shown turning from Main Street into Beach Street, Saco. All were discarded in 1900 after four more modern single truck closed cars, Nos. 10 through 16 even, were acquired by the railway.

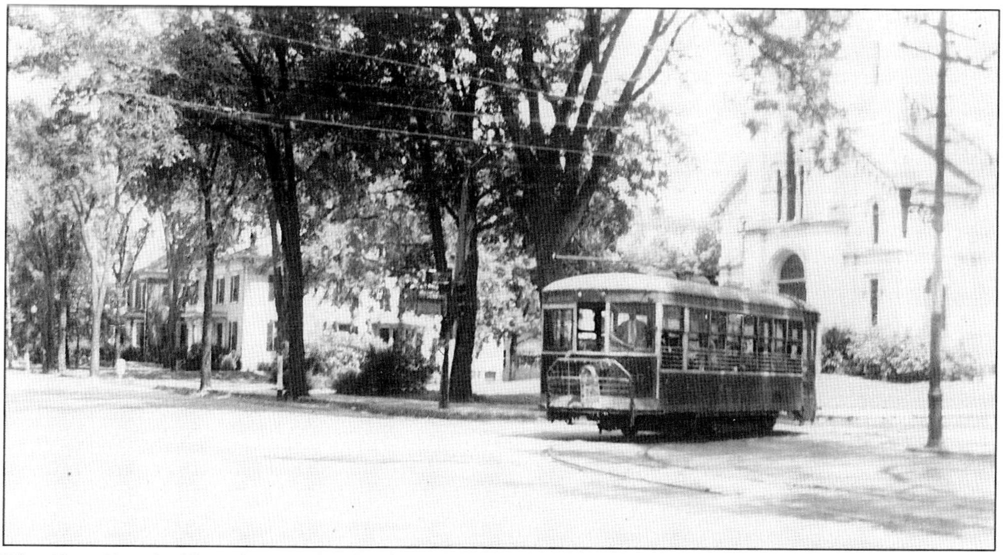

The First Parish Church is in the background as a Birney car turns from Beach Street into Main Street, Saco, on July 21, 1937. Cars of this type had a seating capacity of 32 and their safety equipment included a spring-loaded controller handle, the sudden release of which on a moving car caused the air brakes to be applied, the power to be cut off, sand to be spread on the rails, and the doors balanced so they could be opened manually.

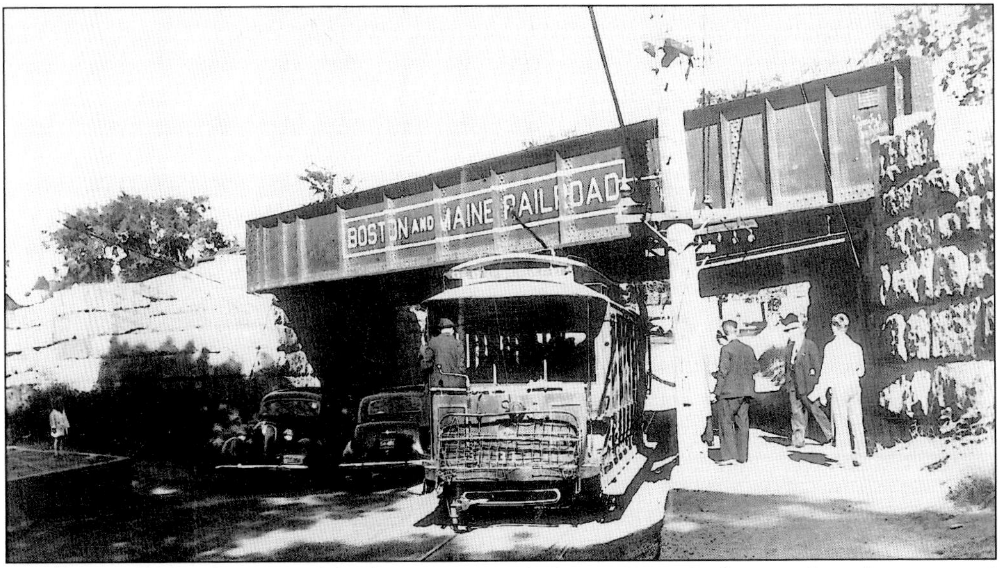

The Boston & Maine Railroad bridge across Beach Street, Saco, had a very low clearance and 12-bench opens were the largest trolleys that could squeeze under the span. Here's No. 31 headed for Old Orchard Beach in the early summer of 1939. Plans to increase the clearance never were carried out because of the cost.

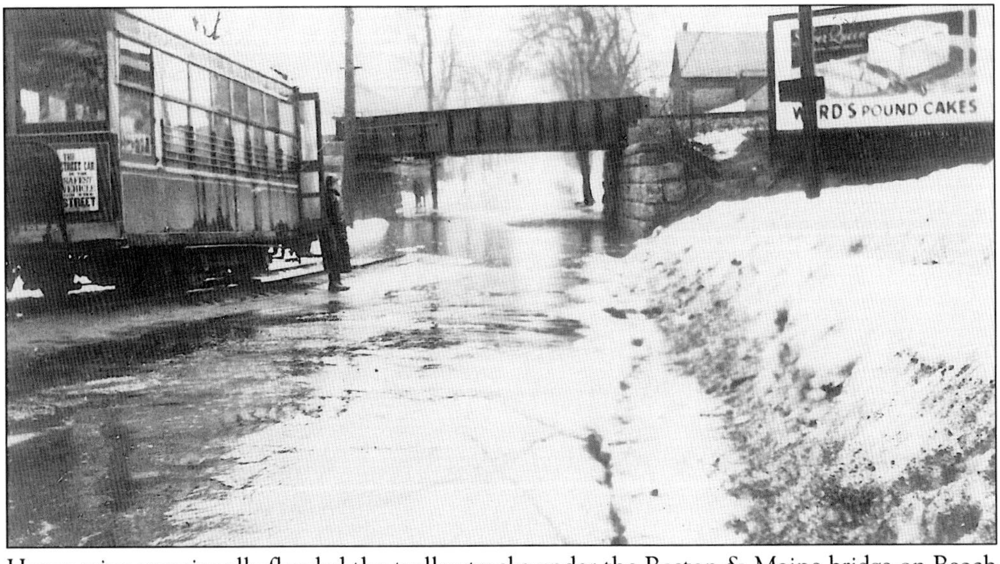

Heavy rains occasionally flooded the trolley tracks under the Boston & Maine bridge on Beach Street, Saco, and raised havoc with Biddeford & Saco schedules. At such times cars were run between Biddeford and the west side of the bridge and between the east side and either Laurel Hill Cemetery or Old Orchard Beach. Passengers changing from car to car had to walk over a sidewalk under the span.

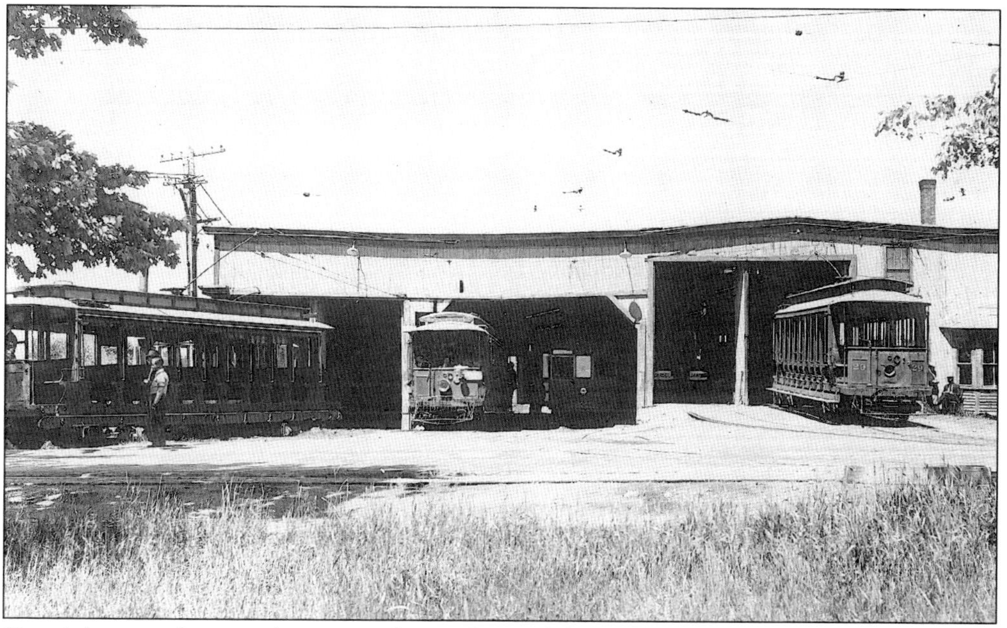

Certainly no architectural gem was the car barn of the Biddeford & Saco Railroad on Beach Street, about opposite the present Promenade Avenue, in Saco. Originally accommodating horsecars and horses, the building was enlarged over the years and eventually had eight tracks and a small office. It was razed after the end of trolley service in 1939.

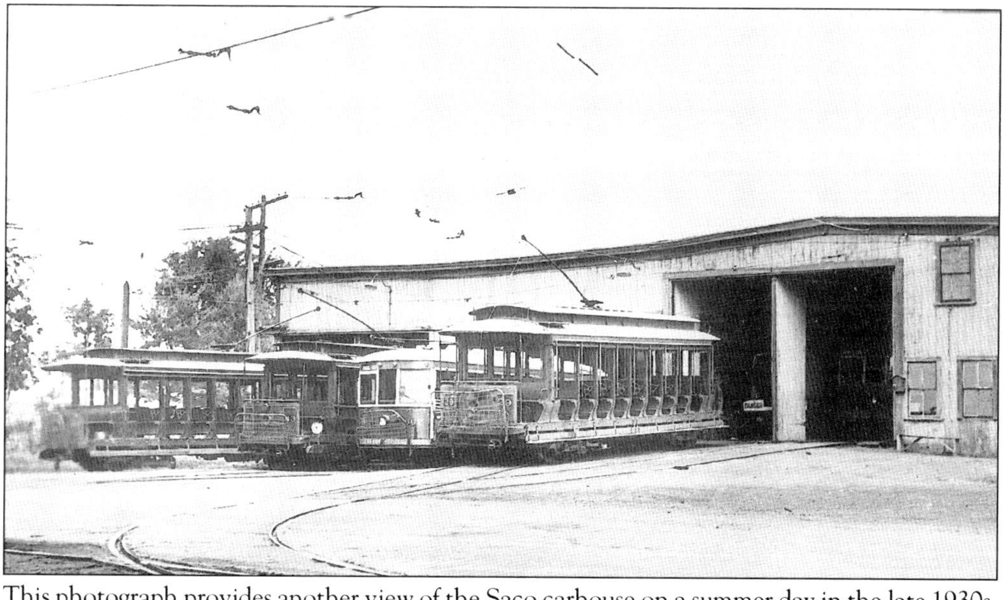

This photograph provides another view of the Saco carhouse on a summer day in the late 1930s. Three 12-bench opens and a Birney car bask in the sun in front of the wood frame building, at the rear of which were a power station and a coal shed. After bus operation began in 1939, the Biddeford & Saco's trolleys were dismantled on the carhouse tracks.

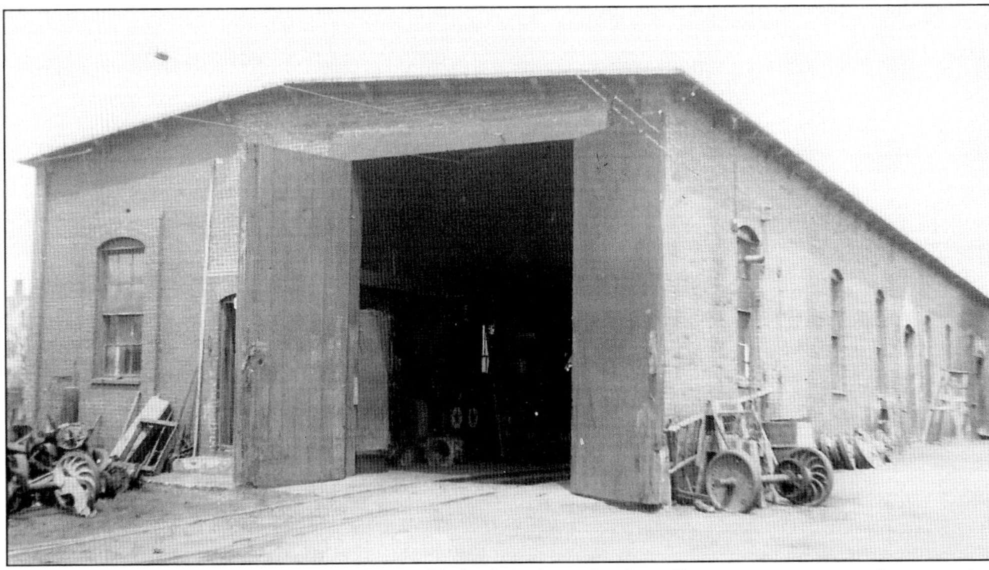

This brick building originally was the Biddeford & Saco Railroad's power station and was active as such from 1892 through 1911. Then the structure was converted to a combination repair shop and substation. After 1939, it was used for maintenance of and repairs to motor buses, which were stored outdoors on the former carhouse site.

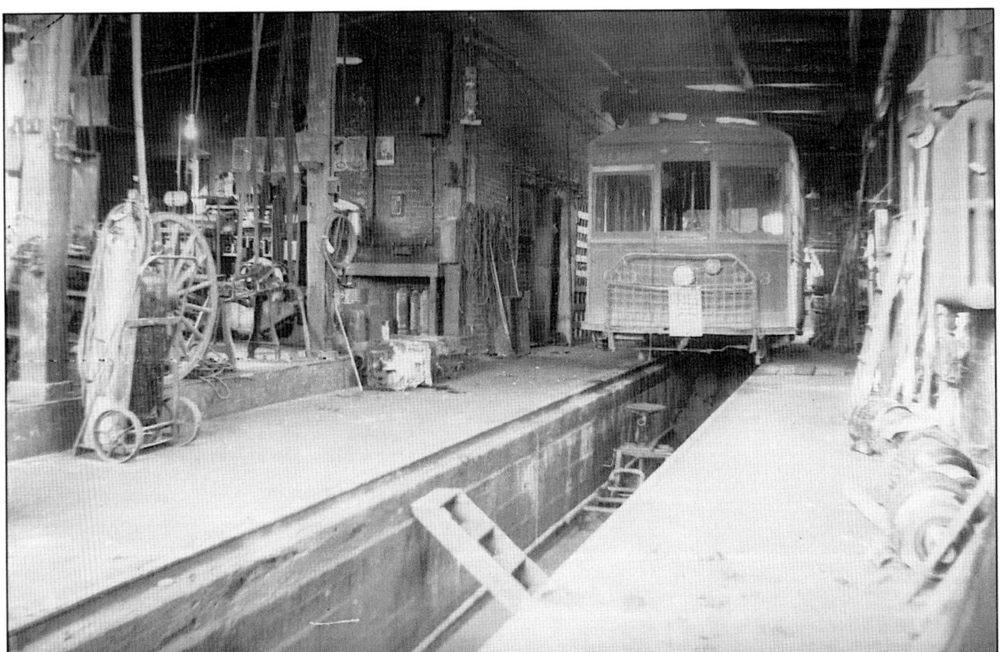

Over the pit in the repair shop is Birney Car 613 on June 29, 1939. Shop facilities were meager, and until 1932 much of the heavy work, such as on wheels and axles, was farmed out to the Portland Railroad Company.

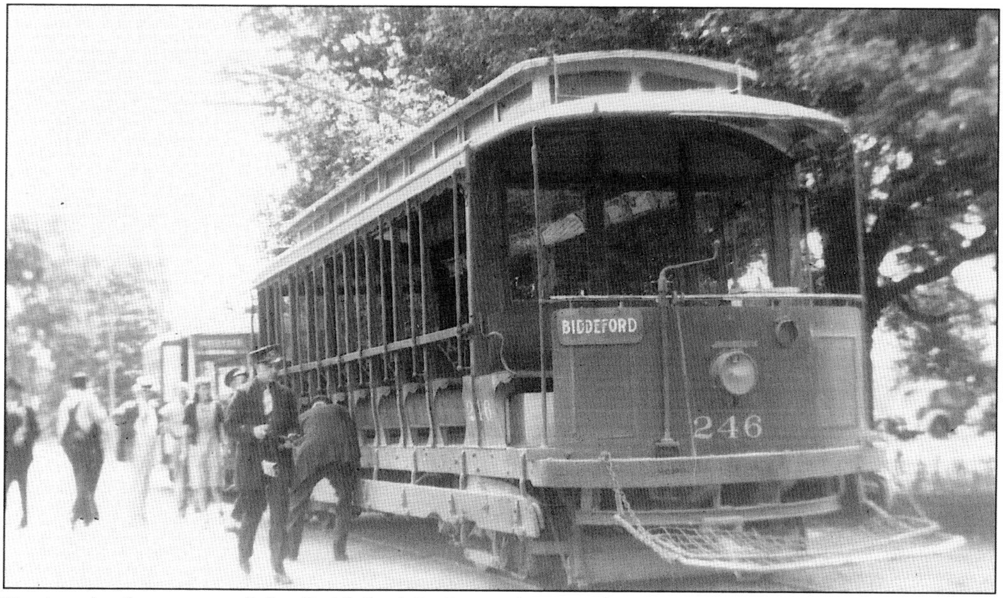

During the last years of the Biddeford & Saco, the popular open "breezers" were run between Biddeford and Old Orchard Beach only in the afternoon and evening, closed cars being in service at other times. Here passengers from the resort arriving at the Saco carhouse around noon transfer to an open car to continue on to Biddeford.

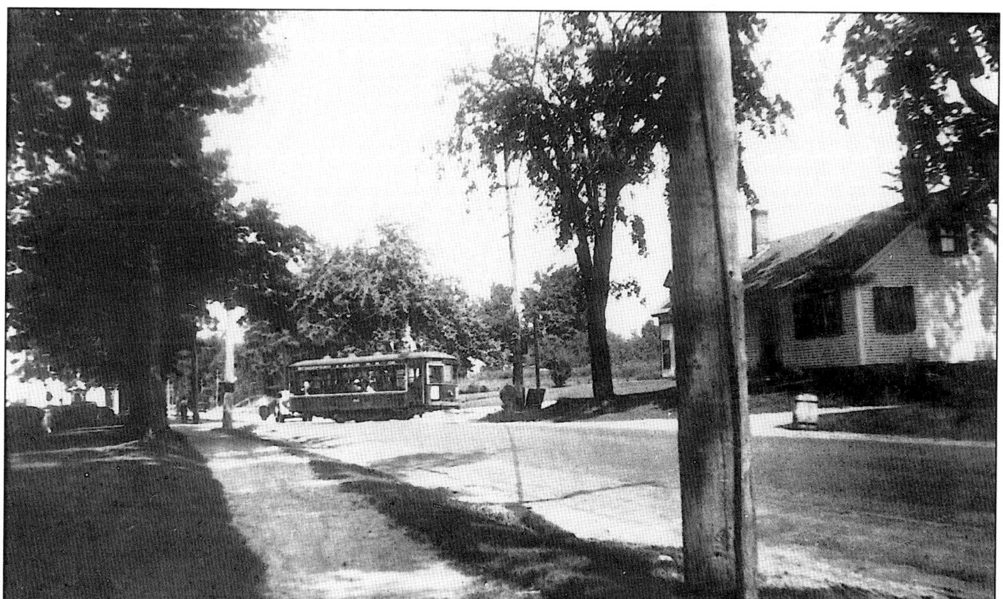

On its way to Old Orchard Beach, a Birney car turns from Beach Street into Old Orchard Road, Saco. During the fall, winter, and spring, every other car leaving Biddeford terminated its run at this intersection, just a stone's throw from Laurel Hill Cemetery, alternate cars continuing on to Old Orchard Beach.

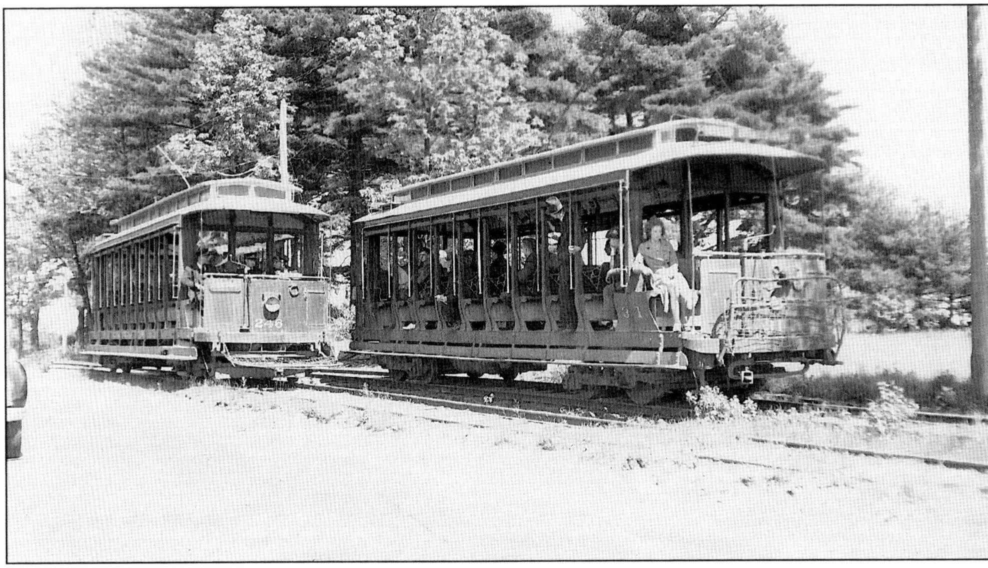

Two open cars, Nos. 246 and 31, meet at Kelley's turnout beside Old Orchard Road, Saco. No. 31 is outbound to Old Orchard Beach while No. 246, a former Portland car, is inbound to Biddeford. The Biddeford & Saco purchased seven 12-bench opens from the Portland Railroad during the 1922-25 period to replace the last of its 10-bench "breezers."

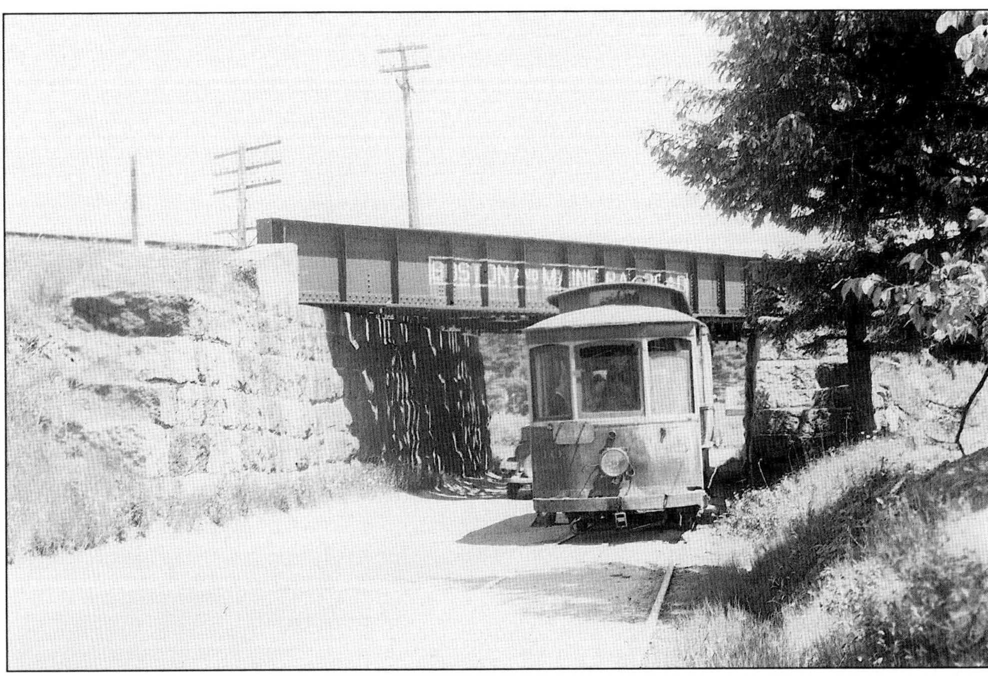

Just a short distance beyond Kelley's was this undercrossing of the Boston & Maine's Portland Division. Biddeford & Saco No. 10 passes under the railroad bridge on June 18, 1939 during a "rail fan" excursion. The enthusiasts also rode on Birney car 607 and open car 31 and paid one dollar for the privilege.

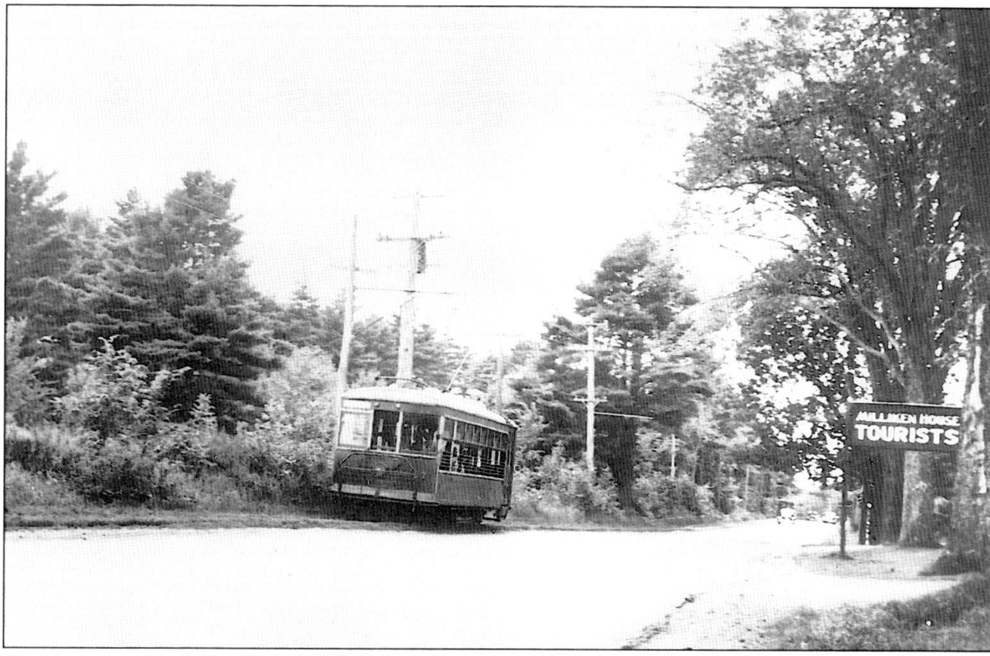

Approaching Old Orchard High School on Saco Avenue, Old Orchard, Car 607 passes the American House on August 14, 1938. Birney cars had poor riding qualities except on smooth track and by 1938 there was little of that on the Biddeford & Saco because of the lack of maintenance.

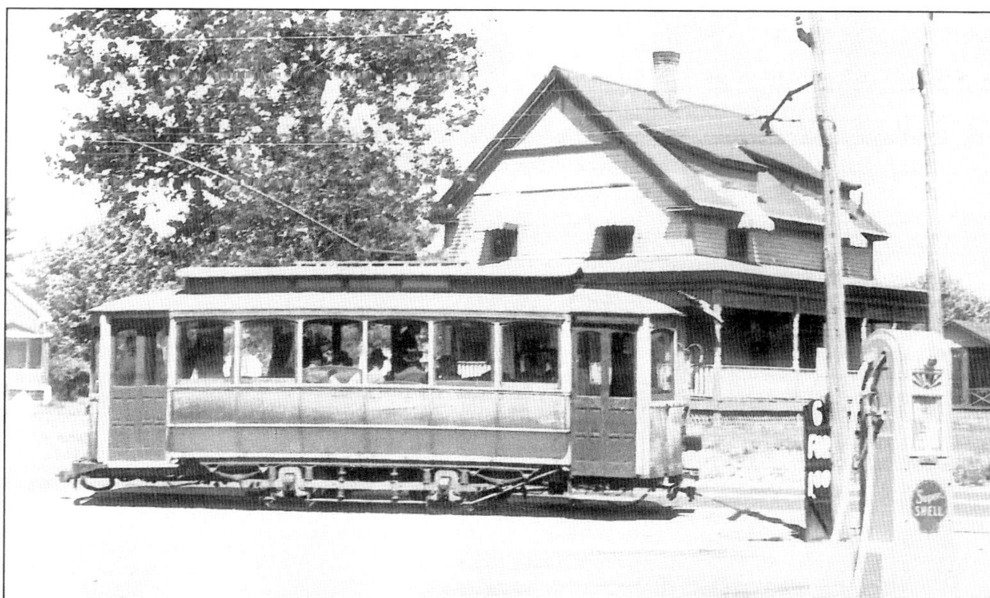

Six gallons for $1 is the gasoline price posted at this Shell station on Saco Avenue, near Ocean Park Road, Old Orchard, on June 18, 1939. The closed car is No. 10, which is being operated on a "rail fan" excursion. When this car was revamped for one-man operation, the compressor for the air brakes was installed on the floor and boarding and alighting passengers had to walk around it.

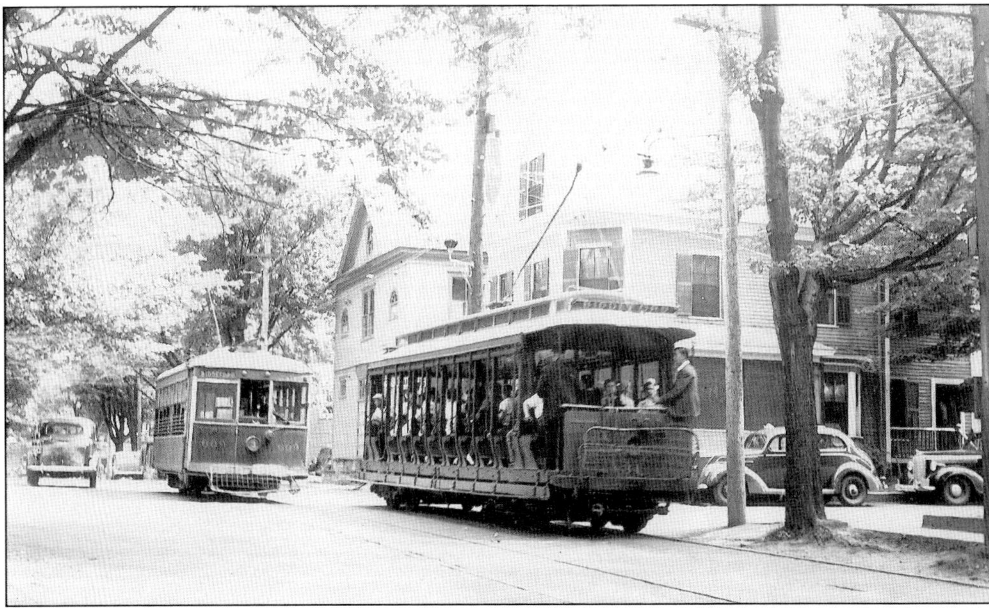

Tabernacle turnout on Union Avenue, Old Orchard Beach, was a regular meeting point for cars running between Biddeford and the resort. Cars 609 and 31 are shown in this photograph taken August 18, 1938 by the late Gerald F. Cunningham.

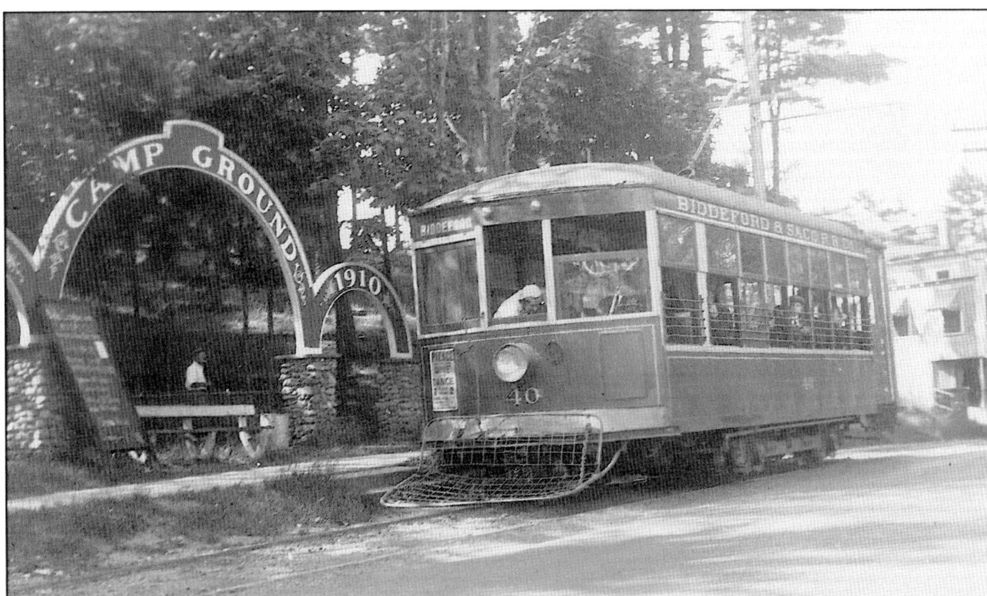

At the Old Orchard Camp Ground's main entrance on Washington Avenue, Car 40 is Biddeford bound on July 14, 1935. The Camp Ground was established in 1873 and was served by horsecars and trolleys from July 15, 1888 through July 5, 1939.

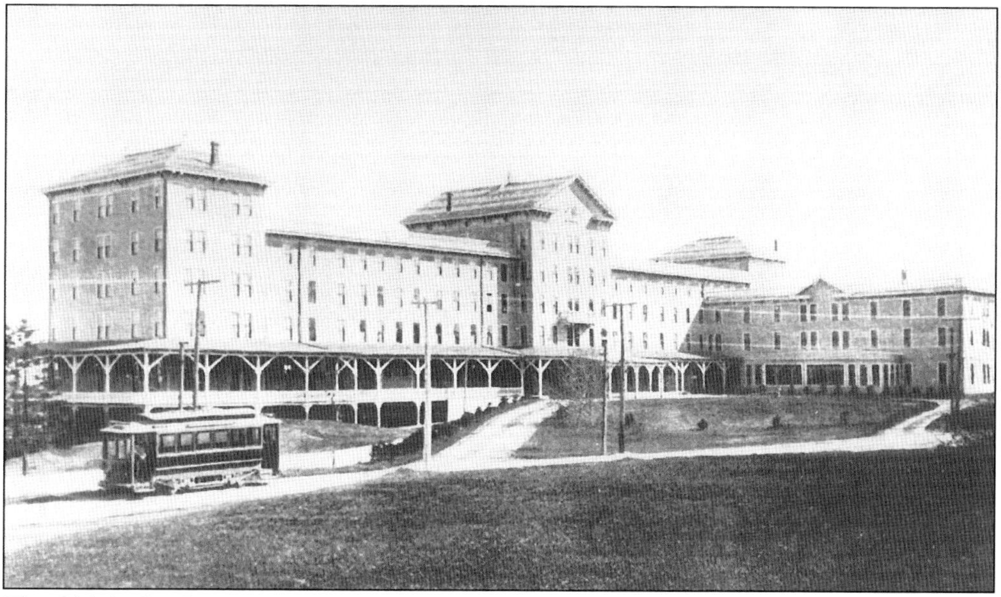

The Old Orchard House on Saco Avenue, Old Orchard Beach, built in 1876, was one of the resort's leading hotels for many years. Apparently the picture was taken during the off season for no people or vehicles are in sight as a Biddeford & Saco trolley passes. The hotel had accommodations for 400 guests and it outlasted the trolleys by four years.

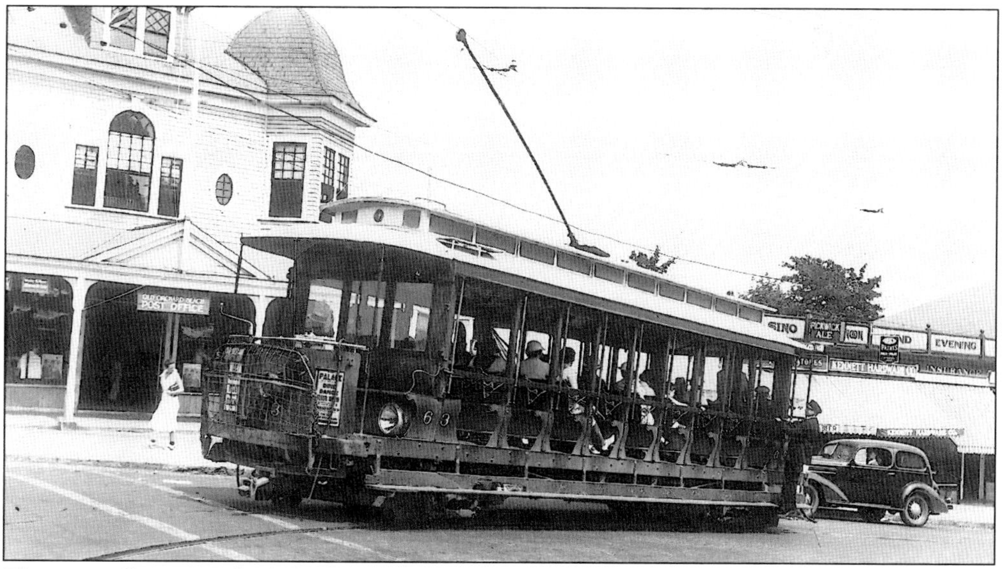

The post office is at the left as Car 63 turns from Saco Avenue onto Old Orchard Street at Old Orchard Beach on July 30, 1936. To the right of the trolley but not shown is St. Margaret Roman Catholic Church. Purchased from Portland in 1925, the open car was of 1910 vintage and was retired at the end of the 1936 summer season.

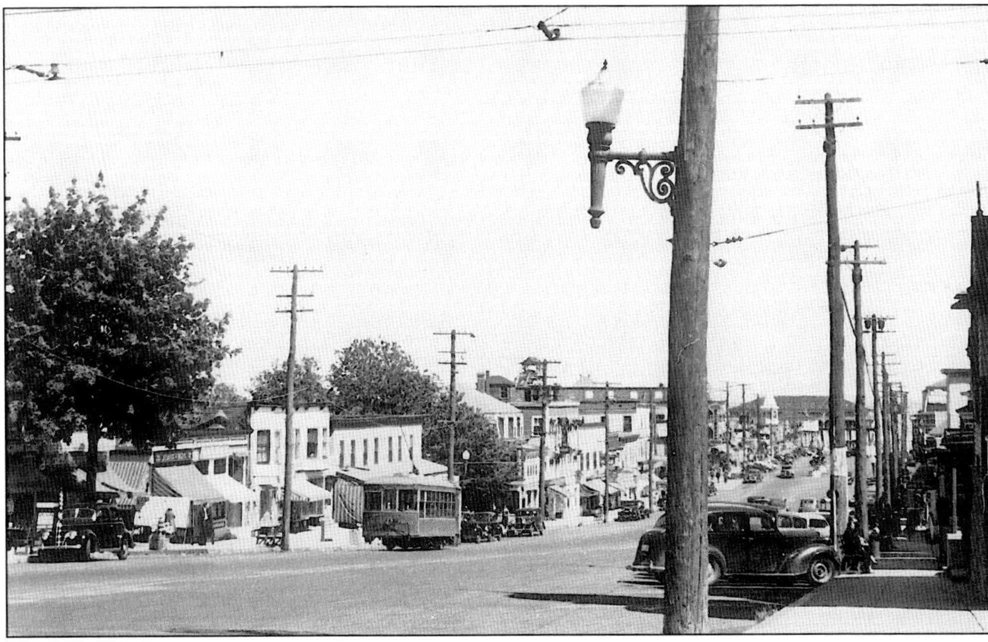

The end of the line is in sight as Birney 603 heads east on Old Orchard Street toward Depot Square, the terminus of the trolley line. This view must have been taken on a weekday because there were so many automobiles at Old Orchard Beach on Saturdays and Sundays during the 1930s that electric cars entering and leaving the resort could only inch along at times.

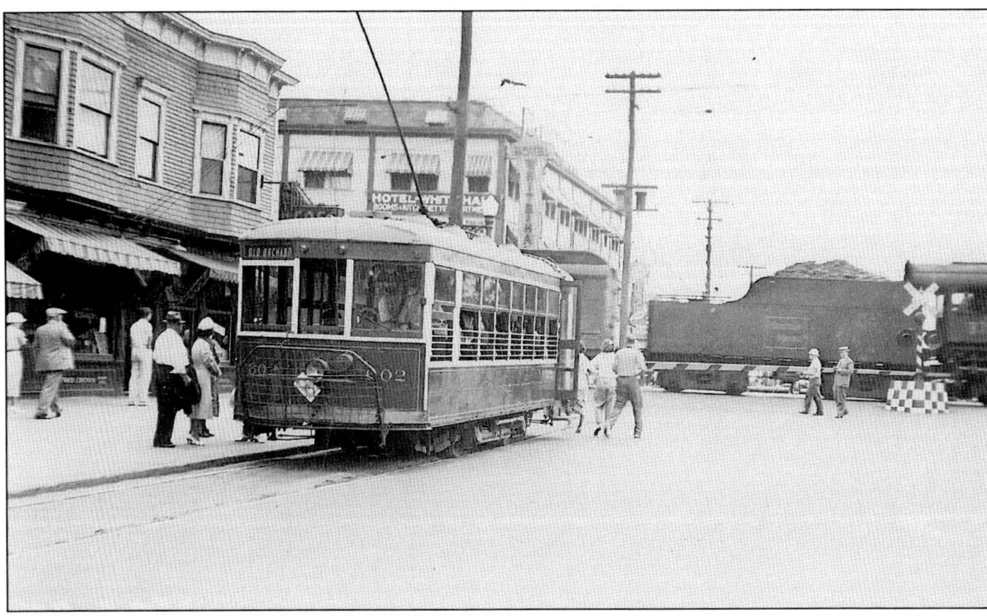

Boston & Maine P-2 class locomotive 3705 crosses Old Orchard Street as Biddeford & Saco 602 discharges its passengers at Old Orchard Beach in 1938. The railroad's Old Orchard Beach depot was on the opposite side of Old Orchard Street and was active until 1963 when the B&M ended passenger service between Boston and Portland.

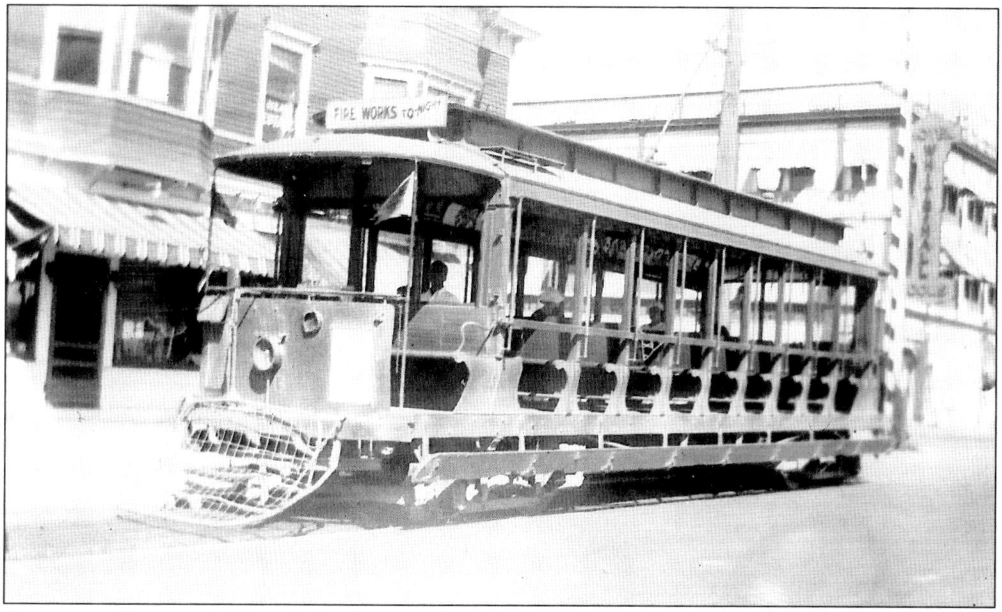

Carrying a "Fireworks Tonight" advertising sign on its roof, a nearly empty open car stands at the end of the line at Old Orchard Beach on July 18, 1934. The fireworks were sponsored by beach merchants to attract mid-week visitors to the resort and the Biddeford & Saco contributed its share because the pyrotechnic displays boosted trolley patronage.

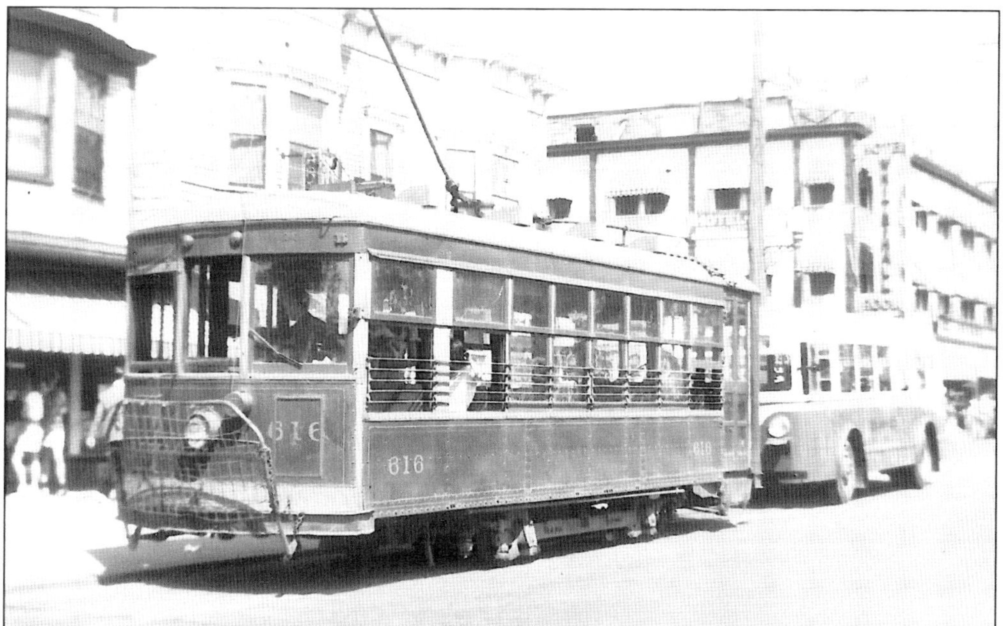

A harbinger of things to come is the Biddeford & Saco bus behind Birney car 616 at Old Orchard Beach in late June of 1939. The last trolleys between Biddeford and Old Orchard Beach were run on July 5, 1939 and bus service started the next morning. Riding was very heavy on the final day of trolley service as many residents of Biddeford, Saco, and Old Orchard Beach took a sentimental farewell trip.

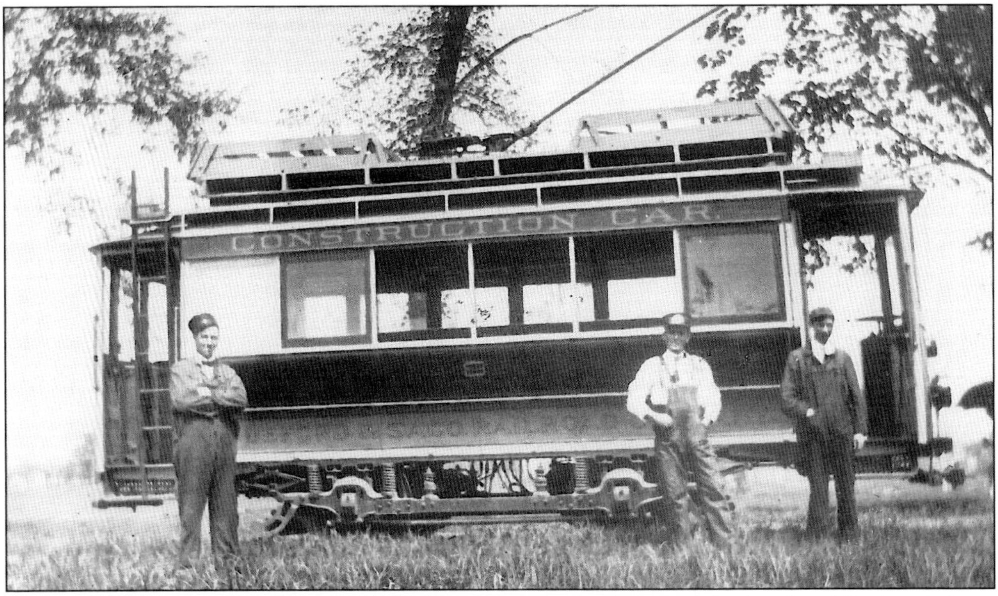

Construction Car No. 8 of the Biddeford & Saco was produced in the Portland Railroad shops about 1902 by rebuilding and electrifying an old Portland horsecar. It survived until 1931 when it was replaced by a former passenger car, No. 16, which had been equipped with a roof platform.

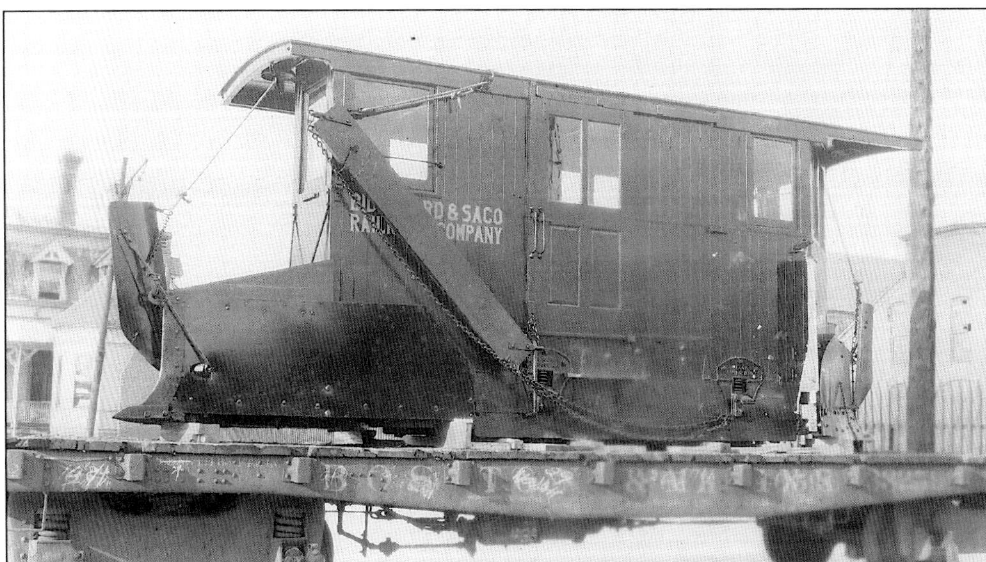

Loaded on a flat car for shipment to Maine is Biddeford & Saco snow plow No. 3. Built in Springfield, Massachusetts in 1914, it survived until the end of the trolley service in 1939.

Seven

The Portland Railroad Company: Saco Division

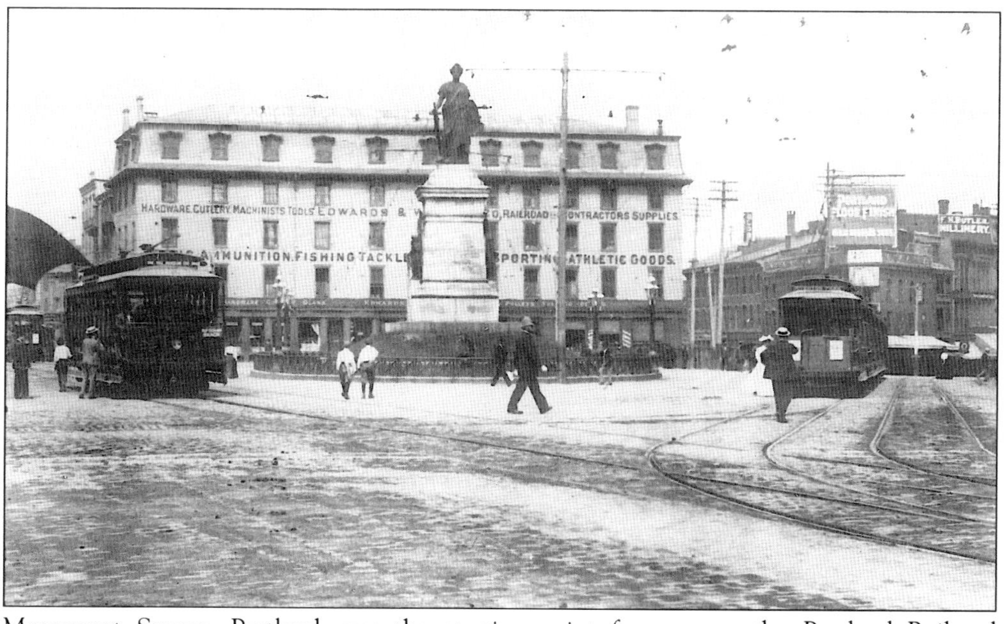

Monument Square, Portland, was the starting point for cars on the Portland Railroad Company's Saco division. At left, No. 182, one of the 14-bench opens purchased in 1902 for operation to Saco and Old Orchard Beach, displays "Oak Hill, Dunstan & Saco" on its front destination sign. The dasher sign reads "Old Orchard Beach." Cars on all routes of the Portland Railroad passed through this square, named after a Civil War memorial monument dedicated in 1891.

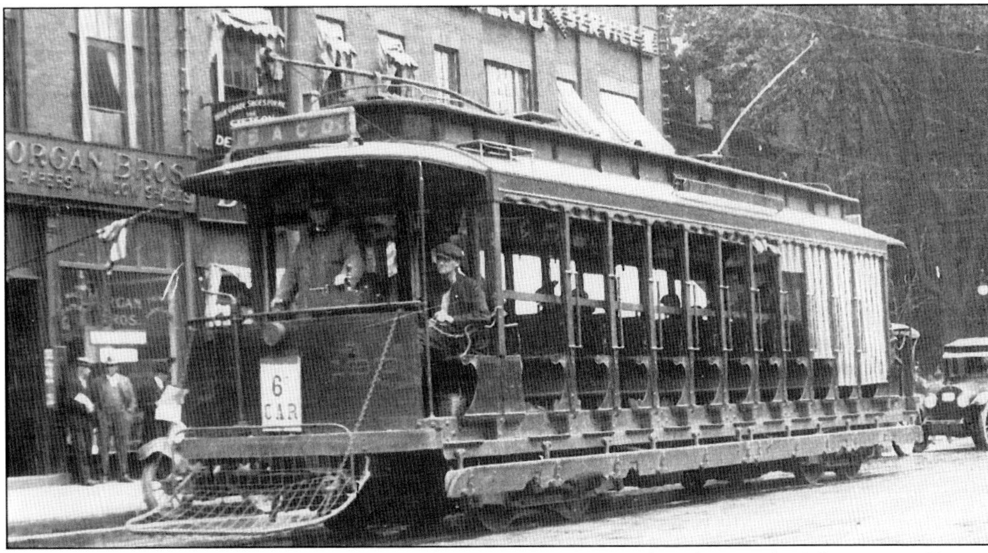

Fourteen-bench open No. 190, which had a seating capacity of 70, leaves the Monument Square waiting room in Portland for Saco in 1918. Above the waiting room were the general offices of the Cumberland County Power & Light Company, which had leased the Portland Railroad Company for 99 years on February 1, 1912.

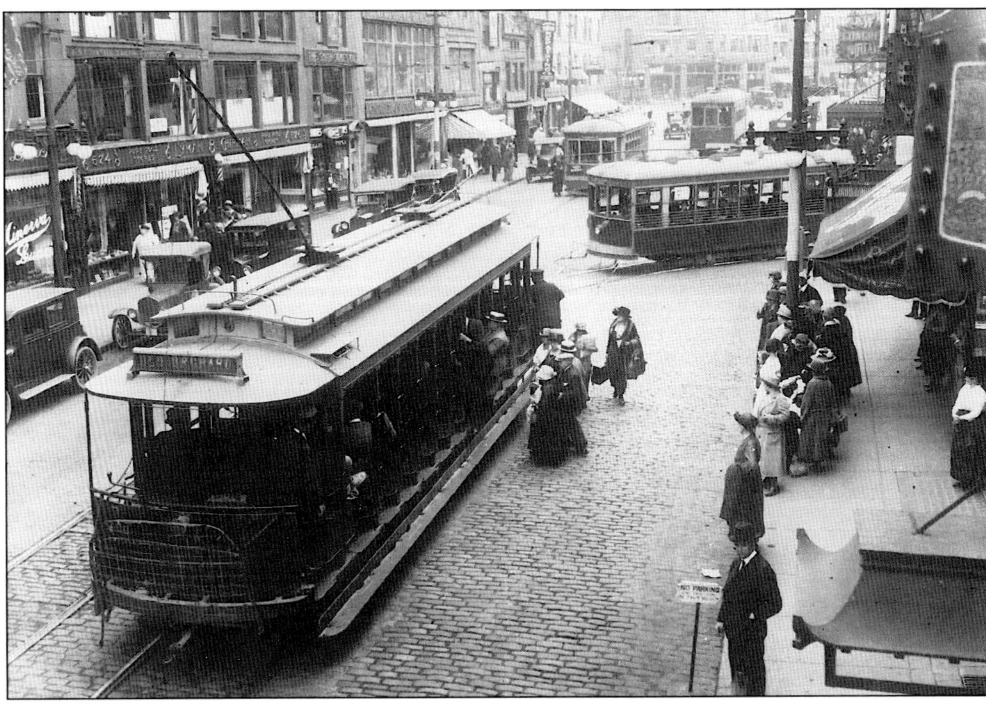

This Old Orchard-bound open car boards passengers at the intersection of Congress Street and Forest Avenue in Portland about 1920. We're looking toward Congress Square - the intersection of Congress, High, and Free Streets. The car was to continue along Congress Street to Railroad Square and then run along St. John Street, past Union Station, to Danforth Street.

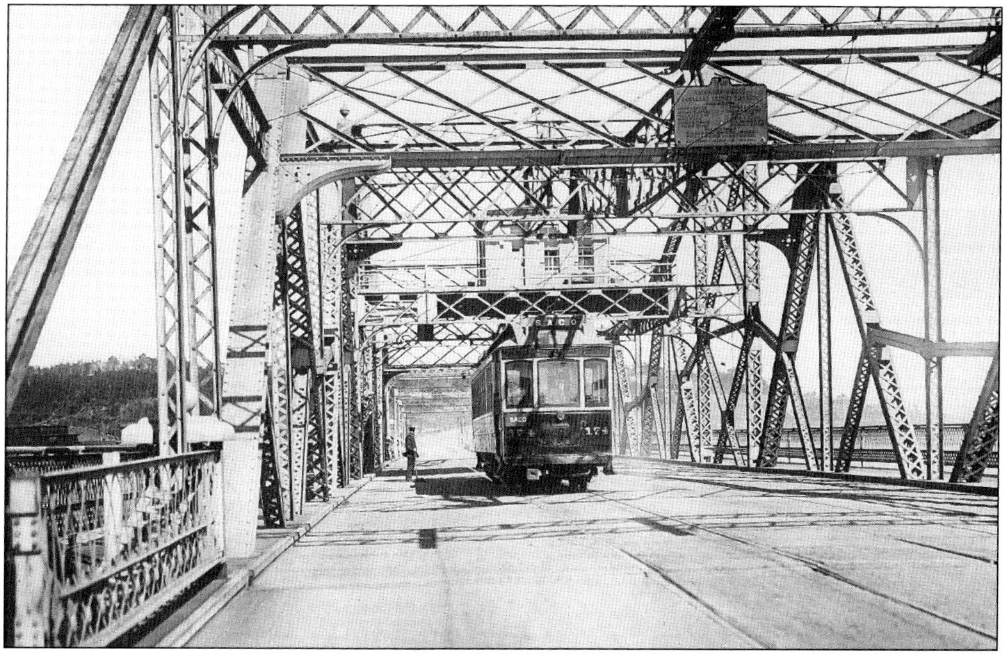

Bound for Saco, Car 174 crosses the new Vaughan's bridge across the Fore River between Danforth Street, Portland, and Main Street, South Portland shortly after the newly built span was opened in August 1909. Through cars were operated between Portland and Saco during the fall, winter, and spring and between Portland and Old Orchard Beach in summer and cars like 174 were run the year round.

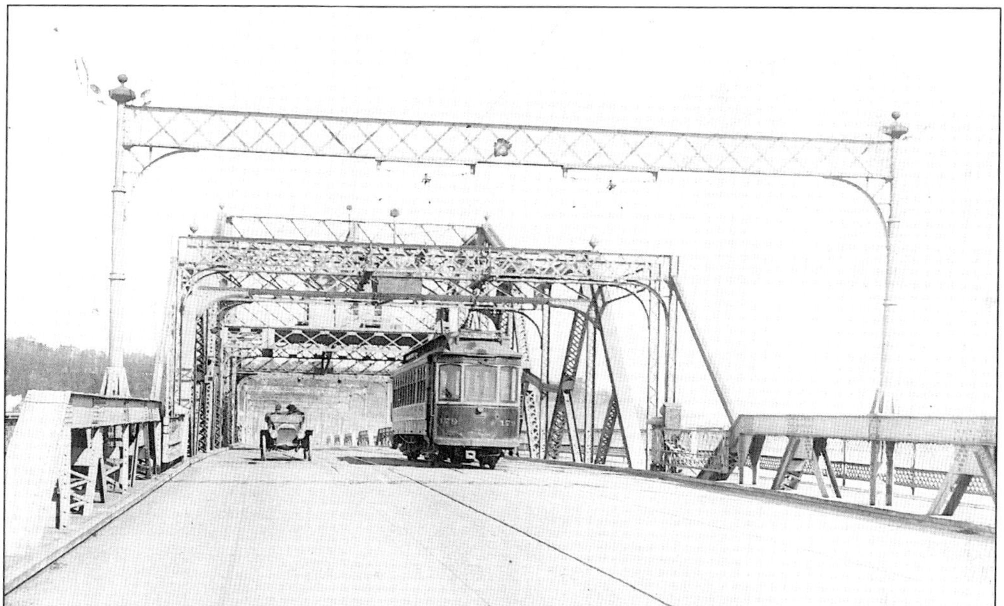

Among the largest closed passenger cars of the Portland Railroad Company were Nos. 173-180, purchased in 1902. These had 34 feet 4 inch bodies with smoking compartments and seating capacity of 48. Interior appointments included overhead luggage racks. Here No. 179 crosses Vaughan's bridge en route to Monument Square.

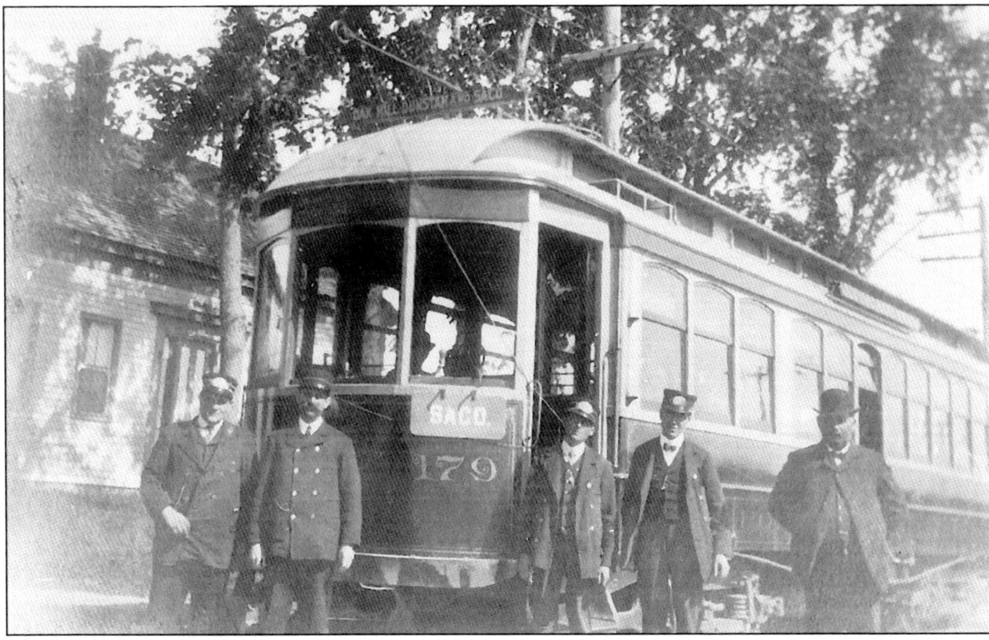

Crews of trolleys meeting at Scottow's turnout near Oak Hill, Scarborough, pose for the photographer in front of Saco-bound Car 179 *c.* 1903. This trolley survived until the end of trolley service in Portland in 1941 and then was scrapped.

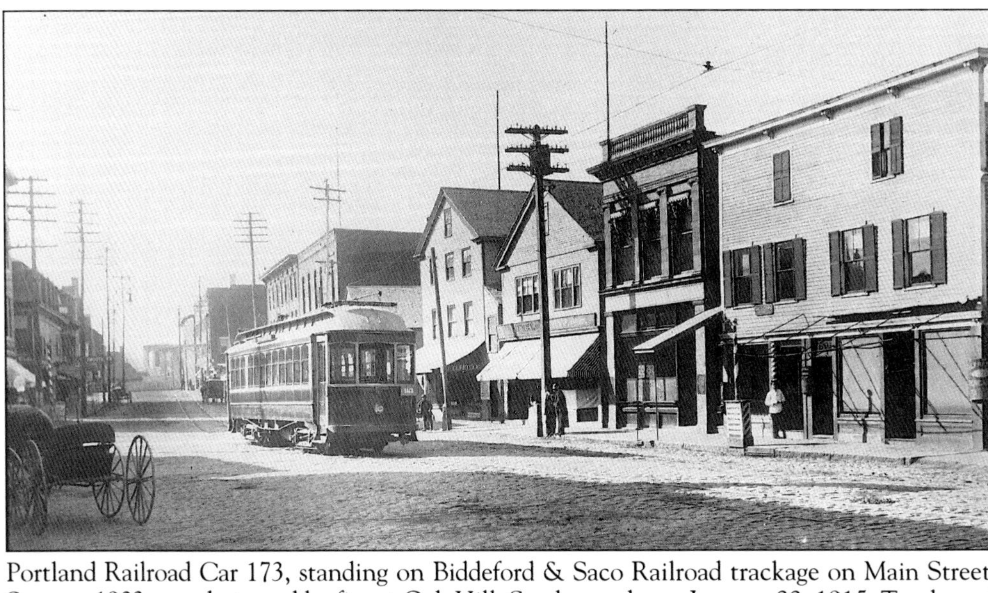

Portland Railroad Car 173, standing on Biddeford & Saco Railroad trackage on Main Street, Saco, *c.* 1903, was destroyed by fire at Oak Hill, Scarborough, on January 22, 1915. Trucks and electrical equipment salvaged from 173 were installed on a replacement car, No. 502, which also lasted until 1941.

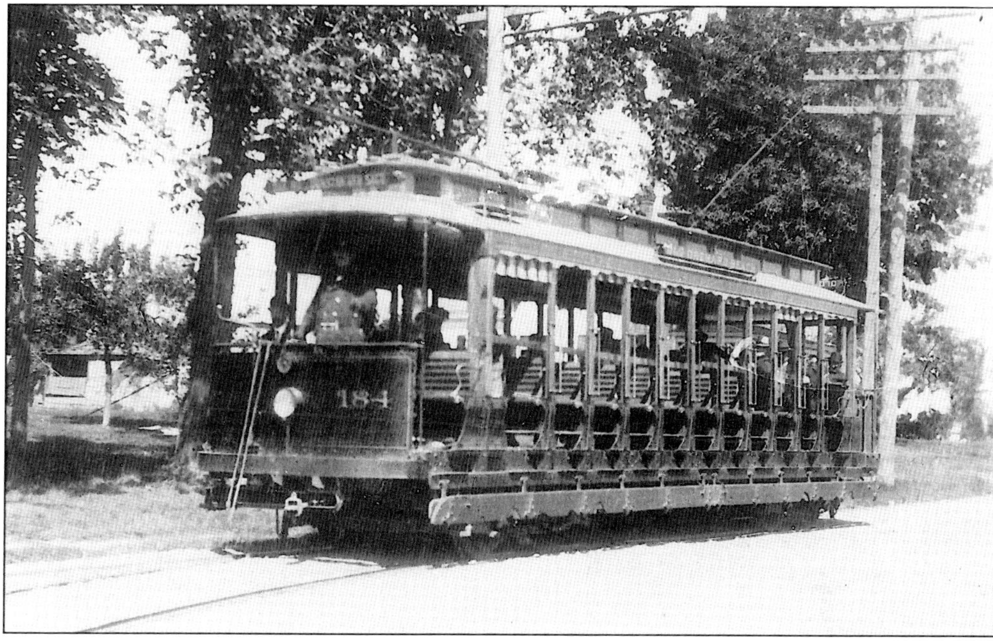

The Old Orchard branch of the Portland Railroad's Saco Division left the main line at Old Orchard Junction near Dunstan Corner, West Scarborough. Car 184 takes the switch at the junction as it heads for the resort about 1905.

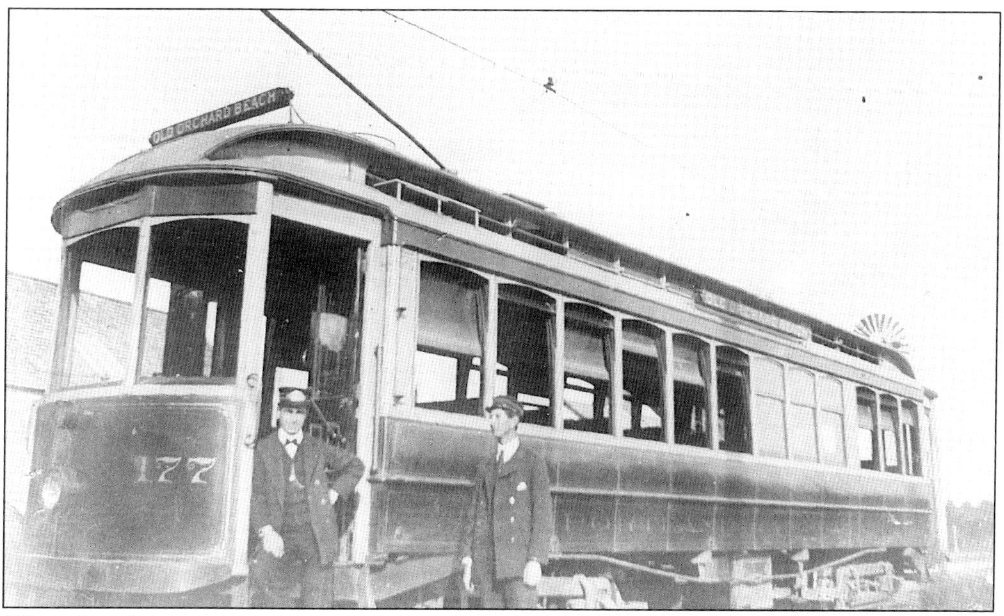

When Saco Division main line cars were running between Portland and Saco, shuttle service was provided between Old Orchard Junction and Old Orchard Beach. No. 177 and its crew, Henry Ward and Fred Shaw, were photographed near the junction as they waited for a connecting car.

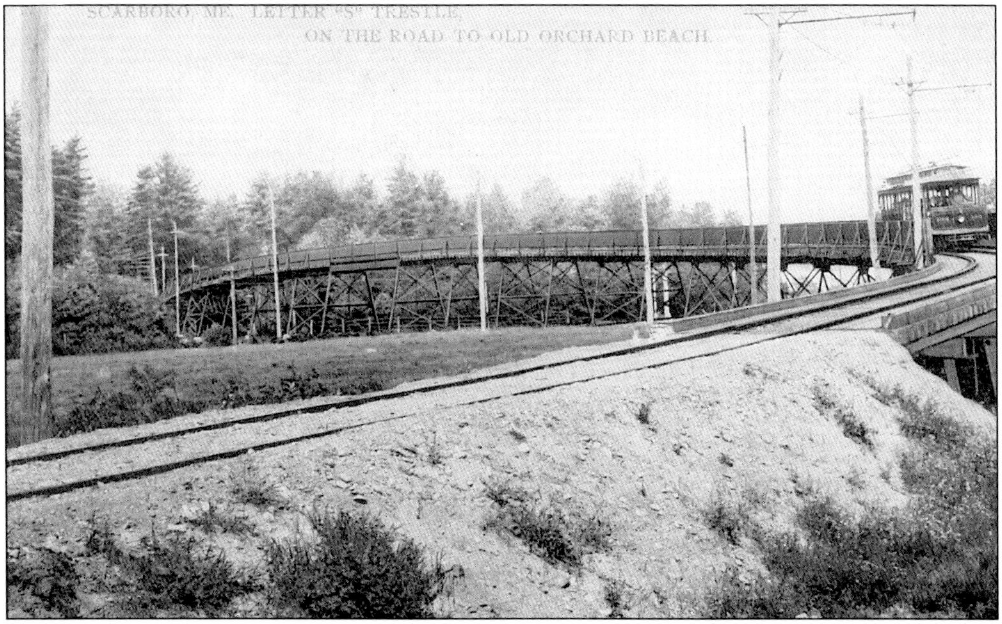

This 700-foot, S-shaped viaduct carried trolleys on the Old Orchard Branch across the eastern division of the Boston & Maine Railroad in West Scarborough. Thirteen passengers were injured when two open cars collided head-on on the easterly approach to the viaduct on August 21, 1910. Both trolleys were extensively damaged and had to be towed back to Portland.

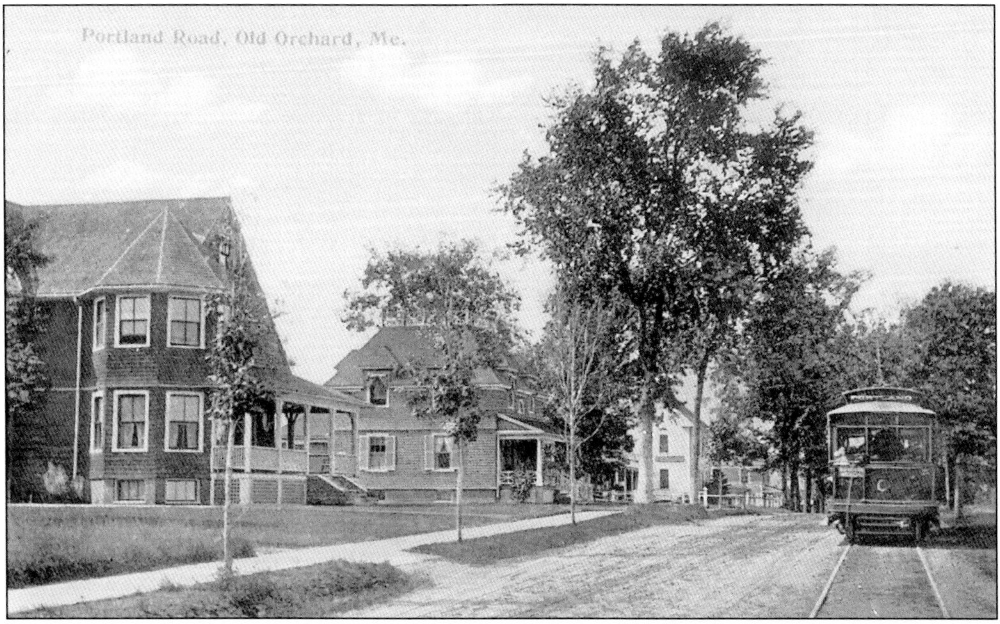

A Portland Railroad open car runs along Portland Road, Old Orchard, en route to Depot Square at Old Orchard Beach. The PRR connected with the Biddeford & Saco at the intersection of Portland Avenue with Saco Avenue and had trackage rights over B&SRR on Old Orchard Street.

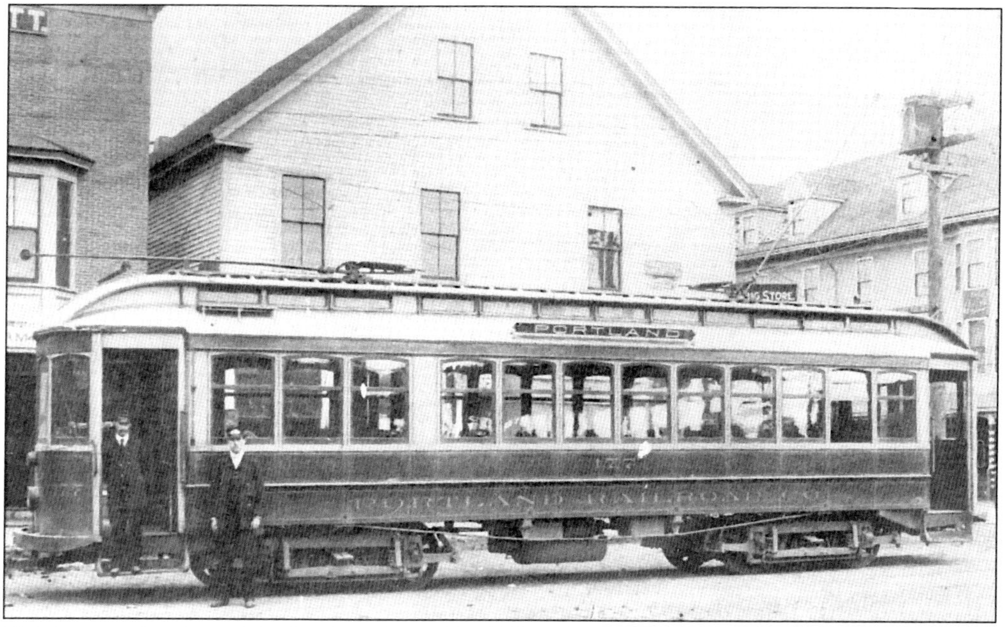

This is an early view of Portland Railroad No. 177 at the end of the line at Old Orchard Beach. The smoking compartment at the front of the car is identified by the wide post between the third and fourth windows. These compartments were eliminated through the removal of a bulkhead when the cars were equipped for one-man operation during the 1920s.

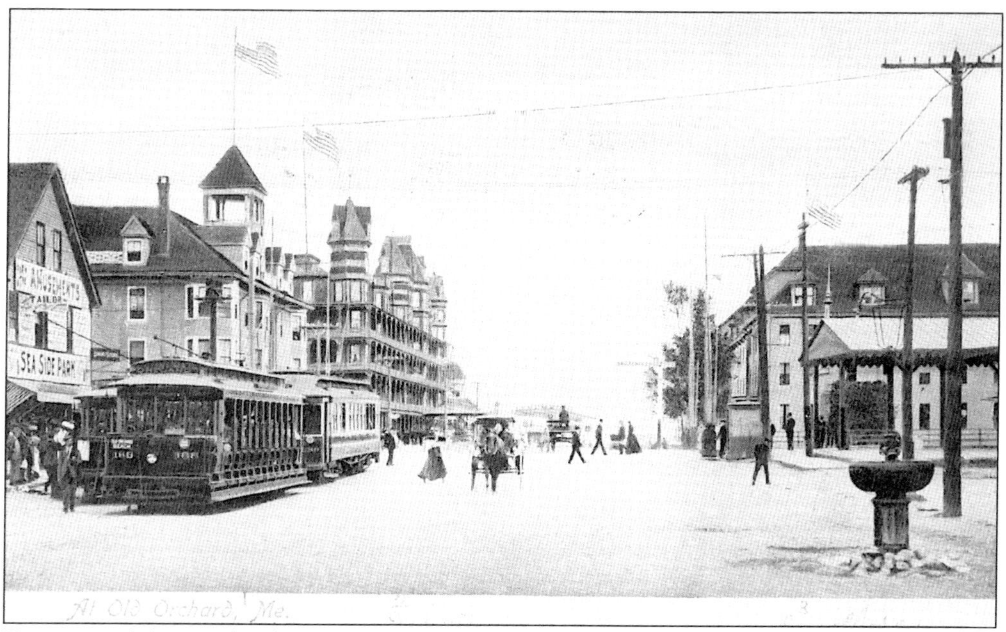

Two cars of the Portland Railroad and one of the Biddeford & Saco are at the end of the line at Old Orchard Beach about 1906. The buildings at the left disappeared during the great conflagration of August 15-16, 1907 when 17 hotels, 20 stores, and 60 cottages were destroyed. Only three lives were lost as flames swept from building to building. Trolleys were jammed on the weekend of August 17-18 as thousands flocked to the beach to view the ruins.

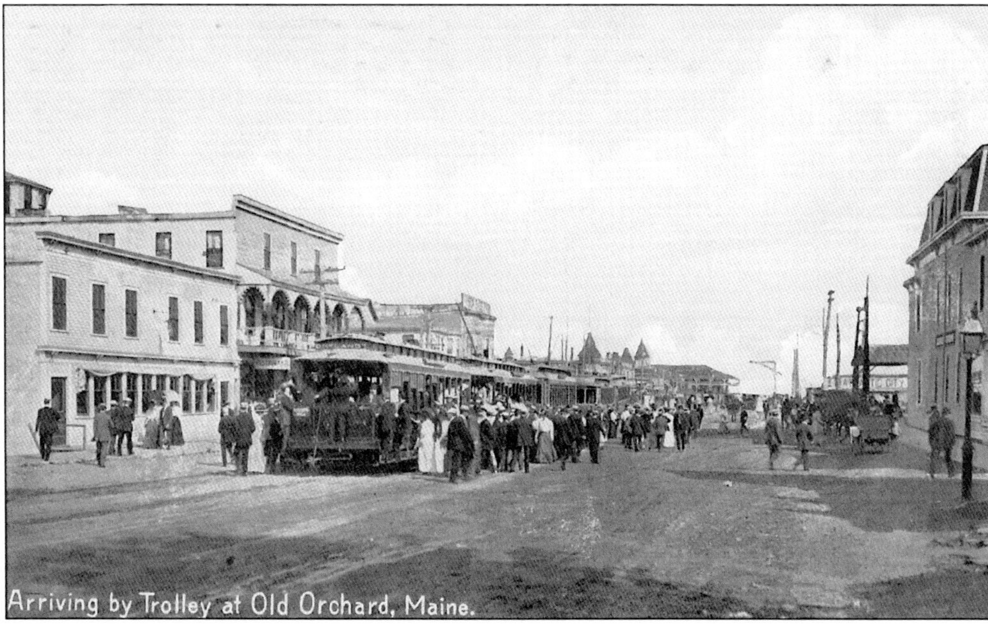

There were days in summer, such as Sundays and holidays, when there was such heavy riding between Portland and Old Orchard Beach that two or more cars had to be run on each scheduled trip. Here four Portland Railroad trolleys discharge passengers on Old Orchard Street at Depot Square.

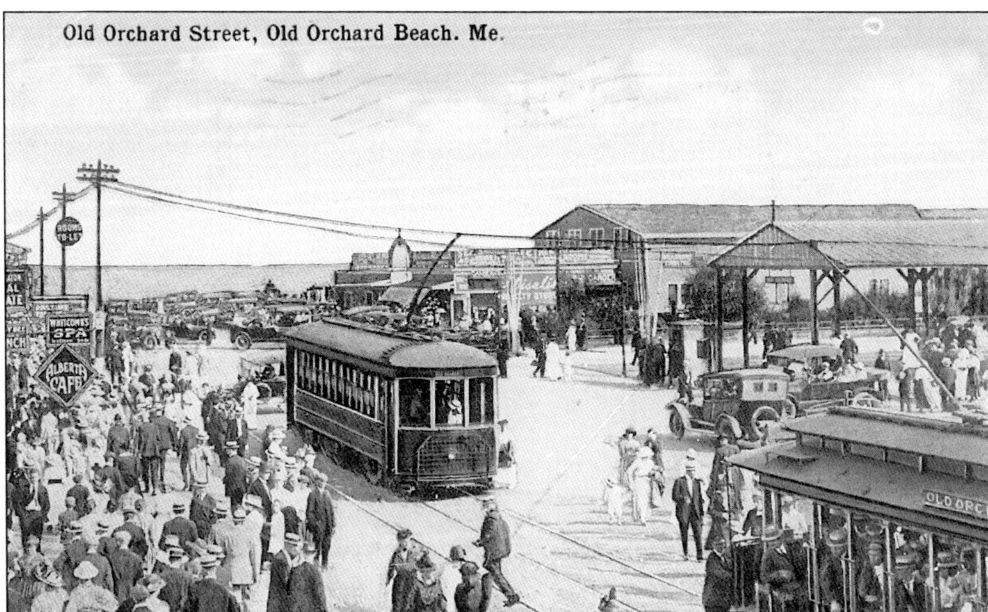

Normally operated on Congress Street line between Union Station and Munjoy Hill in Portland, the closed car at left made a trip to Old Orchard Beach on one busy weekend about 1917. At right is an open car of the 181-190 group.

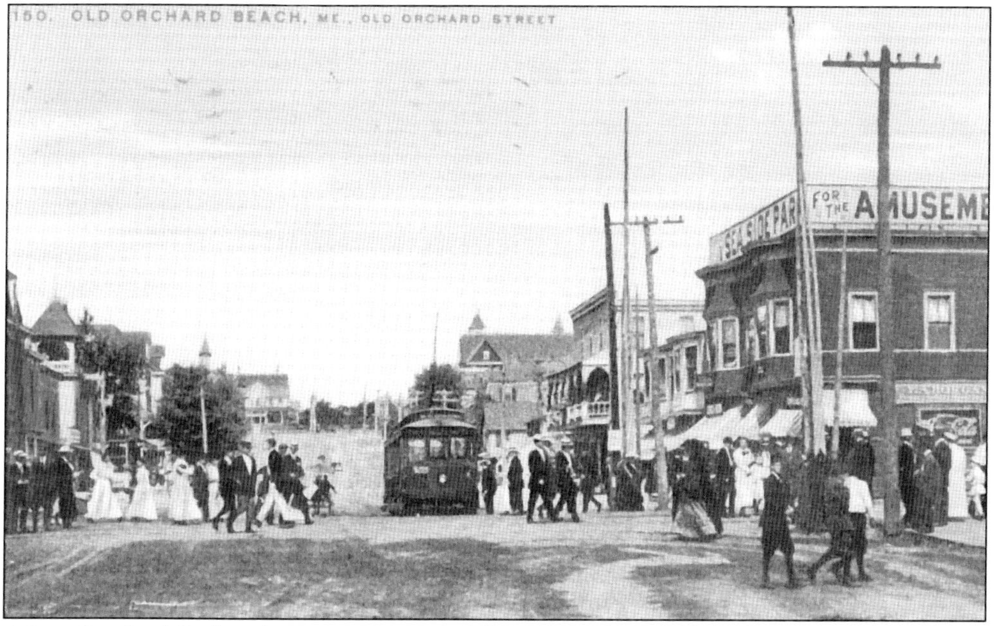

A lone Portland Railroad open car appears in this postcard view of Depot Square, Old Orchard Beach, after the 1907 fire. Sea Side Park, advertised on the building at right, was an amusement complex opened in 1902 off Old Orchard Street.

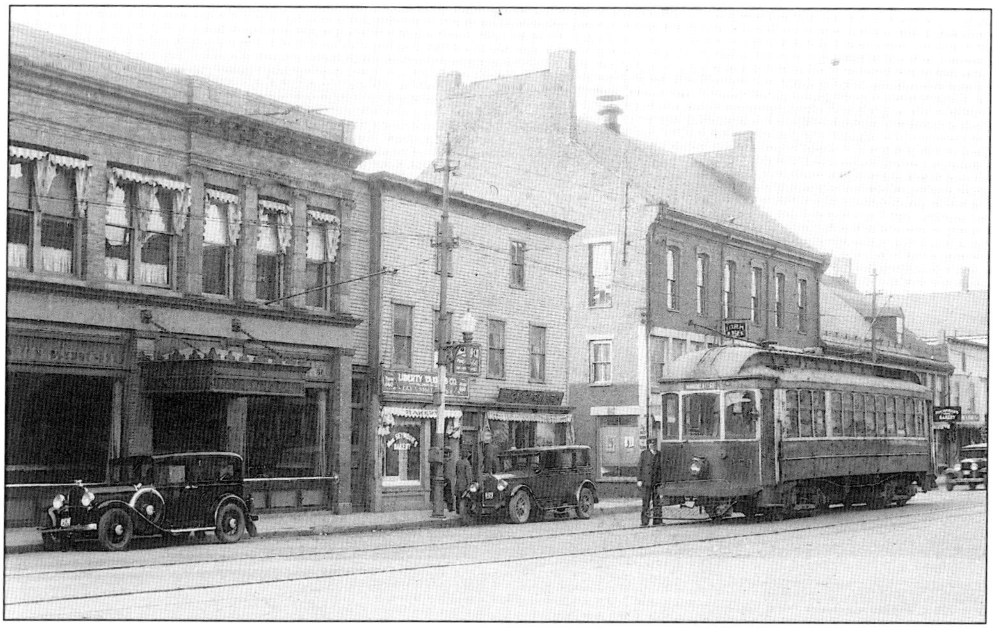

Portland-Saco trolley service ended April 16, 1932, and this view of Portland Railroad No. 179 on Main Street, Saco, reportedly was taken that day. The trolley was to see service in Portland, South Portland, and Westbrook for another nine years.

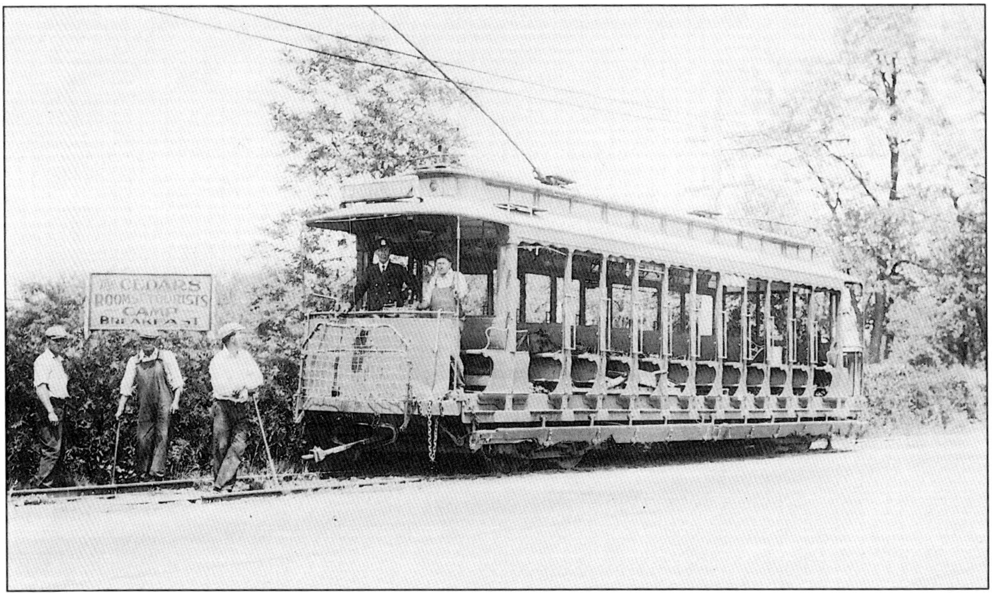

The last use of this 14-bench open car was to carry workmen engaged in tearing up the trolley tracks in Scarborough, Old Orchard, and Saco in 1932. Once the task had been completed, the car was burned for scrap.

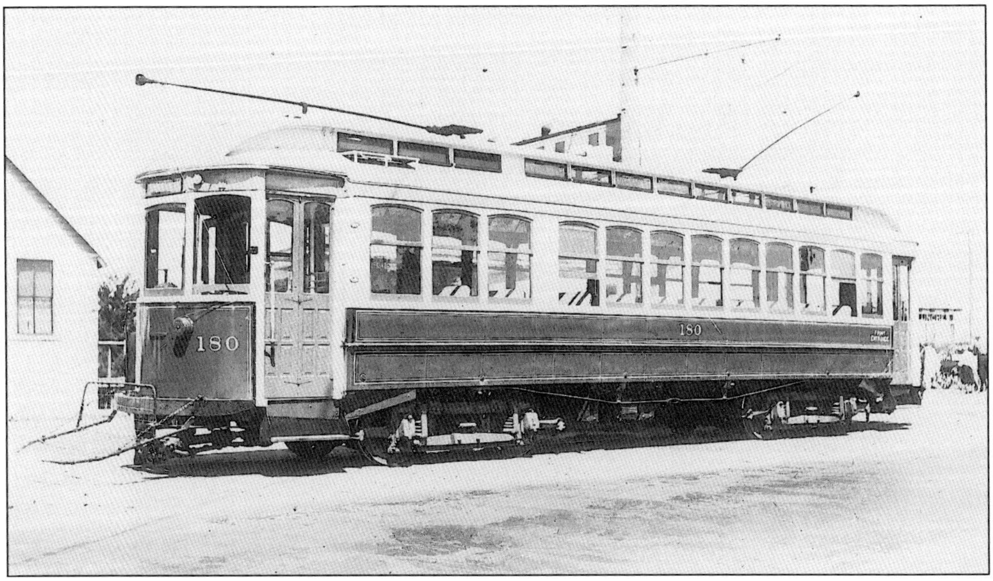

After trolley service to Saco and Old Orchard Beach ended, the Cumberland County Power & Light Company, continued to run trips from Monument Square through Thornton Heights, South Portland, to Nonesuch Corner near the Scarborough boundary until 1939. Car 180 is seen at the end of track about 1938.